Relax. There will be no test.

Museums can ruin a good vacation. Or you can look into the eyes of *David* and see the soul of Renaissance man. And ancient sites can give you goosebumps or heat stroke, depending upon your ability to resurrect the rubble.

Europe 101 sorts Europe's tangle of people and events—from the pyramids to Picasso—into an orderly and fascinating parade to make your sightseeing more meaningful and fun.

Europe 101 connects yesterday's Europe with today's sights—art, museums, buildings, and people. Throughout the book, lists of sights tie your new understanding of Europe right into your upcoming trip plans. This unique approach to art and history, supplemented with maps, timelines, and illustrations, makes this "professor in your pocket" an essential tool in any thinking tourist's preparation for Europe.

Beyond their formal university educations in European history, art, and culture, the authors have spent over eighty months roaming Europe, on their own and as tour guides. These two professional tourists understand what you need to know and, just as important, what you don't.

With *Europe 101*, smart people who slept through their history and art classes before they knew they were Europe-bound can enjoy a fun-to-read, practical book that makes Europe's history, art, and culture come alive.

EUROPE 101

History and Art for the Traveler

FIFTH EDITION

Rick Steves
and
Gene Openshaw

Graphics and Maps by
David C. Hoerlein

JOHN MUIR PUBLICATIONS
SANTA FE, NEW MEXICO

Other JMP travel guidebooks by Rick Steves:
Asia Through the Back Door (with Bob Effertz)
Kidding Around Seattle
Mona Winks: Self-Guided Tours of Europe's Top Museums (with Gene Openshaw)
Rick Steves' Baltics & Russia (with Ian Watson)
Rick Steves' Europe Through the Back Door
Rick Steves' Europe
Rick Steves' France, Belgium & the Netherlands (with Steve Smith)
Rick Steves' Germany, Austria & Switzerland
Rick Steves' Great Britain
Rick Steves' Italy
Rick Steves' Scandinavia
Rick Steves' Spain & Portugal
Rick Steves' Phrase Books: German, Italian, French, Spanish/Portuguese, German/Italian/French

John Muir Publications, P.O. Box 613, Santa Fe, NM 87504

Fifth edition. First printing January 1996

Library of Congress Cataloging-in-Publication Data
Steves, Rick, 1955–
Europe 101: history and art for the traveler / Rick Steves and Gene Openshaw.—5th ed.
  p. cm.
Includes index.
ISBN 1-56261-246-8 (pbk.)
1. Europe—Civilization. 2. Europe—Guidebooks. I. Openshaw, Gene. II. Title.
CB203.S734   1995
914.04'559—dc20   95-18901
                         CIP

Distributed to the book trade by
Publishers Group West
Emeryville, California

Europe Through the Back Door Editor: Risa Laib
John Muir Publications Editors: Elizabeth Wolf, Dianna Delling
Copy Editor: Nancy Gillan
Production: Kathryn Lloyd-Strongin, Sarah Horowitz
Photography: Rick Steves, Dave Hoerlein, and others
Text Design: Kathryn Lloyd-Strongin
Typesetting: Go West Graphics
Printing: Publishers Press

CONTENTS

Owner's Manual

Most history is about as exciting as somebody else's high school yearbook—a pile of meaningless faces and names. This history is different. *Europe 101* throws out the dreary dates and meaningless names. What's left is simple, fast-moving, and essential to your understanding of Europe.

After stripping history naked, *Europe 101* dresses it up with just the personalities and stories that will be a part of your travels. Take Frederick the Great, for instance. Great as he was, he's just Frederick the So-So to the average tourist, so he isn't mentioned in this book. Louis XIV, however, gets special attention because nearly every traveler visits his palace at Versailles or its many copies throughout Europe. Unprepared, bored tourists will wonder why you are having so much fun at Versailles. When you understand Louis, he becomes a real person who pulls his leotards on one leg at a time just like you and me. And his palace comes alive.

Art, like history, can be confusing and frustrating. *Europe 101* carefully ties each style of art to its historical era and relates it to your trip. You can't appreciate baroque art through *Better Homes and Gardens* eyes. You need a Baroque perspective.

Museums can be a drag or they can be unforgettable highlights, depending on what you know. *Europe 101* prepares you. After reading this book, you'll step into a Gothic cathedral, excitedly nudge your partner, and whisper, "Isn't this a marvelous improvement over Romanesque?" Europe, here you come!

No apologies. This book drives art snobs nuts. Its gross generalizations, sketchy dates, oversimplifications, and shoot-from-the-hip opinions really tweeze art highbrows. Our goal is to give you the practical basics (and no more) to make your sightseeing fun and meaningful.

Take a minute to understand the layout. This book covers the essential story of Europe's history and art chronologically through the prehistoric, ancient, medieval, Renaissance, early modern, and modern worlds. Each chapter ends with a timeline that helps you visualize how history and art interrelate. The best examples of this art and history are listed throughout the book in "sightseeing highlights" boxes. These lists are based on fame, accessibility, visitor friendliness, and arbitrary whims because, heck, it's our book. Important topics that don't fit into the chronology are covered in Part II, "Tangents," and in the Appendix.

Take notes as you read this book. Keep your travel plans in mind. Now, raise your travel dreams to their upright and locked positions, and get ready for a fascinating story . . . the story of Europe.

A victim of the Louvre

Part I
Europe's History and Art

Cave painting, 12,000 B.C.

Prehistoric Europe

Civilization was born when nomads settled. Before this, there was no tourism. Uncivilized men and women, armed with crude stone tools and fire, survived by hunting wild animals and gathering plants and fruit. The world was populated by nomads with the munchies.

But even prehistoric nomads had art. In the primitive art of prehistoric Europe, cave paintings and statuettes are magic symbols, not simply decorations. A cave dweller thought he or she could gain control over animals by capturing their likenesses. The paintings and statues were like voodoo dolls: you created a likeness with just enough details to make it recognizable and then stuck pins (or whatever) into it to influence the creature from afar. (It's questionable how much game was actually caught by this method, yet the same theory is used today when Americans strike their TV sets to influence the Super Bowl.)

Paleolithic Art (40,000 B.C.–8000 B.C.)

Europe's first art goes back over 30,000 years. That's five times as old as the oldest pyramid. The earliest art included fertility symbols, decorated pottery, stone circles, burial artifacts, and cave paintings. The most famous and finest early cave paintings (at Altamira in Spain and at Lascaux in France) date back to around 12,000 B.C. The startlingly realistic drawings of animals are made with charcoal, ocher, and other natural pigments. Some of these paintings look like modern art, and in fact, have inspired some modern artists. The Altamira and Lascaux caves are closed to tourists due to the heat and humidity generated by modern crowds. An impressively realistic "copy cave" adjacent to Lascaux is open to sightseers. Made with the same materials and techniques, this is worth a look. The best prehistoric cave painting still open to tourists is the Grotte de Font-de-Gaume, near Lascaux, in France's Dordogne region.

This "hunter style" of art is found throughout Europe. Ancient drawings of animals and, occasionally, drawings of the hunters themselves have been chiseled and sanded onto rocks or dug into hillsides. In many cases, artists expertly incorporated the pre-existing contours of the stone into their art.

As the ice fields slowly receded from northern Europe (beginning around 9,000 B.C.), prehistoric life changed. The frozen plains were replaced by forests and plants. As wandering hunter tribes learned food-gathering, farming, and herding, they began to settle down. Europe entered a new era.

Not all of Europe progressed at the same rate. Scandinavia, enveloped in ice long after the Continent had turned to forest, lagged behind the rest of Europe. Many present-day tribes (the bushmen of Africa, Australia's aborigines, the Eskimos, and England's punk-rockers) still employ some Stone Age technology.

From Hard Rock to Heavy Metal

Historians divide prehistory into ages to show our progression from the use of stone tools (*lith* = stone) to more sophisticated metals.

Paleolithic	40,000–8000 B.C.
Mesolithic	8000–4500 B.C.
Neolithic	4500–2000 B.C.
Copper Age	3000–1800 B.C.
Bronze Age	1800–500 B.C.

Gradually, the scrambling of Europe's prehistoric nomads took on a pattern. People saw the advantages of farming their own plants and raising their own animals in a choice spot. Eventually, more people farmed and fewer hunted. By 10,000 B.C., groups began settling in the most fertile and livable areas near rivers. Their interaction sparked the birth of civilization.

This transition from hunter-gatherer to farmer-herder led to cooperation and leisure time, two elements key to the rise of civilization. People living together and dealing with mutual problems need to get along. This cooperation, or social organization, enabled early societies to accomplish giant projects, such as building irrigation and drainage systems, that no one could do alone. This interaction nurtured governments, a greater exchange of knowledge and ideas, the development of common languages, the rudiments of writing to pre-serve this new knowledge, and paid vacations.

Domestic people were more productive than nomads. In the off-season, they had time on their hands: time to sing songs, tell stories, make decorative pottery, organize religion, and construct permanent buildings.

By 7000 B.C., small independent cities had appeared. Mesopotamia (present-day Iraq, Iran, and the Middle East), ideally located and with a good climate, was the birthplace of Western civilization. At the "Crossroads of the World," where Asia, Europe, and Africa meet, this area was perfect for receiving and spreading through trade all the world's knowledge. This was the age of Jericho, followed by the king-doms of Ur, Uruk, Lagash, and Babylon, each in its time the hub of the known world.

Neolithic Art (4500 B.C.–2000 B.C.)

As art passed from Paleolithic ("Old" Stone Age) to Neolithic ("New" Stone Age), it became less realistic. Figures were simplified and more stylized—symbolic stick figures for that society's magic.

This trend is especially evident in the small goddess statues so pop-ular in the ancient world. People lived at the mercy of nature. They worshiped "Mother Nature," who took the form of a fertile woman. Paleolithic goddesses were realistic portrayals of a female. As time went on, though, artisans began to exag-gerate some of the goddess' most feminine features: breasts, hips, butt, and genitals. By late Neolithic times, goddesses were more stylized still: a goddess might just be a stick with two lumps for breasts.

The Venus of Willendorf, *25,000 B.C.* *(Natural History Museum, Vienna). This 4-inch-high limestone fertility sym-bol was one of many such statues made by prehistoric Europeans who worshiped Mother Nature. This Pillsbury Dough Girl was found in present-day Austria.*

The most impressive remains of Neolithic culture are the massive, megalithic ("big stone") ruins such as Stonehenge in England (2800 B.C.–1500 B.C.). Built of stones weighing as much as 400 tons, these structures amazed Europeans of the Middle Ages, who figured the stones must have been placed by a race of giants.

Megalithic tombs, similar in purpose to the pyramids of ancient Egypt, were burial chambers for the great warrior-aristocrats of the time, carrying them into the next life. Warriors were buried with all their possessions, a boon for modern-day archaeologists. Found throughout Europe, megalithic tombs are most common in western France, which has several thousand.

Some stones (called menhirs) were designed to stand alone, as statues. These are sometimes decorated with a relief carving of a stylized human being.

Stone circles arranged as celestial calendars are the most awe-inspiring and mysterious of Europe's megalithic structures. These circles litter the English countryside. They seem to be designed to determine the date from the sun. Stonehenge's pillars are placed so

Stonehenge, *England. One of Britain's many ancient wonders, Stonehenge is a 4,000-year-old celestial calendar made of giant stones.*

that the rising sun on the longest day of the year (the summer solstice) filters through and strikes the altar stones. An avenue of stones that could accommodate huge crowds leads up to the sanctuary.

Sights of Prehistoric Europe

Britain
  • Stonehenge and Avebury circles

France
  • Lascaux II (re-creation of cave paintings), Les Eyzies, Dordogne
  • Menhirs and Dolmens, Gulf of Morbihan, Brittany

Spain
  • Cave paintings in Pileta caves, near Ronda

Additionally, artifacts in many museums, especially National Museums in Copenhagen, Vienna (Venus of Willendorf), and London

Laocoön, *150 B.C. (Vatican Museum, Rome)*

The Ancient World
3000 B.C.–A.D. 500

The year 3000 B.C., when writing appeared, marks the beginning of recorded history—an historic event that reached its culmination in this book. Egypt was united in 3000 B.C., establishing a great civilization that thrived for 2,000 years.

Egypt

Even if you don't visit Egypt, it's worth knowing about because of its influence on Greek culture and because of the large number of Egyptian artifacts in Europe today. But consider visiting Egypt. Only a 90-minute flight or an all-day boat ride from Athens, Egypt is just about the most exciting side trip you can plug into your European adventure—well worth the diarrhea.

The earliest great civilizations grew up along river valleys (Indus, Tigris, Euphrates, and Nile). Egypt is the Nile. From an airplane, the river looks like a lush green ribbon snaking through an endless sea of sand. By learning to harness the annual flooding of the Nile—its water and its fertilizing silt—ancient Egyptians prospered. The Nile's blessing, combined with relative isolation from enemy civilizations, brought Egyptians contentment and stability.

Except for struggles to unite the two kingdoms of Egypt (upper and lower), Egypt was politically stable. The Egyptian leader, the pharaoh, was believed to be a living god or at least the all-powerful link between the human world and the world of the spirits. To challenge the pharaoh was to challenge everything that held Egyptian society together. Pharaohs ruled a pro status-quo Egypt virtually unchallenged for 2,000 years.

The pharaoh's religion stressed preparation for the afterlife. In those days you *could* "take it with you." Pyramids, built over a period of decades by hordes of (probably willing) slaves, were giant stone tombs designed to preserve a king's or queen's body and possessions so he or she would arrive safely in the afterlife. Many pharaohs even took their servants with them, alive—for a while. The walls were painted with images of earthly things in case the pharaoh's real goodies didn't make it (a primitive forerunner of baggage insurance).

Mummy case, 1290 B.C. (British Museum, London). This mummy case, like much Egyptian art, was funerary: intended for the dead and their baggage back in the days when you could take it with you.

Egypt's art changed little from 3000 through 1000 B.C., reflecting a stable society obsessed with the afterlife. Most Egyptian art is funerary, built for the tombs of the wealthy and found on the Nile's west bank. Since the sun "died" every night on the west bank, it seemed logical for Egyptians to be buried there as well. All the pyramids are on the west bank.

Saqqara is the original pyramid (c. 2700 B.C.). It is a "step pyramid," designed as a series of funerary buildings stacked one on top of the

Tombs and mummification preserved corpses and possessions for the afterlife.

other. The three Great Pyramids at Giza (c. 2500 B.C.) are the most-visited of the pharaoh's stairways to heaven and well worth seeing. These are far from the only pyramids, however. You'll find dozens of them as you explore the Nile region.

Eventually, grave robbers broke into most of the pyramids. Time and time again, pharaohs woke up in heaven with absolutely nothing. Rather than marking their tombs with pyramids, rulers decided to hide them in the "Valley of the Kings," near Luxor. Mounted patrols guarded these hidden waiting rooms for the Eternity Express. Many have been opened as recently as this century, revealing incredible riches and art that looks brand-new even though it's more than 3,000 years old. Tutankhamen ("Tut" to his friends) was just a mediocre pharaoh—an ancient Gerry Ford—who achieved fame only because his tomb was discovered intact. Many more unmarked and hidden pharaohs' tombs wait in silence and darkness.

Egyptian Art

The distinguishing characteristics of Egyptian art—two-dimensionality, strong outlines, and rigid frontality—are explained by Egyptian religion and politics. Egyptian art was symbolic. It was a pictorial roll call of people and things which would be preserved in the afterlife, and it affirmed the divinity of the pharaoh and the relationships of the gods. It was more important for figures to be easily identifiable than to be lifelike.

"Good" art is not necessarily lifelike art. Often artists with great technical skill purposely distorted a subject to make an emotional, social, intellectual, or artistic point. It helps to understand the artist's purpose before judging his work.

The Egyptian artist, a master at portraying details realistically, would paint or sculpt only what was necessary to recognize the subject. Egyptian art consists of picture symbols (like our "Deer Crossing" road signs) showing things from their most characteristic or easy-to-recognize angle.

Nobleman Hunting in the Marshes, *1425 B.C. (British Museum, London). Looking as though he was just run over by a pyramid, this 2–D hunter is flat, as is most Egyptian art.*

For example, while both shoulders may face the viewer, heads are shown in profile.

Painters created unrealistic but recognizable scenes. Fish and birds were shown as if a biologist had stretched them out, trying to capture every identifying trait. This was so effective that scientists today can identify the species of most of the animals found in Egyptian drawings.

When Egyptians died, their souls had to make a long journey to the Egyptian paradise. No normal soul could make this hairy journey without a coffee break. A statue or painting of the deceased qualified as a rest stop. If you were rich, it was worth having your statue on display everywhere you could, to improve your chances of providing your soul with a pit stop on its long journey to salvation.

These were mug shots for eternity: chin up, no funny faces, nothing fancy. Statues were bold, stiff, frontal, and designed according to a rigid set of proportions. The head might be half the height of the body and a forearm as long as a shin. This "canon of proportions" was considered correct and remained unchanged for centuries.

Egyptian statues and paintings, stiff, unrealistic, and forever standing-at-attention, fill several rooms in the British Museum and Vatican Museum.

If any pharaoh made it to heaven, it was Ramses II (the one who wrangled with Moses and the Israelites). Not only did he have more statues than anyone else, but he even had his name chiseled over the names of many earlier pharaohs' statues just in case his soul could read.

The strict hierarchy of Egyptian society is seen in the symbols used in their art. A leopard skin is a sign of priesthood. Anyone barefoot belongs to an inferior class. Important people are shown as bigger than commoners. Portraying a pharaoh as twice as tall as his subjects, while not lifelike, accurately represented his social and political status. Each god and pharaoh had an identifying symbol. A beard was a sign of power. Even Queen Hatshepsut, history's first woman ruler, was portrayed with a beard chiseled on.

The one striking exception to Egypt's 2,000 years of political, religious, and artistic rigidity was the reign of the Pharaoh Akhnaton (1350 B.C.). We owe our knowledge of this period to the recent discovery of the tomb of Akhnaton's son-in-law and successor, Tutankhamen. Akhnaton was Egypt's first monotheist. He startled the conservative nobility and priesthood of his time by lumping the countless gods of the Egyptian pantheon into one all-powerful being, Aton.

Akhnaton, *Egypt's great nonconformist and Tut's father-in-law, promoted individuality. During his reign (c. 1350 B.C.), we see the first real change in 2,000 years of Egyptian art. Note the exaggerated personal features and the sensual curves in this pharaoh's likeness.*

Nefertiti, *1350 B.C. (Egyptian Museum, Berlin). Much of Egypt's greatest art is in Europe, including this masterpiece of Akhnaton's wife.*

In paintings from Akhnaton's reign, we see the royal family painted with a new artistic freedom, with more natural, lifelike, personal settings—a family portrait with Akhnaton; his wife, Nefertiti; and their children. Tut's wife is shown as big as the king, straightening his collar. There is a naturalism and gaiety in these pictures that is radically different from the stiff symbolism of earlier years. Yet after this brief period of freedom, the old rigidity returned.

Egypt's artistic legacy to the rising Greek world was the technical mastery of a formal religious style. Herodotus, an ancient Greek historian, said of the Egyptians, "They are religious to excess, far beyond any other race of men." The statues, wall paintings, coffins, mummies, and tombs you'll see in Europe's museums attest to the Egyptians' obsession with their gods and the afterlife.

Amen-Ra was the King of the Gods, the god of the sun. He is usually shown as a man with a beard, a double-plumed headdress, and a scepter in his right hand. Anubis, with the head of a jackal, was the Messenger of the Gods whose job was conducting the souls of men to the underworld after death. Horus, God of the Sky, has a hawk's head. The pharaoh was believed to be Horus on earth.

Egypt's two halves were represented by a lotus and a papyrus plant. When a pharaoh united Egypt, the art of his reign proudly included a symbol of an intertwined lotus and papyrus, and the pharaoh would be shown wearing the combined crowns of upper and lower Egypt.

Hieroglyphs are essentially pictures

Even Egyptian writing, called hieroglyphs, used pictures to symbolize ideas. They combined two elements: (1) pictures that stood for sounds (phonograms), such as the letters of our alphabet, and (2) pictures representing things and ideas (ideograms), such as the characters used in ancient Chinese writing.

Hieroglyphs were a complete mystery to modern scholars until the discovery of the Rosetta Stone (now in London's British Museum) allowed them to break the code. One hieroglyph you'll see a lot of is the ankh, which represents life. Statues are shown clutching the ankh as though trying to hold onto life.

Several European museums have fine Egyptian collections. The best are London's British Museum (featuring the Rosetta Stone), Paris' Louvre, the Vatican Museum in Rome, and Berlin's Egyptian Museum (starring Nefertiti).

Rosetta Stone, *196 B.C. (British Museum, London). Found on the site of the ancient Hotel Rosetta, this inscription repeated the same message ("Don't wash clothes in the sink") in three different languages, helping modern scholars to break the code of ancient Egyptian hieroglyphics.*

The Pre-Greek World

Minoans

The Minoans created the most impressive pre-Greek civilization. Theirs was a delicate, sensual, happy-go-lucky society that worshiped an easygoing Mother Earth goddess. The Minoans were more concerned with good food and dance than with the afterlife. Life here was an ancient Pepsi commercial.

An isolated location on the island of Crete (a 12-hour boat ride west of Athens) and their great skill as traders enabled Minoans to thrive from

Bull-leaping Fresco, *1500 B.C. (Archaeological Museum, Heraklion, Crete). This wet-plaster painting from the isle of Crete shows the grace of the easy-goin' Minoan civilization that so mysteriously vanished.*

2000 through 1400 B.C. They built their great palaces, Knossus and Phaestus, without fear of attack. The palaces were open and unfortified. Graceful decorations, including tapered columns and lively frescoes, created an atmosphere of intimacy and coziness.

Their art was so free and easy, it's fun to speculate that the laid-back Minoans might have influenced the relaxed art style of Akhnaton's Egypt.

In 1400 B.C., the Minoan civilization vanished without a hint of preceding decline. The great palaces became ghost towns overnight, and no one knows why. Some people think that the eruption of Santorini (home of Atlantis?) caused a tidal wave that swept the Minoan civilization into oblivion. The ruins of Acrotiri on Santorini (more interesting than Crete's Minoan ruins) show the remains of a Minoan-like community destroyed in that same eruption. Today, the island of Santorini is just the lip of a crater (lined with tourists), and the ruins of the Minoan civilization on Crete attract crowds from all over the world.

The Minoans definitely influenced the pre-Greek tribes who lived on the mainland. You can see the unique, inverted Minoan column between the lions atop the famous Lion Gate of the ruined Mycenaean capital, Mycenae (2 hours by bus from Athens). Greek legend has it that

The Lion Gate, *1250 B.C. (Mycenae, Greece). This gateway to the Mycenaean citadel shows the heavy, fortified style of this militaristic society from Trojan War times. Early Greeks, thinking no people could build with such huge stones, called Mycenaean architecture "Cyclopean." Mycenae is 2 hours south of Athens by bus.*

Mask not of Agamemnon, *16th century* B.C. *(National Archaeological Museum, Athens). King Agamemnon's much-sought-after mask was never found. But this was from about the same time and close enough to be known as "the Mask of Agamemnon."*

the Minoans ruled the early Greeks, demanding a yearly sacrifice of young Greeks to the dreadful Minotaur (half-bull, half-man) at the palace of Knossus. The Minoans' domination, however, was probably more cultural than political.

The Greek Dark Ages (1200–800 B.C.)

The end of the Minoans left only the many isolated, semi-barbaric tribes of Greece to fight things out. What we know about the Dark Ages comes largely from the poems and songs passed down over generations and eventually recorded by Homer in the ninth century B.C. in the *Iliad* and the *Odyssey.*

The *Iliad* tells of the Greeks' attack on Troy (on the west coast of present-day Turkey) and the *Odyssey* describes the Greek warrior Odysseus' long journey home after that war. However mythical these stories might be, they reveal the Greeks' desire to establish order in their warring world. The Trojan War is representative of all the wars of this period, and Odysseus' return home to a world filled with anarchy and lawlessness represents the long and difficult rise of a united classical Greece.

Classical Greece

The incredible output of art, architecture, and philosophy during Greece's "Golden Age" set the pace for all of Western civilization to follow. Astonishingly, all this was achieved within the space of a century

Parthenon Metope Panel, *430 B.C. (British Museum, London). This mythical battle between humans and half-human centaurs symbolized Greece's triumph over barbarism and chaos.*

in Athens, a city of 80,000. It was the flowering of many centuries of slow economic and cultural growth.

By 800 B.C., the bickering tribes of the Greek peninsula had settled down, bringing a new era of peace, prosperity, and unification. Great traders, the Greeks shipped their booming new civilization, with its ideas and riches, to every corner of the Mediterranean. As the Greek population multiplied, they established colonies as far away as France, Spain, and Italy. Many Greek ruins remain in those countries today.

A sense of unity (Pan-Hellenism) grew among the Greek-speaking peoples. They developed a common alphabet. They held the first Olympic Games in 776 B.C., during which wars were halted and athletes from all over Greece competed. Political unity grew through conquest and alliance, as the many small, self-contained city-states were brought together.

The individual city-state, or *polis,* was a natural product of Greece's mountainous landscape and of its many islands, which isolated people from their neighbors. An ideal city-state was small enough to walk across in a day but large enough to have the necessary elements of a society: cobblers, a debate team, and a travel agent. It was an independent mini-nation.

Landowners ruled in a generally democratic style. A city-state's typical layout included a combination fortress/worship site atop a hill called the *acropolis* (high city). The *agora,* or marketplace, sat at the base of the hill, with the people's homes and farms gathered around. An important feature of the agora was the *stoa,* a covered colonnade or portico used as a shady meeting place ideal for discussing politics. You can see each of these features today in the ancient center of Athens.

Athens in the Golden Age (450–400 B.C.)

Through alliance, industry, trade, and military might, Athens rose until it dominated the Greek world. Cursed with poor, rocky soil,

Athens turned to craftsmanship and trade for its livelihood. Able leaders stimulated industry by recruiting artisans from throughout the Greek world. By 500 B.C., Athens was the economic and cultural center of a loosely unified Greece.

Persia (present-day Iran and Iraq) posed a threat from the East. Persians ruled Ionia (modern-day Turkey's west coast), a center of high Greek culture. Here, the elegance and riches of Persia and the culture of the Anatolian civilizations mixed with the creative imagination of the Greeks. The Ionian Greeks united under Athenian leadership to protect themselves against the Persians. The Persian invaders even attacked Athens, but the Greeks' superior navy eventually won out, making Athens the protector and policeman of the Greek peninsula.

Old Athens today. _This is the historic core of Athens: the Acropolis (city on the hilltop), the agora (old market at the foot of the hill), and the Plaka to the left (the 19th-century town and now the tourist, hotel, restaurant, shopping, and nightlife center)._

In less than 100 years, Athens had risen from a stable, small-crafts city-state to the cultural, political, and economic center of an empire. Athens demanded payment, or tribute, from the other city-states for her defense of the peninsula. The new wealth in Athens set off a cultural volcano whose dust is still settling.

After the Persian War, the Athenians immediately set about rebuilding their city, which had been burned by the invaders. Grand public buildings and temples were built and then decorated with the greatest painting and sculpture ever. Giant amphitheaters were built to house dramatic, musical, and poetic festivals. During all this cultural growth and public building, average citizens remained hard workers, living modest but comfortable lives.

In schools and in the agora, under the shade of the stoa, the Greeks debated many of the questions that still occupy the human mind. Both Plato (who wrote down many of Socrates' ideas) and his student Aristotle organized schools of philosophy.

Plato (c. 380 B.C.) taught that the physical world is only a pale reflection of true reality (the way a shadow on the wall is a poor version of the three-dimensional, full-color world we see) and that rational thinking is the path to understanding the true reality. Aristotle (c. 340 B.C.) believed only in the physical realm—what you see is what you get. An avid biologist, he emphasized study of the physical world rather than the unseen one.

These two divergent ideas resurfaced again and again, especially in Christian theology centuries later.

In the fifth century A.D., St. Augustine believed (like Plato) in a realm beyond the material world. To Augustine, this unseen world was the "City of God." Thomas Aquinas, a 13th-century follower of Aristotle, attempted to reconcile Christian faith with Aristotelian reason, and viewed the physical and spiritual world as one inseparable whole.

The Greeks studied the world and man's place in it. They weren't content with traditional answers and old values. (Similar ideas were popping up all over the world at this time: Buddha in India, Confucius in China, and the Old Testament prophets in Palestine were all trying to relate everyday life to some larger scheme of things.)

The Greeks' "Golden Mean" was a new ideal that stressed the importance of balance, order, and harmony. Ideally life was balanced. In school, both the mind and the body were trained. Olympic athletes were lauded for being well-rounded. Rather than being just the fastest runner, a true Olympian was also a musician and a poet.

Greek Architecture

Greek art is known for its symmetry, harmony, and classic simplicity. It strikes a happy medium (or golden mean) between the rigidly formal Egyptian art and the unrestrained flamboyance of later Hellenistic art.

In architecture, this ideal of "nothing to excess" is best seen in Greek temples. There were two different styles, or orders: Doric and Ionic. Although the easiest way to identify these styles is by their columns, the columns themselves are only the tip of this architectural iceberg.

Doric columns are strong and simple, following the earliest styles of temple building. (The Doric tribe, of whom the Spartans were members, was known for its austere lifestyle.)

A Greek temple housed a god's statue. Since the people worshiped

Life Slice—Ancient Greece

Imagine a Greece without rubble, without ruins; when statues had arms and buildings had roofs; when the gray marble columns were painted bright colors; when flesh-and-blood people went around saying, "Know thyself." This was the time when ancient Greece was alive—farming, trading, voting, and going to the theater.

Farming was a tough row to hoe in rocky Greece, so the Greeks learned to trade with people in more fertile areas. Greeks produced wine, olive oil, and crafts (like pottery) which they traded for grain. They had lots of slaves. As many as one-third of the people in Athens were slaves.

As well as being slave-owners, the ancient Greeks were great democrats. Greece was divided by mountains and water into many small, self-governing, democratic city-states run by the common vote of the citizens. In Athens, any landowning adult male could vote. (Thomas Jefferson added that you also had to be white.)

With all their slaves and wealth, the Golden Age Athenians still lived quite simply. For dress, men and women wore simple, loose tunics and heavier wool wrappings for decoration and warmth. The children learned the three Rs, music, and athletics. The favorite leisure activities were sports and the theater.

Greek Theater, *350 B.C., Epidauros, Greece*

outside, its exterior was the important part and the interior was small and simple. The earliest temples were built of mud, brick, and wood. With greater prosperity, stone came into use. The Greeks kept the old style with the new material. The stone columns were shaped like timber supports; and formerly wooden beam ends, now in stone, divided the square panels on the eaves. The tops, or capitals, of Doric columns are also simple: just little sailors' caps of stone between the columns and the roofs they support.

The Parthenon, in Athens, is the greatest Doric temple, a masterpiece of Greek order and balance. The columns are thick but much more graceful than those of the massive Egyptian temples. These Doric columns swell slightly in the middle to give the impression that the roof is compressing them just a little.

The designers of the Parthenon used other eye-pleasing optical illusions. The base of the temple, which appears flat, actually bows up in the middle to overcome the illusion of sagging that a straight horizontal line would give. (If you and your partner stand on the same step at opposite ends, you'll see each other only from the waist up.) Also, the columns bend inward just a hair. If you extended the outer columns upward a mile, they would come together. These design elements give a more harmonious, cohesive feel to the architectural masterpiece of Greece's Golden Age.

Whereas Doric beauty was austere, the later Ionic style reflected grace, ease, and freedom while retaining balance and simplicity. An Ionic column is more slender than a Doric column and has deeper vertical grooves. The capital, with its scroll-like curls sticking out of either side, is more decorative. These curls give the impression of splaying under the weight of the roof. This style reflects a conscious effort to decorate and beautify the temple, but the ornamentation is never extravagant.

THE **PARTHENON**

AS IT APPEARS   AS IT WAS BUILT   AS IT WOULD LOOK
WITHOUT OPTICAL
CORRECTIONS

The Parthenon, 450 B.C., Athens. A "classic" example of Doric simplicity that stood nearly intact until the 17th century, when it was partially destroyed by an explosion during a Venetian-Turkish war. Today its greatest threat is 20th-century pollution.

A third order, the Corinthian, was developed during the Hellenistic period and was passed on to Roman architecture, where it is often seen side by side with Doric and Ionic. The Corinthian is the next step in the path from simplicity to decoration. A Corinthian column's flowery capital of acanthus leaves doesn't even pretend to serve an architectural purpose; it is blatantly ornamental.

The purpose of the capital is to fool the roof into thinking that the columns are fatter than they are. They shorten the distance the stone roof "planks" need to span. Capitals let the columns be slimmer and farther apart—the mark of a more elegant building. As temples evolved to more graceful styles, columns became more slender. There was a canon of proportions: Doric columns were to be eight times as tall as

DORIC   IONIC   CORINTHIAN

*Classical Architecture: Doric, Ionic, and Corinthian. The easiest way to iden-
tify the classical "orders" is by the columns. Doric is the earliest, simple and
stocky. Ionic is fancier, thinner, with more pronounced grooves and a rolled
capital. Corinthian (Roman style) is the most ornate, with a leafy capital. As
temples evolved, columns grew skinnier and more widely spaced. Memory
aid—the orders gain syllables as they evolve: Doric, Ionic, Corinthian.*

their base width, Ionic were to be ten times as tall as their base width, and Corinthian were to be 11 times as tall as their base width.

Temples of all the orders had similar features. Groovy fluted columns are an architectural echo of the days when the columns were logs with their bark gouged out. Columns were made of stacked slices of stone, each with a plug to keep it in line. They held up the roof and provided a pleasant, shady stoa under the broad eaves.

In the old days, when timbers spanned the roof, the ends of the beams divided the roof into little, fun-to-fill-with-carving squares called metopes (MET-o-peez). When builders began to use stone, the metopes were retained. The "pediment" is the triangular gable that was the artistic focus of the ancient sculptors. They filled these narrow, awkwardly shaped spaces with some of ancient Greece's best art. The "frieze," the panel under the eaves, was usually filled with low-relief carvings of mythological battles and scenes. The famous Elgin Marbles, now in the British Museum, are the sculptures that decorated the Parthenon's frieze, metopes, and pediments.

Much post-Greek architecture, from Roman to 20th century, utilizes the classical orders for decoration.

Greek Sculpture and Painting

The Greeks believed that the human body expressed the human spirit. Greek sculptors tried to catch it in all its naked splendor, depicting even gods as having human bodies. They sculpted accurate, posed, balanced, idealized, and beautiful physical specimens. Greek sculpture evolves in clear steps from rigid to balanced to exuberant.

The evolution is so distinct that college art professors can reasonably expect their students to look at a piece of Greek art for their first time and say, within ten years, when it was made.

Statues from the archaic period (750–500 B.C.) feel Egyptian. This stiff, posed frontality is seen in the Greek *kouros*, statues of naked young men from the sixth century B.C. They are strongly outlined and remarkably realistic, but not lifelike. A kouros looks like a human, but like no human in particular because there are no individual details. The body appears to have been made on an assembly line, with universally interchangeable parts.

Greek society honored individuality and admired the human body. This attitude, combined with technical mastery of the skills of sculpture, freed the subject from those archaic, rigid poses. Artists began to relax their subjects and portray life more realistically. Sculptors showed lively subjects from different angles. Artists paid closer attention to

Geometric-style vase, 700 B.C. (detail of Dipylon vase, National Archaeological Museum, Athens). This earliest stage of Greek art shows wasp-waisted figures pulling their hair out to symbolize their sadness at this funeral procession.

*Evolving from stiff, Egyptian-type poses,
Greek sculpture spun and whirled into lifelike action. The **Auxerre Goddess**, the oldest (7th century B.C.), resembles a column.
The 6th-century B.C. **Kouros** (boy) has legs
but doesn't move. His younger friend is
loosening up for the Golden Age. The
Discus Thrower (450 B.C.) is utterly realistic. Caught at the moment just before the
frisbee is thrown, he is full of energy but
still perfectly balanced. Like most great
"Greek" statues, this is a Roman copy of a
long-gone original.*

detail. Robes drape down naturally from these statues, and the intricate folds become beautiful in themselves.

Remember that the "Greek" statues filling Europe's museums are mostly chalky, lifeless Roman copies with blank stares and Vatican fig leaves. When you see an original, you'll be impressed by its vibrancy. Athens' National Archaeological Museum, by far the greatest museum for ancient Greek art, has many good and original examples of each stage of Greek sculpture.

For 2,500 years Greece has been a good-time destination.

Greek painting was also revolutionized by the discovery of foreshortening. (You foreshortened the last time you drew receding lines to turn a square into a three-dimensional box.) Now a subject could be shown from any angle, not just from the most convenient frontal pose. The artist could record things as they happened, even putting his individual stamp on the work by showing it from his personal perspective.

In their day, Greek painters were more famous than their sculpting counterparts. The best Greek painting you're likely to see will be on the vases that fill art museums from Oslo to Lisbon. (The vases were used to hold oil or wine rather than flowers.) Sample a slice of Greek life by studying these vase paintings.

Even with this exciting, new-found freedom in their mastery of the arts, the Golden Age of Greece is best characterized by the Golden Mean: restraint and a strong sense of harmony and balance.

The famous statue *The Discus Thrower* illustrates this balance. It's a remarkable study in movement, yet the body is captured at a moment of non-movement, just before he hurls the discus. The human form is posed but natural, perfectly balanced, with nothing in the extreme; it reflects the Golden Mean. Previously, the body had been the sum of its parts. Now, it was an organic whole.

The brief Golden Age of Greece (450 B.C.) was the balancing point between archaic and Hellenistic Greece. Both society and its art evolved from the aristocratic, traditional and stiff Archaic age (c. 600 B.C.) to the democratic, original, realistic, and wildly individual Hellenistic age (c. 300 B.C.).

Hellenism (330 B.C.–First Century A.D.)

Single-handedly, Alexander the Great spread the ideas of the small Greek peninsula throughout the Mediterranean and Near East. Alexander ushered in the Hellenistic period. (*Hellene* is Greek for "Greek.")

As Athens declined in power through costly wars with Sparta and other neighboring city-states, the Macedonians to the north (present-day Serbia) swept in. Their leader was 20-year-old Alexander, a former student of Aristotle. By the time Alexander died, at the age of 32, he had created the largest empire ever, stretching as far east as India. (What have you accomplished lately?)

Alexander was a military genius, a great administrator, and a lover of Greek culture. He went to bed each night with two things under his pillow: a dagger and a copy of the *Iliad*. While he conquered Greece politically, Greece ruled Alexander's empire culturally.

During the Hellenistic era, Greek was the common language of most of the civilized world. Cities everywhere had Greek-style governments and schools. Their citizens observed Greek holidays and studied Greek literature. Public squares throughout the Mediterranean looked Greek. Alexandria (Egypt) was the intellectual center of the world, with more than a million people, a flourishing arts and literature scene, and the greatest library anywhere. No ship was allowed to enter the port without surrendering its books to be copied.

Hellenistic sculpture was "ancient Baroque," reflecting the exuberance of Hellenistic civilization. Dramatic, emotional, and unbalanced, it showed rough-and-tumble scenes such as the one depicted

Altar of Zeus, *170 B.C. (Pergamon Museum, Berlin)*

in the Altar of Zeus (in Berlin's Pergamon museum). A typical example, this tangle of battling gods and giants is literally falling out of the relief scene and onto the monumental stairway. These action scenes replaced the "soccer team portrait" formality of earlier reliefs.

When Alexander died in 323 B.C., his political empire crumbled. But the Greek civilization fostered during his rule lived on for centuries. This Hellenistic culture featured a passion for creativity. A group from this period called the "cynics" were history's first hippies, rejecting all authority and institutions. The focus was on the individual.

As the Romans conquered Alexander's empire, they found the ready-made centralized government and economy of Hellenistic Greece easy to administer. Hellenistic Greeks were more

Laocoön, *150 B.C. (detail, Vatican Museum, Rome). A textbook example of the Hellenistic style, it's a rocket of exuberance. Unearthed near Rome in 1506, this work astounded and inspired Michelangelo and the Renaissance sculptors.*

Venus de Medici, *Roman copy of Praxiteles' third century B.C. Greek original (Uffizi Gallery, Florence). Greek art evolved to a Golden Age balance. This copy of a Greek masterpiece served as the ideal of classical beauty through the ages. Nineteenth-century tourists used to swoon in ecstasy at her loveliness.*

"civilized" than their Roman conquerors. The Romans absorbed what was profitable into their own culture, and civilization took one more step westward.

Athens' National Archaeological Museum

Preface a visit to the ancient wonders of Greece with a visit to the National Archaeological Museum in Athens.

Athens, like Mexico City and Cairo, has hoarded the lion's share of its artistic heritage under one grand and obligatory roof. Take this museum as seriously as you can. Trace the evolution of Greek art, study a guidebook, take a guided tour, and examine the ancient lifestyles painted on the vases. After gaining a rudimentary knowledge of Greek art here, you can head for the hills and resurrect all that B.C. rubble.

Five Favorite Greek Ruins

Just because something is B.C. doesn't mean it must be seen. There's plenty of mediocre B.C. stuff. Be selective. Visit the top few sights, then move on to the sun, food, and drink of a country with many dimensions.

Here are our five favorite Greek ruins. For maximum goosebumps and minimum heat stroke, see these and skip the rest.

Top Five Ancient Greek Sights

The Acropolis, Athens (artist's reconstruction)

Athens' Acropolis

This is the biggie. While the city of Athens might be overrated, its historic hilltop is not.

Study the Parthenon. This is the climax of the Acropolis and Greece's finest Doric temple. The statuary and carving of the temples of the Acropolis have fled Athens' acidic air. You can see them in the museum on the Acropolis, in Paris' Louvre, and—best of all—in London's British Museum.

Below the Acropolis is the ancient agora, ancient Athens' civic center and market. Most important among many sights here is the Temple of Hephaistos, or Theseum, the best-preserved classical Greek temple anywhere.

Delos

Without Delos, Athens' Acropolis might not have been built. During Greece's Golden Age, the treasury of the Athens-dominated Greek alliance was located on this little island near Mykonos. The Athenians financed the architectural glorification of their city by looting this treasury.

Delos, an easy half-day side trip from Mykonos, was the legendary birthplace of Apollo and therefore the most sacred Cycladic island. Today it's uninhabited except for the daily boatloads of visitors. See the famous "Lions of Delos," wander through nearly a square mile of crumbled greatness, and climb to the island's summit for a picnic. From the peak of Delos, you'll enjoy a grand, 360-degree view of the Greek Isles, with the Fort Knox of ancient Greece at your feet.

Europe 101 mapmaker Dave Hoerlein on starting block at Olympia

Olympia

For more than a thousand years, the Olympic Games were held in their birthplace . . . Olympia. Once the most important sanctuary of Zeus in all of Greece, the site is now a thought-provoking and popular tourist attraction.

Most tourists sail to Greece from Italy. The boat (free with a Eurailpass) lands in Patras, and the hordes stampede on into Athens. Be different. Head south from Patras to Olympia and then explore the Peloponnesian interior on your way to Athens.

Olympia's Temple of Zeus was one of the great tourist traps of the ancient world, boasting a then-world-famous 40-foot statue of Zeus by the great sculptor Phidias. It was one of the Seven Wonders of the Ancient World.

Olympia can still knock you on your discus. Get there early to avoid the tour-bus crowds. The local guidebook and the Olympia Museum can bring the ruins to life. Crank up your imagination and refill the stadium with 40,000 fans as you line up on that original starting block.

Delphi

Once upon a time, Zeus, the king of all the gods, threw out two eagles. Where they met after circling the earth was declared to be the world's navel. This was the center of the universe and the home of the Oracle of Delphi. In the days of Socrates, this was where the gods spoke to the people.

From throughout greater Greece, people would come here with lavish gifts to exchange for wisdom from the gods. The priests surveyed whoever came. Organizing this knowledge, they actually had a good idea about the political, military, and economic situation of the entire area. Their savvy advice was good enough to be accepted as divine. Delphi grew politically powerful, religiously righteous, and very rich.

Today, its staggering setting does more than its history to make this 4-hour side trip from Athens worthwhile. Along with plenty of photogenic ruins to explore, Delphi has one of Greece's best archaeological museums.

Ephesus

The ruins of Asia Minor's largest metropolis, once the home of the Ephesians of New Testament fame, are unforgettable. Ephesus is actually on the Turkish mainland, only a 90-minute boat ride from the beautiful Greek island of Samos.

Ephesus was at its peak at about 100 B.C., when it was the capital of the Roman province of Asia. Its theater seated 25,000. Using the art historian's method of estimating an ancient city's population by multiplying the capacity of its theater by ten, the city was home to 250,000 Ephesians. You can marvel at the giant theater, park your

Top Ten Ancient Greek Sights (in order)

1. Athens' Acropolis and agora (Greece)
2. Delos, treasury of Athenian League (near Mykonos, Greece)
3. Olympia, site of first Olympic Games (Peloponnese, Greece)
4. Delphi, site of oracle (Greece)
5. Ephesus—as exciting as Athens, but it's more Roman than Greek
6. Paestum temple (just south of Naples, Italy)
7. Mycenae (south of Athens, Greece)
8. Epidauros theatre (Peloponnese, Greece)
9. Aphrodisias (near Pamukkale, Turkey)
10. Acrotiri ruins, from Minoan time (Santorini, Greece)

Temple of Neptune, 450 B.C., Paestum (south of Naples), Italy. You don't need to go to Greece to see great Greek ruins. Five hundred years before Christ, southern Italy was Magna Graecia . . . Greater Greece.

chariot outside a grand library, and hike up the marble-cobbled main street—an ancient can-can of elegant ruins casually surviving just another century. You can even sit on a 2,000-year-old toilet.

A trip to Efes (Turkish for Ephesus) is a great excuse to enjoy a slice of Turkey. Remember, you experience more cultural change by taking the short boat ride from the Greek islands to Turkey than you get by flying all the way from the USA to Greece. If you can just bust out of Europe for a while, you won't need museums . . . they're living in the streets.

Beware. Greece is the most touristed, but least explored country in Europe. It seems that at any time, 90 percent of its tourists are packed into its top dozen or so sights marveling at the crowds.

Greece is peppered with ancient sights, each offering something unique. But as with Gothic cathedrals, German castles, or Scandinavian blondes, you can't and shouldn't try to see and appreciate them all.

Top Museums of Ancient Greece

Greece
* National Archaeological Museum, Athens

Britain
* British Museum (Parthenon sculpture), London

France
* Louvre (*Venus de Milo*, *Victory of Samothrace*), Paris

Italy
* Vatican Museum (*Laocoön*), Rome

Germany
* Pergamon Museum (altar from Ephesus), Berlin

Victory of Samothrace,
190 B.C. (Louvre, Paris)

Who's Who of Ancient Greece

The great sculptor Phidias (around 450 B.C.) was responsible for the statuary of the Parthenon. He was the first one to let the body show through the robes. Praxiteles (around 350 B.C.), the greatest Athenian sculptor, mastered realism in his statues. Top philosophers were Socrates, Plato, and Aristotle. Leading playwrights were Aristophanes, Euripides, and Sophocles. Euclid and Pythagoras were the first math teachers.

Rome

Rome is history's supreme success story. By conquest, assimilation, and great administration, Rome rose from a small Etruscan town to the ruling seat of a vast empire.

Classical Rome lasted for a thousand years, from 500 B.C. through A.D. 500. In a nutshell, it grew for 500 years, peaked for 200, and fell for 300. For the first 500 years, Rome was a republic; for the second 500, an empire. Today, armies of tourists endure the hot Roman sun and battle its crazy traffic to see what's left of that greatest of civilizations.

Legend says that Rome was founded in 753 B.C. by twin brothers Romulus (hence "Rome") and Remus (hence "Uncle Remus"). They are said to have been orphaned as babies and raised by a she-wolf before

Etruscan She-Wolf, *500 B.C. (Capitoline Museum, Rome). Long after the Etruscans sculpted this statue, Romulus and Remus were scooted under, and it became the symbol of Rome. You'll see copies of this everywhere, but the original is in the museum on Capitol Hill in Rome.*

starting the greatest empire ever. This story must have seemed an appropriate metaphor for the Romans, explaining how such a "civilized" people (as they considered themselves) could have grown out of such "barbarian" surroundings.

Rome was situated at the first bridge on the Tiber River, as far upstream as boats could navigate. Ruled by Etruscan kings, Rome linked the advanced Etruscan civilization to the north with the agriculturally rich Greek colonies to the south.

The Etruscans thrived in much of northern Italy during Greece's Golden Age. Excavations of Etruscan tombs indicate that the Etruscans were peaceful, religious, easygoing, and prosperous craftspeople and merchants. With a good map, you can track down many interesting Etruscan sights between Rome and Florence.

Etruscan Museums and Sites

Italy
- Necropolis, Tarquinia (near Rome)
- Etruscan museum, Orvieto (near Rome)
- Tombs and frescoes, Cerveteri (near Rome)
- Etruscan museum and gate, Volterra (near San Gimignano)
- Vatican Museum, Rome

Denmark
- Carlsberg Glyptothek, Copenhagen

France
- Louvre, Paris

Etruscan sarcophagus (detail), 6th century B.C., Louvre, Paris

Beginning of the Roman Republic

In 509 B.C. the local Romans threw out their Etruscan king, establishing a plutocratic (rule by the rich) republic. From the start, war was the business of state, and Rome expanded. The Roman conquests were cemented by a well-organized, generally enlightened, benevolent rule. People knew that when they were conquered by Rome, they had joined the winning team, that political stability would replace barbarian invasions, and that they would enjoy free trade and public building projects: roads, baths, aqueducts, theaters, and great games. With contented subjects, the empire continued to expand. By 260 B.C. it included Italy, and by 100 B.C. the Roman "Republic" controlled the entire Mediterranean world.

This giant empire strained a government that had been designed to rule only a small city-state. During the first century B.C., while still growing and prospering, Rome had to deal with civil strife, class struggles, corrupt politicians (back then . . . all Republicans), and the corrosive individuality of Hellenism.

Julius Caesar, an ambitious general, cunning politician, and charismatic leader, outmaneuvered his rivals and grabbed the reins of Rome in about 50 B.C. Supported by his armies, Caesar suspended the constitution and replaced the republic with a no-nonsense empire. His dictatorial rule restored order and reformed the government.

He further consolidated his power by naming a month, July, after himself. He rammed through many reforms, but underestimated the conservatives in the senate and those who loved the old republic. He was assassinated (*Et tu, Brute?*), and a struggle followed between would-be dictators and republicans. A decade later the political vacuum was filled by Julius' adopted son, Caesar Augustus. (This family name became a title: Caesar, Tsar, Kaiser.)

Arch of Titus, A.D. 81 (Forum, Rome). *Emperors milked their military victories for propaganda purposes. Grand triumphal arches glorified their exploits. Today you'll find these arches scattered from Germany to Morocco.*

Pax Romana: The Roman Peace (A.D. 1–200)

Augustus, known as the architect of the Roman Empire, established a full-blown monarchy and ushered in the "Pax Romana." This "Roman peace" was a period of 200 years of relative peace and prosperity with an enlightened and generally benevolent rule throughout the vast empire. While Augustus, like Julius, had an appetite for power and also named a month in his honor, he was more sensitive to the senate and its traditions. Still, he reformed the government, restored temples, undertook huge public building projects, and even legislated morality. He declared himself the *pontifex maximus* (high priest) and boasted that he "found Rome a city of brick and left it a city of marble."

The Pax Romana's unprecedented political stability was made possible by a smooth succession of leaders. Historically, accession to the throne was hereditary, but just as historically, emperors' sons made lousy rulers. The great rulers of the second century (Nerva, Trajan,

Roman maps called the Mediterranean "Our Sea" (Mare Nostrum). The empire stretched as far north as the Danube and Rhine rivers and the southern border of Scotland. At this time, the word "Rome" meant the entire civilized world.

Augustus of the Prima Porta,
A.D. *14 (Vatican Museum, Rome).*
Here, the first emperor, Augustus
(the very-much-in-command
founder of the Pax Romana),
teaches Rome how to hail a cab.

Hadrian, and Antoninus) had no blood sons. Instead, each adopted as a son the man he deemed most capable of ruling. Then, when the ruler died, the "son" inherited the throne and ruled well. This worked fine until Marcus Aurelius had a blood son, Commodus. As emperor, this palace brat—who ran around dressed in animal skins and carrying a club as if he were Hercules—ushered in a period of instability and decline.

The Pax Romana saw a well-governed Rome reach its zenith, stretching from the Nile to the Danube and from the Rhine to the south border of present-day Scotland, where the Romans decided to call it an empire and built Hadrian's Wall from coast to coast across northern England. Everywhere the Roman army went, it built roads, aqueducts, and cities on a grid plan. Trade thrived. Roman maps labeled the Mediterranean "Mare Nostrum" (Our Sea). At its peak, the word "Rome" meant not the city, but the entire civilized Western world.

Roman Religion

Religion permeated Roman life. The gods were powers you bargained or dealt with. If you wanted a favor, you prayed and sacrificed to the proper god, either at home on a small altar or at the local temple. For guidance, you might see a seer who'd rip open an animal to check the shape of the entrails for predictions of the future.

Jupiter was the king of the gods. Like all the Roman gods, he was based on his Greek counterpart, Zeus. Each profession had its patron god or goddess. Betty Crocker would pray to Vesta, the goddess of the hearth. You worshiped the gods not out of moral obligation, but to gain a favor. Here's one prayer that has survived: "I beseech you to avenge the theft committed against me. Punish with a terrible death whoever stole these articles—six tunics, two cloaks, etc."

Life Slice—Ancient Rome

Let's look at a typical well-to-do Roman citizen and his family over the course of a day.

In the morning, Nebulus reviews the finances of the country farm with his caretaker/accountant/slave. He's interrupted by a "client," one of many poorer people dependent upon him for favors. The client, a shoemaker, wants permission from the government to open a new shop. He asks Nebulus to cut through red tape. Nebulus promises to consult a lawyer friend in the basilica.

After a light lunch and siesta, he walks to the baths for a workout and a little steam. There, he discusses plans for donating money to build a new aqueduct for the city.

Back home, his wife, Vapid, tends to the household affairs. The servants clean the house and send clothing to the laundry. Usual dress is a simple woolen tunic: two pieces of cloth, front and back, sewn together at the sides. But tonight they'll dress up for a dinner party. She'll wear silk, with a wreath of flowers, and Nebulus will wear his toga, a 20-foot-long white cloth. It's heavy and hard to put on, but it's the rage.

The children, Raucous and Ubiquitous, say good-bye to the pet dog and head off to school in the Forum. Nothing funny happened on the way. At school, it's down to business. They learn their basic three R's. When they get older, they'll study literature, Greek, and public speaking. (The saving grace of this dreary education is that they don't have to take Latin.)

At the dinner party, Vapid marvels over the chef's creation: ham soaked with honey, pasted in flour and baked. The guests toast each other with clay goblets bearing inscriptions like "Fill me up," and "Love me, baby!"

The legendary Roman orgy was just that—legendary. Romans advocated moderation and fidelity. If anything, stuffiness and business sense were the rule. The family unit was considered sacred.

The good life, frescoed on a wall at Pompeii (A.D. 79). Many of Pompeii's frescoes are in the National Archeological Museum in Naples.

The Pantheon, *with its famous skylight, gives you a feel for the magnificence and splendor of Rome better than any other sight. This concrete structure, 142 feet high and 142 feet wide, was built in 27 B.C. by Agrippa, then rebuilt by Hadrian in A.D. 126. A domed temple dedicated to all Roman gods, it was the wonder of its age and an inspiration for Renaissance artists. The huge domes of the Florence cathedral and St. Peter's in Rome were modeled on this early architectural triumph.*

Roman Art and Architecture

While they could be inventive and delicate in their art, the Romans were better engineers and administrators than artists. The Greeks loved beauty and intellectual stimulation, but Rome's artistic accomplishments were big and functional, designed for accommodating the masses with roads, colosseums, and baths rather than portraying beautiful gods. If offered a choice of a ticket to a symposium on the nature of truth or a ticket to a gladiatorial battle to the death, a Roman would go for the gore.

Rome's greatest contributions to history are in law and engineering. Her legal and administrative traditions were the basis for all Western

Greek architects were limited by the width a stone beam could span.

By developing the round arch, Rome was able to build circles around the Greeks.

governments that followed. In engineering, the Romans developed the use of the arch and concrete, enabling them to build structures that dwarfed anything built by the Greeks.

Maybe it's lucky that the Romans weren't great innovators in art. As a result, they admired, preserved, and copied the precious Greek art that otherwise might have been lost or destroyed. In fact, most of the examples of Greek Golden Age sculpture you'll see during your trip are excellent Roman copies. The originals are long gone, but all high-class Romans wanted quality copies of Greek originals in their villa. It's these 2,000-year-old copies of 2,500-year-old originals that fill today's museums.

Roman art and architecture are characterized by utility and grandeur. (A Roman tourist in modern America would buy postcards of a Los Angeles freeway interchange.) The Romans focused on functionality and purpose. Decoration was secondary.

The Colosseum is a good example of functional Roman engineering that accommodated the needs of the masses. To double the seating capacity, they put two theaters together, making a circular amphitheater. A canvas awning could be drawn across the top to make it a "domed" stadium. It could seat 50,000 fans.

The Colosseum's essential structure was Roman, built with arches, barrel vaults, and concrete. The three orders of Greek columns on the exterior—Doric, Ionic, and Corinthian—were

The Colosseum, A.D. 80, Rome

simply decorations, pasted on because the Romans thought Greek things were cool.

On opening day at the Colosseum, Romans enjoyed the slaughter of 5,000 animals. About a thousand years later, the Colosseum was appreciated only as a quarry offering free, pre-cut stones to anyone who could carry them away.

Roman Busts

One art form in which the Romans actually surpassed the Greeks was the making of portraits. The Greeks were simply concerned with sculpting or painting idealized human "10s" without distinguishing individual characteristics. But Roman ancestor worship and family solidarity required realistic portraits of the father and his ancestors. Also, since good Romans worshiped the emperor as a god, his portrait was nearly everywhere.

Roman portraiture (especially the common "bust," a statue showing just the chest up, minus arms) reached a new level of naturalism. Of course, many portraits were idealized and prettied

Roman Portrait Busts, Capitoline Museum, Rome. *Since the Romans worshiped the father and the emperor, there was a great demand for portrait busts. The museum on Rome's Capitol Hill has more heads than a Grateful Dead concert in a cabbage patch.*

up despite their stern dignity, but many are startling portraits of downright ugly people. We have a living history in the busts of the famous emperors: they come alive as people, not just as faceless names from the past.

When Rome faded as a political empire, much of her art lay dormant, ignored until the Renaissance (rebirth) of classical ideals a thousand years later.

Rome Rots

In the third century A.D., known as the "Age of Iron and Rust," the great empire started to unravel. Taxation rose to oppressive levels, people abandoned the cities, inflation (1,000 percent over twenty

Top Roman Sights Outside of Italy
France
  • Pont du Gard, near Avignon
  • Colosseum, theater, and arena; Nîmes and Arles
  • Theater and arch, Orange
Spain
  • Aqueduct, Segovia
Britain
  • Aquae Sulis spa and
    museum, Bath
  • Hadrian's Wall (best
    near Haltwhistle)
Germany
  • Porta Nigra and Con-
    stantine's basilica, Trier
Turkey
  • Ephesus, near Kusadasi
    (on west coast)
Croatia
  • Diocletian's Palace,
    Split
Switzerland
  • Avenches (Aventicum)

Pont du Gard, late first century B.C., *near Nîmes, France. This impressive Roman aqueduct, built without mortar 2,000 years ago, carried water to the citizens of a nearby Roman town.*

years) demoralized people, and barbarians were closing in on the borders. Politically, the government was more like a banana republic than a great empire. During one fifty-year period, 18 Roman emperors were assassinated. The army was no longer a provider; it was an expensive problem.

Like most ancient civilizations, Rome had a false economy based on slavery and booty. When Rome stopped expanding, the flow of booty (cheap resources) and slaves (cheap labor) that had fueled the empire for so long dried up. When a society reaches this point, it must do one of three things: begin living within its means, rot out at the core, or build up a big deficit. Hmmm.

Rome's tumble was a gradual process delayed by two strong rulers. Diocletian (ruled 285–305), recognizing that the empire was overextended, split it into an eastern half and a western half. He established a strict economic and political order after a century of chaos. In 304, Diocletian became notorious for carrying out the worst-ever persecution of Christians. Later, Constantine (285–340) moved the capital eastward to present-day Istanbul (named Constantinople in his honor). He ruled the eastern half, while Rome was left holding the crumbling West.

Christian Rome

Constantine (who witnessed the torture of many martyrs as a boy) made Christianity not only legal but also the official religion of Rome. He supported the Church with money and privileges. For its last 150 years, Rome was officially Christian.

Roman Art and Architecture in Italy

Rome
  • Colosseum, Forum, Circus Maximus, and Pantheon

Ostia Antica
  • Rome's ancient seaport

Pompeii and Herculaneum
  • Volcano victims (south of Naples)

Tivoli
  • Hadrian's Villa (near Rome)

Verona
  • Theater and Arena

People debate whether Constantine sanctioned the religion in a pragmatic move to gain the support of a growing, prosperous, and potentially law-abiding minority, or whether he really had, as he

A Roman relief of Jesus as the good shepherd.

claims, a Christian vision that helped him defeat his rival and co-emperor Maxentius in battle in A.D. 312. (The huge Arch of Constantine next to the Colosseum marks his victory.)

His mother was a devout Christian, famous within the church for her search for the actual cross of Jesus. Rome's embrace of Christianity was made easier by the scripture that explains how Jesus said to "give to Caesar that which is Caesar's and to God that which is God's."

A later emperor made Christianity Rome's only legal religion. In the year 300 you could be killed for being a Christian, and in 400 you could be killed for not being a Christian.

As you travel today, you'll see plenty of early Christian art. Common symbols include the good shepherd (Jesus carrying a lamb on his shoulders) as well as the fish (the Greek letters of which stand for the words: "Jesus Christ, son of God, Savior"). The Vatican Museum has a huge collection of such art.

But Rome's downfall was inevitable. In 476, the last emperor was tossed out by invading barbarians, and the Roman Empire's long terminal illness was over.

Rome's ghost lived on. Her urban nobility fled from the cities, establishing themselves as the feudal lords of medieval Europe's countryside. Latin, the Roman language, was the language of the educated and ruling classes throughout the Middle Ages. And the Roman Catholic Church inherited the empire's administrative finesse and has been ruled by a "pontifex maximus" ever since.

Top Museums of Ancient Rome

Rome
- Vatican Museum
- National Museum
- Capitoline Museum
- EUR Museum (scale model of ancient Rome)

Naples
- National Museum

Paris
- Louvre

Köln, Germany
- Romisch-Germanisches Museum

Timeline of the Ancient World

You've just absorbed 3,500 years of history and art. That wasn't so bad, was it? Before you shake the dust of the ancient world off and plunge into the Dark Ages, review what we've covered by perusing the timeline on the next page.

You can look at the march of history two ways: horizontally and vertically. Before you lie down, let us explain. The timeline shows civilizations moving horizontally (left to right) as they travel through time. But it also shows vertical history: related events that occur at the same approximate date. Look both ways to see how civilizations and artistic trends interact and relate.

Grauballe Man, A.D. *300 (Forhistorisk Museum Moesgard, Arhus, Denmark) Wallowing in the Stone Age*

Horizontally, we can see how each of the ancient cultures influenced the following one. The early Mesopotamian cities came first, followed by the stable agricultural civilization of Egypt. The Minoans from Crete influenced the mainland Mycenaeans, who slowly progressed economically and politically into the Golden Age of Greek culture. Alexander the Great spread this culture by conquest throughout the Hellenistic world, where it was later adopted by the growing Roman Empire. The sacking of Rome marks the end of the ancient world.

Notice that while culture moved progressively westward from Mesopotamia to Rome, Central and Northern Europe remained populated by barbarian tribes wallowing in the Stone Age.

Looking at vertical history, we see that political events (the upper half of the timeline) intertwine with art and architecture trends (lower half). For example, look up and down the chart around the year 500 B.C. and see how the Greek era of productive colonization and the successful war against Persia (in the upper half) financed the building of the Acropolis and the Golden Age of art (lower half).

ANCIENT WORLD

DCH

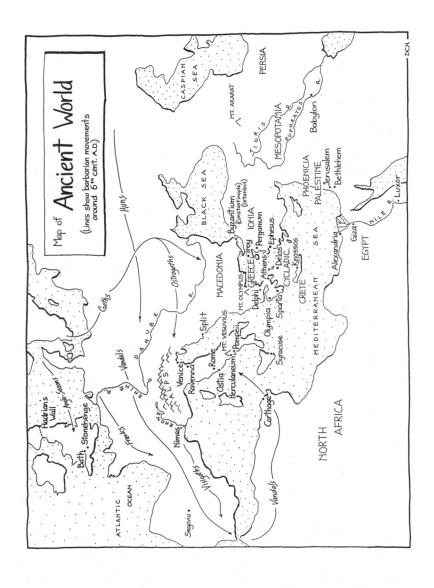

Map of **Ancient World**

(Lines show barbarian movements
around 6th cent. A.D.)

CASPIAN SEA

PERSIA

MT. ARARAT

MESOPOTAMIA

TIGRIS

EUPHRATES

Babylon

R.

Huns

BLACK SEA

Byzantium
(Constantinople)
(Istanbul)

IONIA

Pergamum

Troy

Ephesus

PHOENICIA

PALESTINE

Jerusalem

Bethlehem

Goths

Ostrogoths

R.

MACEDONIA

MT. OLYMPUS

GREECE

Delphi

Athens

Delos

CYCLADIC.

Knossos

Sparta

Olympia

CRETE

MEDITERRANEAN SEA

Alexandria

Gizα

EGYPT

NILE R.

Luxor

DANUBE

Vandals

RHINE R.

Split

ALPS

Venice

MT. VESUVIUS

Ravenna

Rome

Pompeii

Ostia

Herculaneum

Syracuse

Carthage

Hadrian's Wall

Bath

Stonehenge

Anglo-Saxons

Franks

RHONE R.

Nimes

Visigoths

Segovia

ATLANTIC OCEAN

Vandals

NORTH AFRICA

DCH

The Middle Ages
A.D. 500–1500

A thousand years separate the ancient and the modern worlds. These "Middle Ages" lasted from about A.D. 500 to 1500. The first half of the Middle Ages were the Dark Ages (500–1000) and the second half were the High Middle Ages (1000–1500).

The castles and cathedrals that fill the average tourist's scrapbook are the great physical accomplishments of medieval Europe. Nearly all of these came from the High Middle Ages. When you understand the religious fervor that built these cathedrals and the brutality that built the castles, they come alive. But first let's wallow in the darkness for about 500 years.

The Dark Ages (A.D. 500–1000)

By A.D. 500, Rome had collapsed. Three realms filled the power vacuum: the Christian church, the Byzantine Empire, and the barbarians of Northern Europe. While each of these helped kill Rome, they also helped preserve it.

Two of these realms, the church and the Byzantine Empire, are actually extensions of the old Roman Empire, dating from the reign of Emperor Constantine (A.D. 300). In trying to revive his fading empire, Constantine recognized the rights of the Christian church, a body that had grown, despite persecution, into one of the stabilizing institutions of the empire. Later, Christianity became Rome's official state religion.

The Church

The church bridged the ancient and modern worlds by carrying Rome's classical learning and administration through the Middle Ages and passing it along to the rising secular world during the Renaissance.

Church government was organized with the same hierarchies as the Roman government. Roman governors became Roman Catholic bishops, senators became cardinals, scholars became priests, and the pope even adopted the supreme title originally held by the emperor—Pontifex Maximus.

The Dark Ages, A.D. 500–1000

Monasteries preserved classical literature and the Latin language in Dark Age Europe. When Benedict set up what later became the most influential monastic order of the Middle Ages, he scheduled a daily program of monks' duties, combining manual labor with intellectual tasks such as translating and copying ancient texts, including works that were purely secular and even heretical.

Until the popes got the church organized into a central system (around A.D. 1000), the loose chain of monasteries was the center of Christianity. Monks were also the keepers of technological knowledge—about clocks, waterwheels, accounting, wine-making, foundries, gristmills, textiles, and agricultural techniques. Cistercian monasteries were leaders of the medieval industrial revolution of the later Middle Ages.

Intellectual life survived the Dark Ages in monasteries. Copying and translating Greek and Roman writings were common tasks for monks.

The Christian church preserved some of Rome's sheer grandness. Its great wealth, amassed from tithes and vast landholdings, was invested in huge church buildings, decorated as ornately as anything Rome had ever seen. The pomp and pageantry of the church rituals you might see in your travels is reminiscent of the glorious days of Caesar. For a taste of Caesar's Rome, visit Rome's lavish Christian basilicas (such as

Santa Maria Maggiore). As you stand in the shade of the huge ruined arches of the Basilica Maxentius in the Roman Forum, remember that houses of justice such as this one served as the architectural model for almost all Christian churches to follow.

The Byzantine Empire

The eastern Roman Empire, which became the Byzantine Empire, was another great preserver of Roman culture. In a desperate attempt to invigorate his failing empire, Constantine, around A.D. 330, moved his capital from Rome to the new city of Constantinople (modern-day Istanbul).

In a sense, this was the real end of Rome. The center of the civilized West packed up and moved eastward, where it remained for a thousand years while Europe struggled to establish itself. The emperor and his court—scholars, artists, and all—moved to the East, leaving the self-proclaimed emperors in Rome with no real power outside Italy.

We think of the Eastern Empire as Byzantine rather than Roman because it quickly took on an Eastern flavor. Its language, literature,

Byzantine Sights

Italy
- Churches and mosaics, Ravenna
- St. Mark's, Venice

Turkey
- Hagia Sophia Museum and Chora Church, Istanbul

Greece
- Mystra (near Sparta on the Peloponnesian Peninsula)
- Meteora pinnacle monasteries
- Mt. Athos monasteries (for men only)

Germany
- Charlemagne's Chapel, Aachen

France
- Sacré-Coeur (neo-Byzantine church), Paris

St. Mark's Basilica in Venice is covered with intricate Byzantine-style mosaics. Imagine paving a football field with contact lenses.

Byzantine Mosaic, A.D. *550,
Ravenna. The top Byzantine
art was mosaics made from
patterns of small stones and
glass. Mosaics in Ravenna,
Venice, and Istanbul (once
Constantinople) still glitter
with the glory of Byzantium.*

and art were Greek. The church followed "Eastern Orthodox" ways,
eventually splitting with the pope's Latin church.

Nevertheless, the Byzantine Empire had a great influence on the
West. Throughout the Dark Ages, the emperor in Constantinople
was considered by Christians and barbarians all over Europe to be the
civilized world's supreme ruler. Constantinople was the Christian
world's leading city for centuries.

After the Crusades lubricated communication between the East and
West, the long-forgotten classical Roman and Greek knowledge
returned to Europe. When Constantinople was finally overrun by the
Turks, scholars and artists fled to the West, where their knowledge
spurred the growing spirit of the Renaissance.

Constantinople, today's Istanbul, is an exciting brew of ancient past
and cosmopolitan present, Moslem East and Christian West.

Barbarian Europe

The third realm of the Dark Ages was a scattered and chaotic compost
pile of barbarian tribes from which modern Europe was to sprout. It
had no effective government and no sense of state, just small
autonomous tribes and peasant communities. Local life was isolated,
fragmented, dreary, illiterate, superstitious, and self-sufficient at best.
People lived like animals in huts, wearing the same homespun clothing
all year and rarely flossing.

Rome had shrunk to a ramshackle town of less than 50,000 people.
Wild beasts and outlaws flourished throughout the countryside.
Forests replaced cultivated land. Thoughts of an afterlife concerned
people more than secular growth. Money, trade, and progress had little to do with the "Dark" Ages (as we, with such an opposite outlook,
have termed those times).

Quietly, the seeds of modern Europe were planted. There was no
nation of France or England, but there were barbarian tribes of

Franks and Angles. The Dark Ages saw the emergence of local nations no longer dominated by Roman culture. The Franks were becoming France, and Angleland was to become England.

Life in the Dark Ages

The Fall of Rome was like a great stone column crashing across the Continent, burying Europe and scattering civilization like so much dust. It was 500 years before dazed Europeans began to pick themselves up from the rubble and build a new world. In the meantime, they lived lives of hardship, fear, and ignorance.

Skeletons unearthed by archaeologists show a people chronically undernourished, partly because of ineffective farming techniques. Infant and child mortality rates soared. Wise elders of a village might have been only in their thirties.

Whatever civilization the Romans had brought to the barbarians of Northern Europe died. Roads and cities, pillaged as quarries by local peasants, crumbled. There were few large towns and little trade; the economy was based on subsistence farming clustered around small villages. A bad harvest was a sentence for famine and death to a community isolated from outside help.

The Roman communication grapevine withered as fewer and fewer people learned to read and write. Priests and monks alone were literate or capable of simple arithmetic at a time when letters and numbers were believed by the unlearned to have magical powers. (Our modern word "clerk," someone who works with words or numbers, comes from "cleric.")

Feudalism

Dark Age Europe had no effective government. "King" was more an honorary title than a position of power. Government was in the hands of local nobles, barons, dukes, knights, petty lords, and the NRA.

A strict social and economic system called "feudalism" evolved to give this chaotic world some order and security. Feudalism carefully defined the duties of each class. Like chessmen, each group could move only a certain way. Each class was dependent on the other for its livelihood. The peasants pledged part of their crop to a local noble, who in turn gave them land to work and the promise of protection and a system of justice. This noble was in the service of a more powerful noble, and so on up to the king, the pinnacle of the feudal hierarchy.

The currency of feudalism was loyalty and land. A lower nobleman (vassal) promised loyalty (fealty) to a higher-up (lord) in return for use

```
┌──  Feudal terms: ──────────┐
│  fealty = loyalty                    │
│  fief = land, in return for fealty   │
│  lord = man above on feudal ladder   │
│  vassal= man below on feudal ladder  │
│  king = top rung of feudal ladder    │
│  serfs= near slaves who worked the   │
│        land of the lowest lord. This │
│        was manoralism. The manor     │
│        house was the lord's palace.  │
│  knight= moves up two and over one.  │
│        Worth about as much as a      │
│        bishop.                       │
└──────────────────────────────┘
```

of some land (a fief). One man's vassal was another man's lord. A strict code of honor cemented this two-way deal.

The feudal nobility played war for kicks. On sunny afternoons the knights suited up, trampled their peasants' crops, and raided the neighboring nobles' domains in an attempt to kidnap the lord. Most of medieval Europe toiled to survive while sons of the rich spent their leisure hours playing chivalrous games. The perennial pawns in this feudal chess game were, of course, the peasants.

Nobles hardly lived lives of luxury, though. Their castles were crude structures: cold, damp, and dark, with little privacy or warmth. Nobles were illiterate and proud of it. They looked down on educated people. The younger sons of nobles (who received no inheritance) were forced to become clergy. The rest lived lives that revolved around war, training for war, hunting, and feasting. Their feasts often became week-long bouts of drinking and rowdiness. "Medieval life was regulated by a calendar of feasts which governed the relations between the living and the dead, old and young, men and women, blending technology, magic, work, religion, workdays, and feast days into a satisfying whole" (Friedrich Heer, *Medieval World*).

Barbarians, Christians, and Medieval Justice

Life in the Dark Ages was clouded by the fear of barbarian invasions. Vikings from Scandinavia, Magyars from Hungary, Huns from Central Asia, and Moslems from Spain all threatened Europe. In the days before hard and firm political boundaries, the demographic map of Eurasia was in constant flux. Tribes everywhere were migrating away from danger and resettling in more hospitable lands. It wasn't until centuries later that the invaders were defeated or absorbed, and Europeans stopped finishing off their prayers with "and deliver us from the Norsemen, amen."

In a time when there was no effective central government, might made right. Basic protection was essential and expensive. Some estimate that 75 percent of Europe's total income was spent paying soldiers for protection. A king achieved autonomy only if he could organize protectors and keep them satisfactorily paid.

Europeans also had to contend with demons, devils, spirits of the woods and rocks, mischievous saints, and a jealous god. Magic and local folklore were woven into Christianity. Witches were burned. A sword could be put on trial for falling off the wall, as if a spirit had inhabited it. The hideous gargoyles that adorn Romanesque churches come straight out of the imagination of these superstitious and frightened people.

Justice was meted out in "trials by ordeal." The accused might have been forced to grab a red-hot iron or to pull a stone from a caldron of boiling water. If he was unharmed or the wound healed miraculously in a few days, he was innocent. If not, he was really punished. A woman accused of being a witch might have been bound and thrown into a lake. If she drowned, she was believed to be innocent. If she floated, she was believed to be guilty and burnt accordingly. These ordeals were usually held in or near the church, with a priest in attendance.

Trial by Ordeal. *The ancient "trial by ordeal" survived well into the Middle Ages. Here, two bishops lead a queen barefoot over a red-hot grate to determine whether she has been true to her husband (left). Notice the hand of God overseeing things.*

Medieval crime and punishment museum poster, Rothenburg, Germany

Look at a ninth-century history book and you can see the mix of magic, fear, fantasy, harshness, and ignorance of the Dark Ages. The years are boiled down to a few terrible and miraculous events, all told matter-of-factly. Some excerpts:

Account of the year A.D. 837: A gigantic whirlwind broke out and a comet appeared, emitting streams of light three cubits long before the amazed spectators. The pagans devastated Walicrum and abducted many women there, taking also huge sums of money.

The year 852: The steel of the pagans grew white-hot; an excessive heat of the sun; famine followed; there was no fodder for the beasts, but the feeding of pigs flourished.

The year 853: Great hunger in Saxony, with the result that many ate horses.

The year 857: A great plague with swelling of the bladder raged among the people and destroyed them with horrible festering, so that their limbs dropped off and fell away before death.

The church was the refuge from this awful and fearful world. God was a god of power, like an earthly noble, to fight the forces of evil. God's weapons were prayer, the Mass, and other rituals which, in the minds of the peasants, had magical power. Romanesque churches stood like fortresses in the war against Satan. To peasants, the church was a refuge from a dreary life and a hint of the glories that awaited them in heaven. If ever religion was "the opiate of the masses," it was in medieval Europe.

The church dominated every aspect of medieval life. A sin was a crime and vice versa. Religious authorities were the civil authorities. Tithes were taxes. God brought prosperity and He brought plagues. The Bible was the final word on all matters scientific, economic, social, and political. This began a thousand-year period during which theology was the leading science.

Throughout the Middle Ages, monasteries were a necessary institution to mediate intellectually between God and man. The year 529 was pivotal: Christian thought triumphed over secular thinking as the Emperor Justinian closed the Platonic Academy in Athens and the first monastic order, the Benedictines, was founded. From this point on, Europe's best minds struggled with the interpretation of God's word. Every sentence needed to be understood and applied. Answers were debated in universities and contemplated in monasteries. Since contemplation was considered the "highest service to God," the best and the brightest European minds remained silent.

In spite of the high-thinking monks, the folk religion changed little with the coming of Christianity. Old folk gods got new names. Christian churches were built on holy pagan sites. The good spirits of folklore became the saints of the church, but remained the powers to be bargained with for earthly favors. The church calendar, which established holy days (hence the word "holiday"), patterned itself after old pagan feast days. Even today, we celebrate Christmas much as the Druids of Britain celebrated the winter solstice, with trees and mistletoe.

While the Roman Empire was Christian from the time of the Roman Emperor Constantine, Christianity was slow to penetrate the northern countries. The Viking and Hungarian invasions in the eighth and ninth centuries slowed its spread. Not until A.D. 1000 could Europe be considered thoroughly Christian.

Viking Sights
Britain
  • Jorvik Exhibit, York
Norway
  • Ships at Bygdoy, Oslo
Denmark
  • National Museum, Copenhagen
  • Viking Ship Museum, Roskilde

Candles in the Wind: Dark Age Bright Spots

A few brave individuals nursed the flickering flame of civilization through the Dark Ages. They preserved the learning of the classical world until later economic prosperity allowed it to blaze again in society at large.

Of course, the whole world wasn't in a Dark Age. In Central America, the Mayans and Toltecs were building great cities and doing complex astronomical work. In China, the T'ang dynasty was flourishing. Many of the technological inventions that spurred Europe's recovery from the Dark Ages came from China: paper, clockwork, looms, tiger balm, spinning wheels, and gunpowder.

On the fringes of Europe, other cultures kept Greco-Roman learning alive. Byzantium was a stronghold of culture during Europe's Dark Ages. The Islamic countries, from the Middle East to North Africa to Spain, fostered science and literature while Europe was still groping for the light switch.

Even within Europe, not all areas were in complete darkness. Italy, closest to the source of Roman influence, kept in touch with the classical world even after its fall to the barbarians. Always linked by trade with the enlightened Byzantine world, Italy was even united briefly with the Eastern Empire under the Emperor Justinian (A.D. 550). The churches of Ravenna from this period are as magnificent as anything in Istanbul.

Spain and the Moors (711–1492)

When most of Spain and Portugal fell to the Moors (Moslem invaders from North Africa), the region's importance as an intellectual center increased. Islam was more tolerant of other religions than was medieval Christianity. In Spain, both Christians and Jews were allowed freedom and relative equality (for a fee). The interaction among the three cultures sparked inquiry and debate, producing some of the Middle Ages' finest scholars.

In 950, the library at Cordoba, Spain, held some 600,000 manuscripts. In the same year, there were only 5,000 manuscripts in all of France. As Christians gradually reconquered Iberia, Europe rediscovered a wealth of knowledge from ancient Greece and Rome.

All over Spain and Portugal, but especially in Cordoba and Granada (the last Moslem stronghold), you'll see impressive Moorish buildings.

Ireland

Fleeing the barbarian chaos of Continental Europe as Rome fell, missionary monks carried civilization to the western fringe of the known world. Ireland was the northern intellectual capital. When St. Patrick, a fifth-century Christian monk from Romanized England, established his faith in Ireland, he found excellent schools run by the native Celtic tribes that taught classical subjects. Patrick and his successors kept these schools open, mixing Christianity into the curriculum. Latin learning was re-infused into England and the Continent (as far inland as Switzerland) by Irish missionaries. Sights such as the evocative ruins of the church at Cashel, near Tipperary, remind us of the importance of Ireland during this period.

The Book of Kells (Trinity College, Dublin) and the Lindisfarne Gospels (British Museum) are the best examples of this monastic flowering from 500–900. Both are illuminated (illustrated) gospels showing classical, Celtic, and even Byzantine influences.

Symbolic of the darkness of the Dark Ages, illuminated manuscripts merely kept alive a flame that had been kindled long ago. Few ideas were flowing into or out of medieval Europe. The monks, keepers of the flame, were the conscientious objectors to the chaos of the Dark Ages. Checking into monasteries, they earned their keep by copying texts. It was a tedious task. To vent their creative spirits, they would decorate title pages or chapter headings. Illuminated manuscripts became the top art form of Dark Age Europe.

Page from **Book of Kells,** A.D. *9th century (Trinity College, Dublin). The illuminated manuscript was Dark Age Europe's greatest pictorial art form. Other fine illuminated manuscripts are exhibited at London's British Museum.*

Charlemagne and the Holy Roman Empire

Throughout the Middle Ages, popes and kings struggled to establish their power. While the popes were undisputed spiritual leaders, they needed a military alliance to effectively wield power. And being crowned by the pope wouldn't look bad on a king's résumé either. The alliance was born as the pope crowned Charles the Great, emperor of a "Holy Roman Empire," on Christmas day in the year 800.

The reign of Charlemagne (SHAR-luh-mayn)—Charles the Great, King of the Franks—was a bright light in the Dark Ages. He united most of the Western Christian world, from Germany to Sicily, and established what we call the Carolingian Empire, the largest since Rome. He was the protector of Christendom.

This was a mini-Renaissance. Drowsy Europe quivered and drooled with excitement at this "Roman revival." Charlemagne's capital city of Aix-la-Chapelle (present-day Aachen, Germany; well worth a visit) became the first capital of Europe. Trade and communication increased, and the court became a cultural center where artists and scholars worked to revive Roman ideals. Academia flourished, and classical works were studied and copied. It's said that Charlemagne could read a little (a rarity at the time) and went to bed each night with a slate to practice his writing.

Charlemagne personally set about to improve the lot of his people. He instituted trial by judge, replacing the barbaric trial-by-ordeal; revised the monetary system; built schools and churches; and advanced the Christian faith. Perhaps most important, *his* foot became *the* foot, a standard form of measurement (according to tour guides).

Despite the "Carolingian Renaissance," these were still the Dark Ages. Charlemagne was an enlightened but ruthless leader, responsible for the conversion of the pagan German tribes to Christianity. His chosen instrument of persuasion was the same used by later Crusaders—the sword. He invaded Germany, conquered it tribe by tribe, and gave the leaders a choice: convert or die. The Franks built churches that were really military outposts in the conquered lands. Resistance died hard, and the resisters died even harder; it's said that Charlemagne once ordered the decapitation of 4,500 pagans in one day.

Charlemagne was the top-dog ruler, but the Franks who succeeded him were wieners. When he died, his empire was divided among his three sons into realms that became Germany, France, and the smaller countries. His successors returned to their quarreling ways, and as they bickered, the light of the Carolingian Renaissance flickered out.

Later kings in Germany and Austria claimed to rule a revived "Holy Roman Empire" like Charlemagne's; but their kingdoms, as Voltaire pointed out, were neither holy, nor Roman, nor an empire. It was to be a long time before Europe enjoyed being ruled by another leader of Charlemagne's stature and shoe size.

Charlemagne's reign was a turning point in the early Middle Ages. Before his time, it seemed that darkness might dominate forever. Afterward, hope in the restoration of learning and civilization was rekindled.

End of the Millennium

Much of Europe figured life would come to an end in the year 1000. After all, the Biblical book of Revelation says an angel came down and bound the devil for 1000 years "after which he must be loosed a little season." In the 990s, business stopped and people focused only on salvation. The streets were filled with people whipping themselves in remorse.

The year 1000 came and went. So did 1001. Europe breathed a sigh of relief and set about preparing for the best millennium ever. With a burst of energy, a 300-year-long boom time began.

The High Middle Ages (1000–1500)

At the turn of the first millennium, Europe began waking up. It made some basic economic, political, and ideological changes that culminated a few centuries later in the Renaissance. For the previous 500 years, progress could have been graphed as a straight, horizontal line. Now that line soared upward, carrying Europe into the modern age.

Barbarian invasions were no longer a great threat, and people settled down. Feeling secure, Europeans built and planned for the future. Natural power sources were harnessed by the windmill and water-wheel. Agricultural advances such as improved plows and harnesses and crop rotation increased productivity. Fewer farmers were needed to feed the society. Towns grew up, offering newly upwardly mobile peasants ("numpies") an exciting alternative to life under their feudal masters. Urbanization increased trade and improved communication. Europeans were no longer hopelessly isolated in a dark feudal struggle for subsistence. Europe perked up, experiencing the same enthusiasm that marked the United States' westward movement. Land was cleared and roads and bridges were built as Europe flexed its muscles.

Dark Age thought was anchored in Augustine's City of God notion that there is one truth for both heaven and earth. New thinkers were accepting Aristotelian reason and rising above Dark Age mysticism. After 700 years of "theology rules," scholars were now fascinated by the natural world. The City of Man became as worthy of study as the City of God.

Romanesque Art (1000–1200)

Whether you like it or not, you'll probably spend a lot of time in Europe's churches. They're huge, free, usually open, and right on the main square. With a little background, they come alive.

Medieval life revolved around the church. Typically the only stone structure in town and a landmark for miles around, the church was the political, religious, and even recreational center of the town. The lavish churches, surrounded by bleak hovels, offered the medieval peasant a glorious promise and an escape from the almost endless drudgery of feudal life.

The Romanesque style is the first real "European" art form, named for its Roman features—columns and rounded arches—which create an overall effect of massiveness and strength. Romanesque churches are like dark fortresses with thick walls, squat towers, big blocks of stone, few windows, dark interiors, and a minimum of decoration. Over the years, the massive "tunnel" vaults lightened up into the graceful ribbed vaults of the Gothic style.

Romanesque church. Called "Roman"-esque for its round arches and columns. Considered Europe's first real architecture, it featured fortress-of-God designs, small windows, and dark interiors.

Medieval churches were based on the ancient Roman "basilica" floor plan. The pagan temples of Rome were designed to house only the image of the god, not crowds of worshipers. But Christians worship together and the Mass requires a large meeting hall. So when Christianity became Rome's adopted religion, new churches were modeled not after her temples, but after the largest Roman secular structures: Roman law courts, or basilicas. The same basilica floor plans that you'll see in the

Roman Forum (Basilicas Aemilia, Julia, and Maxentius) were used in nearly every medieval church.

A basilica has a long central hall (nave) with narrower halls on either side, and at the far end, a semicircular area (apse) around the altar. An aisle that forms a cross with the main hall, called a transept, was added so that the building looked more Christian, but the basic pre-Christian basilica plan remained.

This floor plan was ideal for accommodating large congregations, especially the massive processions of pilgrims who came to worship Christian relics (such as a piece of Jesus' cross or the bone of a saint). Pilgrims would amble up one side aisle, around the altar, and out the other aisle, worshiping at each chapel along the way. Columns separated the walkways (ambulatories) from the long central nave where the congregation stood (sitting in church hadn't been invented yet).

Medieval churches are like a compass, always facing east, toward Jerusalem. The portal (entry) is therefore the "west portal," the transepts point north and south, and the altar is at the east end. Memorizing the terms used in the last few paragraphs will make you an informed medieval churchgoer.

Medieval Religious Art

Although the floor plan of churches was essentially Roman, the Romanesque decorations were strictly Christian. Theologians wondered, "What is art's place in the church?" The Bible stated explicitly that no "graven images" should be made for worshiping. Did that include paintings? Craftings of nature? Illustrated Bible stories? The debate lasted for centuries. By the year 600, it was generally agreed that art had great value in worship as a way of educating and inspiring the masses of illiterate Christians. Remember, most Middle Age Europeans couldn't read, write, or speak Latin, the language used in church services. They went to church to "read" the stories of their religion as told in sculpture, stained glass, tapestries, and paintings.

The images carved into the walls and doors of churches were every bit as effective as the priest's sermon. Typically, devout peasants could look at scenes of lost souls, naked and chained, being dragged off to Hell. On Jesus' right would be the blessed faces looking to heaven, hands obediently folded, content with the promise of a happy afterlife. Escapist theology was as attractive to feudal peasants (and their overlords) in medieval Europe as it is to 20th-century peasants (and their overlords) in Central America.

Basilica Aemilia, *179 B.C. (Forum, Rome). The floor plan of pre-Christian law courts became the model for churches throughout the Middle Ages. Notice the central nave (where the tourists are walking) flanked by narrower side aisles.*

Church architecture, the designing of God's house, was the most respected medieval art form. Arts such as sculpture and stained glass were okay because they embellished the house of God. Statues were tucked into niches carved in the church wall. Stories were told in low-relief, protruding only slightly from the wall or surrounding material (as opposed to freestanding statues).

MEDIEVAL CHURCH FLOOR PLAN

European churches have basilica-style main halls with transepts added to give the rectangular basilicas the shape of a Latin cross. Note: A "cathedral" is not a type of church architecture. It's simply a church that's a governing center for a local bishop.

Tympanum (the semicircular area above the door) of a Romanesque church. Here you'll find a Romanesque church's most interesting sculpture. Notice how cluttered these narrative reliefs look—a far cry from the bold, freestanding statues of ancient Rome and the coming Renaissance.

A church's most interesting and creative sculpture is often found in the tympanum (the arched area above the door) or hiding in the capitals of the columns along the nave. Sculptors were allowed a little craziness here, and it's fun to see their grotesque fantasies peeking through the capital's leaves, filling nooks, and sticking out of crannies.

Because medieval art is mostly Christian art, realism and classical beauty took a back seat to getting the message across. Artists concentrated on inspiring and uplifting the peasants by boiling their subjects down to the essential details—just what was necessary to convey the point of the story. Pictures became symbols that stood for ideas and actions rather than representations of real things. A lion was meant to be a symbol of the resurrection, not a lesson in zoology.

Classical techniques that made art realistic were forgotten. Medieval art was stiff, unreal, and two-dimensional. Figures looked as if they'd been cut out of paper and pasted into random groups. Background, shading, depth, and proportion didn't matter. Scenes were often overcrowded.

When considered in its context and for its narrative function, there's plenty of very good and creative Romanesque art. The artist wanted to teach and inspire the viewer, and being freed from the

Hell, *13th century (San Giovanni baptistery, Florence)*

constraints of realism enabled the medieval artist to experiment with new (and often bizarre) color schemes, compositions, and proportions, sometimes exaggerating them to enhance the spiritual effect.

Top Romanesque Art and Architecture
Britain
- Cathedral, Durham

Germany
- Aix-la-Chapelle (Charlemagne's church and relics), Aachen
- Cathedrals of Trier, Worms, and Speyer

France
- Bayeux Tapestry, Bayeux
- Cathedral, Vezelay
- Basilique St. Sernin and Augustins Museum, Toulouse
- Carcassonne (medieval walled town)
- Sarlat (medieval town)
- Many small village churches in Burgundy

Spain
- Santiago de Compostela (cathedral), Santiago

Italy
- Cathedral, Leaning Tower, and Baptistery, Pisa

Bayeux Tapestry *(detail), about 1080 (Tapestry Museum, Bayeux, France). This 900-year-old embroidery tells the story of the Battle of Hastings when, in 1066, the Normans under William the Bastard—soon to become "Conqueror"— of France invaded and began their conquest of England. Typical of Romanesque art, realism takes a back seat to narration. Bayeux, a pleasant town, is only 2 hours by train from Paris.*

The final product, although far from "classical," is impressive, inspirational, and beautiful on its own terms.

Medieval art, like Chinese, Byzantine, and Egyptian art but unlike our culture's art, had no need to be original. A donor would commission an artist to create a replica of an existing piece of art, possibly with finer materials but with no demand for particular originality. The artist would have no problems with copying someone else's work. It's like our notion of music. For your wedding you hire an organist and a singer, not to come up with new music but to redo nicely something you already know you like.

While most medieval art was religious, plenty of secular art decorated castles. Unfortunately, little survives. While churches and church art were respected, protected, and saved, secular work was destroyed, abandoned, or built over.

Crusades (1100–1250)

With the new millennium, Europe was feeling its oats. This new progressive spirit showed itself in the aggressive "holiness" called the Crusades, a subject you'll encounter often in your sightseeing.

The Crusades were a series of military expeditions promoted by various popes and kings to recapture or protect the holy city of

Jerusalem from Moslem invaders (who also considered it holy). Although Crusades began as religious missions, nearly anyone could find a self-serving reason to join these holy wars of prophets and profits.

The East enjoyed luxuries dreamed about by many Europeans. As merchants hoped, the Crusades reopened lucrative trade routes from Europe to the East. Nobles enjoyed this opportunity to conquer new land for fiefs, while their knights sought adventure, glory, and spoils in the Crusades. The pope's prestige and authority seemed to soar with each Moslem killed, and Christians chased salvation by converting "heathens" and protecting Jerusalem.

Although the Crusades finally failed with the Moslem capture of Jerusalem (and, later, Constantinople), they did have a great effect on Europe, giving it a broader, more cosmopolitan outlook. They opened a floodgate of new ideas from the East and brought back many classical ideas that the West had lost during the Dark Ages. The Crusaders also learned important stoneworking skills that helped Europeans build the great castles and churches of the Middle Ages. And the majestic flavor of sacred Byzantine art showed up clearly in Western art.

Venice emerged from the Crusades the big winner. Europe's appetite had been whetted by the East's luxury goods, and sea-trading Venice

Canaletto, Doge's Palace in Venice (Uffizi, Florence)

established itself as the dominant intermediary. The Venetians prospered, expanding to control the entire Adriatic area politically and to become Europe's economic powerhouse until new trade routes to the East were developed several hundred years later by Vasco da Gama and others. Today Venice's past glory decays elegantly and her lavish architecture reflects her former lucrative position at the crossroads of East and West.

Castles and Sieges

Like a tortoise fighting a stone—that was medieval warfare when impregnable castles dotted Europe's landscape. War was a drawn-out, costly struggle as one side laid siege to the other. The only good thing to be said was that casualties were few and far between. Boredom was the common enemy of attacker and attacked.

The medieval castle was a simple stone structure consisting of a central "keep," or main building, surrounded by a wall. The keep was usually built on a hill, cliff, or mound of earth. The wall enclosed the castle yard where the people lived. This mound and yard (or "motte and bailey") pattern was the basis of all medieval castles.

Later castles were much bigger, with more rings of walls as much as twenty feet thick. The Crusaders had been impressed by the massive castles and walled cities of the Byzantines and applied many of their techniques to their castle-building back home.

Outside the wall was the moat, a ditch filled with water (they put alligators in them only in fairy tales). The main gate was made of oak, plated with iron, and often protected by a portcullis, or iron grill. Above the gate were twin towers, often four stories high, with small windows for shooting at the enemy.

The keep was the headquarters and home of the lord, used as a dining hall, ballroom, and as a last bastion if/when the outer walls fell in an attack. Despite their impressive architecture, castles were cold, damp, and uncomfortable. A lord who commanded thousands had fewer creature comforts than a 20th-century suburban dog.

Against such a formidable structure as a castle, an attacker's main weapon was hunger. The enemy camped around the castle and waited for supplies to run out. This often took years, and given the poor communication and supply lines of the period, the attacker might well run out of supplies first.

During a siege of Carcassonne (Europe's greatest walled fortress city) in southern France, the city ran desperately low on food and was about to surrender. The attackers (who happened to be the

Carcassonne, *Europe's greatest medieval fortress city*

army of Charlemagne), after waiting for years, were getting really restless. In a stroke of genius, a townswoman fed the last of the food to the last pig and threw the pig over the wall. Splat. When the invaders saw how well-fed the pig was, they figured the people inside had plenty of food, so they packed up and headed home. The town was saved.

But the patience of military men wears thin, and later on, castles were stormed with a number of ingenious weapons. Catapults, powered by tension or counterweights, were used to fling huge boulders or red-hot irons over the walls. Under cover of archers armed with crossbows and 6-foot longbows, armies would approach the castle and fill the moat with dirt. Then they would wheel up the "storming towers," built of wood and covered with fire-resistant wet hides, and climb over the walls. They battered weak points in the wall and gate with a wood-and-iron battering ram. They even tried tunneling beneath the walls.

The defenders poured boiling water and burning pitch onto the invaders. From the turrets, archers fired arrows, flung missiles, and hurled insults. Others were stationed along the walls to overturn ladders and storming towers. Once the attackers got inside the castle, battle was fierce hand-to-hand combat. More likely, though, the

The Siege: *Medieval castles gave defenders the edge. Any decent castle was a pain to attack. Some castles were simply avoided, written off as unconquerable. The "starve 'em out siege" approach was the most common. Some sieges lasted years, until hunger or boredom won out. The advent of gunpowder ended the days when the best offense was a good castle.*

Rheinfels castle *(artist reconstruction), b. 1245, Germany*

defenders simply retreated behind the next inner wall to start the process over again.

Warfare changed dramatically with the coming of gunpowder. When the Turks besieged Constantinople in 1453, they had a new weapon: a 19-ton cannon that fired 1,500-pound rocks more than a mile in the air. The era of gunpowder had arrived, and the castle walls of Europe fell. Within a century, the siege style of warfare that had gone on almost unchanged for 2,000 years was a thing of the past.

Early castles evolved from primitive ditch and stockade fortifications. Sites offering natural fortification, like a hilltop surrounded by a river, were preferred. As ditches became moats and stockades became stone walls, castles took the form we think of today.

Many of the castles you'll see in Europe today never had a military function. After 1500, lords built castle-forts for protection and castle-palaces for domestic life. In the romantic era of the 1800s, many castles, like those of Bavaria's Mad King Ludwig, had no practical purpose and were merely fantasy abodes.

Top Medieval Castles

Germany
- Burg Eltz and Cochem Castle on the Mosel River
- Many castles along the Rhine (Rheinfels and Marksburg are best) from Mainz to Koblenz

Italy
- Reifenstein Castle, Vipiteno

Britain
- Tower of London, London
- Warwick Castle, Warwick

Switzerland
- Château Chillon, Lake Geneva

France
- Langeais and Chinon, Loire Valley
- Beynac, Dordogne
- Carcassonne, Languedoc

Burg Eltz, on Germany's Mosel River

Knights, Ladies, Love, and War

King Arthur and the Knights of the Round Table—Lancelot, Galahad, Perceval, and company—are the ideal of medieval life, where men are always chivalrous and women are always kidnapped by dragons. Even though Arthur and the knights are pure fiction based on a minor historical figure, the myth played a big role in medieval thinking.

Knights of the Middle Ages followed an unwritten code of honor and chivalry that demanded valor in battle and service to their king, God, and ladylove. Originally intended for knights alone, it was quickly accepted by all nobility in Europe, whose lives revolved around war, religion, loyalty, and (occasionally) love.

Knights were warriors who pledged their fighting skills to some powerful lord in return for land, a title, or money. Knights on horseback were much more important than the average mercenary foot soldier. With the invention of stirrups, the rider could dig in and put force behind the lance he carried. A single knight could charge and break the ranks of dozens of foot soldiers. Dressed in a heavily armored suit (so heavy that if he fell off he was as helpless as a belly-up turtle), a mounted knight was like a tank among infantry.

Later descendants carried the title of "knight" earned by their warrior forefathers, even when they themselves took no part in war. The code of chivalry still applied to these gentlemen of high society. In fact, the word for "gentleman" in several languages (French, *chevalier*; Spanish, *caballero*; Italian, *cavaliere*), like the word chivalry itself, comes from the Latin word for "horseman."

When there were no real wars in which they could demonstrate their courage and skill, knights held tournaments, fighting each other individually or in teams. The most common event, the joust, sent two knights charging at each other on horseback, each determined to unseat the other by using his lance. Sure enough, many knights died in these "sporting" contests. In later tournaments, an attempt was made to try to minimize injury by using blunted or wooden weapons, saving the sport but diminishing the danger (like modern fencing). Still, as late as 1559, France lost a king (Henri II) when a wooden splinter pierced his visor during a joust.

Medieval pageantry and contests such as jousting are reenacted energetically in many of Europe's colorful festivals. Try to work a few of these festivals into your itinerary (such as the Saracen's Joust in Arezzo, Italy, on the second Sunday in September, or the medieval Children's Fest in Dinkelsbuhl, Germany, in mid-July).

The heroic deeds of knighthood were proclaimed in story and song by troubadours, wandering poet-singer-storytellers of the Middle Ages. These men were not journalists by any means; they didn't tell of real men performing real deeds. Instead, they created an ideal world of loving knights and lovely ladies. Their stories set the pattern of behavior for medieval lords and ladies.

Camelot: Henry, Eleanor, and Courtly Love

The closest Europe ever came to a real "Camelot" was the court of King Henry II and Queen Eleanor of Aquitaine, rulers of a united England and France during the short-lived Angevin Empire (1150–1200). Henry was the perfect Arthur—strong and intelligent, with a dominating personality. Eleanor was the refined, strong-willed, and beautiful Guinevere with a healthy dose of political savvy thrown in. Their son Richard the Lionhearted had, by contemporary accounts, the attributes of all the Knights of the Round Table rolled into one.

Their court was Europe's center for troubadours and young knights, for days spent in jousting and nights under the stars listening to stories and songs.

It was here that a new element was added to the old warrior's code of chivalry and love. The knight of this period had to be not only valiant in war but gentle in love as well. The new code was known as "courtly love."

Love was a radical notion in a society where marriages were arranged by parents, primarily for monetary and political gain. It was the brainchild of highly educated ladies of the court tired of being treated as bargaining chips in the marriage game. They insisted that both parties, the man and the woman, had to consent for a marriage to be valid.

Queen Eleanor had strong personal reasons for supporting romantic love and opposing arranged marriages. She and Henry had become estranged when Henry took a mistress (no big deal) and insisted on being seen with her in public (big deal). She was also aware of the fate of a young kinswoman, Alais, who had been given to young Richard for a bride. Because Richard was away on Crusade, Henry thought nothing of taking Alais for his own, keeping her a prisoner for 25 years. At his death, she was freed only to be married off to a lesser courtier.

The new code of chivalry demanded that the knight serve his lady first; next in importance came service to God and king. In tournaments and battles, it was customary for the knight to wear a token from the lady, perhaps a handkerchief or a flower.

The main theme of the troubadours' songs of love (*chansons d'amour*) was unconsummated love. The knight is head over heels for the lady but, alas, she is married or somehow beyond his reach. Nevertheless, the knight accepts this hopeless situation, pining for his true love and doing all in his power to please her, while knowing she can never be his. The songs alternate between the ecstasy of love and the bitterness of longing.

In the court of Queen Eleanor, "rules" of love were drawn up to "educate" the young men about how they should act toward the ladies. Knights had to give up their baser passions, thinking always of what would please their beloveds. Here are some of the court's "Twelve Rules of Love" (from a 12th-century book, *The Art of Courtly Love*):

—Marrying for money should be avoided like a deadly pestilence.

—Thou shalt keep thyself chaste for the sake of thy beloved. (A radical idea for the time.)

—In practicing the solaces of love thou shalt not exceed the desires of thy lover.

—Thou shalt not be a revealer of love affairs.

—Thou shalt be in all things polite and courteous.

—Thou shalt be obedient in all things to the command of ladies, and strive in the service of Love.

Historical fact shatters any illusions that Henry and Eleanor created a real-life Camelot. But the ideals of chivalry lived on long after knighthood lost its warring function. The 17th-century English gentleman and the *gentilhomme* of France owed much to the medieval code. The duel replaced the tournament as a test of courage.

The last gasp of true romantic chivalry in literature was the tragi-comic fictional figure of Don Quixote (written in 1610). Ridiculed by his contemporaries, he held fast to the old ideals, jousting with wind-mills when there were no other true knights left to fight.

Birth of Nation-States

During the High Middle Ages, feudalism gave way to urbanism. Cities broke the rural feudal mold. Merchants were natural allies of a national government, which offered political stability, uniform laws, coinage and measurements, freer trade, and independence from the whims of feudal lords.

An hour's cruise down the Rhine River, lined with castles (each a separate "kingdom" in its day), tells the story. In earlier times, a trad-ing ship might have crossed 35 "national" boundaries and paid 35 customs duties just to take a load downstream. The urbanites wel-comed a king who could keep the peace between the feuding feudal nobles, creating a larger political unit more conducive to efficient business and trade.

The time was ripe for the emergence of Europe's large states. England and France appeared in something like their modern form. When William the Bastard (of Normandy) crossed the English Channel in 1066 and became William the Conqueror, he set up a strong central government and forced a greater unification of England's feudal lords.

England became part of the Angevin Empire, which, by the time of Henry II and Queen Eleanor of Aquitaine, stretched from Scotland south through western France to the Pyrenees. However, when Henry's and Eleanor's son Richard the Lionhearted died, England returned to fragmented rule by local nobles. An assembly of nobles cemented their newly recovered autonomy by forcing the new King John to sign the Magna Carta (1215), which constitu-tionally guaranteed that the king was not above the law. This set the stage for hundreds of years of power struggles between strong kings and strong nobles (who later formed the Parliament).

The French bits of the shattered Angevin Empire were conquered and united, and France emerged as Europe's superpower.

Church versus State

Throughout the Middle Ages, kings and popes played tug-of-war with temporal power. After the year 1000, on the crest of a spiritual revival, a series of energetic popes reformed the church, the monasteries, and communications networks, establishing the papacy as a political power to rival the kings.

In many ways, the medieval church operated like a nation without borders. It was Europe's greatest landowner, taxed through tithes, influenced political decisions on all levels, and attracted Europe's most talented men to work in its service. Local kings and princes saw this rich and powerful so-called spiritual organization as a meddler in their material realm.

This pope–king thing came to a head in the debate over who had the right to appoint bishops. The pivotal battle of wills was between Pope Gregory VII and "Holy Roman Emperor" Henry IV of Germany.

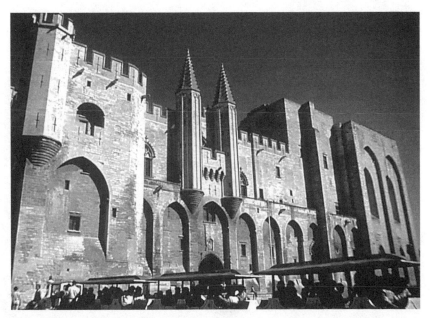

Papal Palace in Avignon

The powerful German king appointed a bishop against the pope's will and was excommunicated. Despite his military might, Henry learned that his people supported him only if he was in good with the pope. Fighting for his political life, he "went to Canossa" (Italy, 1077) to beg forgiveness of the pope. The famous image of the Holy Roman Emperor kneeling for hours in the snow outside Gregory's window reminded later leaders that the pope was supreme.

As explained earlier, the Vatican endorsed the Holy Roman Empire in return for its protection of papal interests around Europe. In the 14th century, the balance of power tipped away from both the emperor and the pope. The pope was moved to a palace in Avignon where he "ruled" from 1309 to 1377 as a puppet of the French king. A second pope was installed in Rome during this "Babylonian Captivity." The papacy never recovered from this humiliation, and as powerful nation-states emerged, the power of the Holy Roman Empire also ebbed.

Note that earlier, the church and nobles shaped European history. Later, popes and kings joined in. Coming up, we'll see how the city class (French Revolution) and the working class (Socialist Revolution) were dealt onto the card table of European history.

Monasteries

While the church played power politics and grew rich and corrupt, monasteries worked to keep the focus on simplicity and poverty. Two strong orders of monks, the Dominicans and the Franciscans, emerged in the 12th and 13th centuries. The image from the movie *Brother Sun, Sister Moon* of a Christlike St. Francis walking down the Vatican aisle to ask an Oz-like pope to consider the possibility that the Church had lost its way is a powerful one. But even determined Franciscans and Dominicans dressed in sackcloths couldn't resist the rich mortals of Europe throwing their wealth at them in hopes of a better chance at salvation. Monasticism peaked in the 13th century.

Gothic Art (1150–1400)

The combination of church wealth, political stability, and a reawakened spiritual fervor brought Europe a new artistic style—Gothic. Centered in rich, stable northern France, this style replaced the gloomy, heavy Romanesque with an exciting lightness and grace.

From the first page of the Bible, it's clear that light is divine. Abbot Suger, who "invented" the Gothic style in 1144 at St. Denis outside Paris (rebuilt, and not worth visiting today), wanted to create a cathedral of light. Europe followed suit, building churches with roofs held up by skeletons of support, freeing the walls to become window holders. Now when Christians went to church, they were bathed in the light of heaven.

Gothic architecture began with certain technical improvements over Romanesque. In a Romanesque church, the heavy stone roof arched over the supporting pillars like a bridge. These pillars had to be fortified into massive walls to support the weight, leaving only tiny windows and a dark place of worship.

Gothic architects, masters at playing one form against another, knew that while round arches send the weight of the roof straight down, pointed arches would send it outward. With pointed arches, churches could be built higher than ever while buttresses—rather than thick, fat walls—did the supporting. By using pointed arches in a crisscross pattern, spanning diagonally from column to column, the architects increased the strength still more.

To counteract the outward pressure, Gothic architects reinforced the walls with buttresses. "Flying" buttresses project away from the church several meters, offering even greater support while taking up even less wall space. In the end, the church was supported by a skeleton of columns, ribs, pointed arches, and buttresses. The roof became taller than ever and glorious stained glass windows lit the place of worship.

Stained glass became a booming new medium for artists and an excellent opportunity for more narrative art to be "read" by the devout but illiterate peasants.

The basic arches of medieval architecture

SCHEMATIC GOTHIC SECTION
(ARROWS SHOW BALANCING STRUCTURAL FORCES)

It takes 13 tourists to build a Gothic church: six columns, six buttresses, and one steeple.

The Gothic style evolved from a simple start to an elaborate finale. The basic supportive ribs of the kitty-corner arches (vaulting) were surrounded by a web of purely decorative arches called "tracery." Over time, this tracery became fantastically elaborate and complex and was often covered with gold. The last, most overripe stage in Gothic is called "flamboyant" (flamelike). You'll see the English version of flamboyant Gothic, called "perpendicular" Gothic, in the Henry VII Chapel of London's Westminster Abbey or King's College Chapel in Cambridge.

The Gothic style was very competitive. With architects, sculptors, and painters traveling all over Europe to compare and study new churches, Gothic church design was remarkably consistent.

Italy tempered the tense verticality inherent in Gothic architecture (pointy spires) to make it more compatible with the horizon-

Sainte Chapelle, *b. 1246, Paris. Supine view.*

King's College Chapel, (b. 1446–1515), Cambridge, England. The Gothic style evolved into a very ornate "flamboyant" (flamelike) stage known as "perpendicular" in England. Here nearly all the wall space is devoted to brilliant stained glass. The essential ribbing on the ceiling is decorated with extra tracery, or purely ornamental riblets. This is aptly called "fan vaulting."

tal stability (domes) that came with her classic roots. This is particularly evident in the great Italian Gothic cathedrals of Florence (capped by Renaissance domes), Siena, and Orvieto—not so tall, no flying buttresses, and more likely to please a Caesar. These churches make up for their stubbiness by sporting more colorfully decorated facades.

But there was more to Gothic than church architecture. There was a delight in things of beauty. Abbot Suger's favorite saying, "Man may rise to an understanding of the divine through the senses," is the intellectual basis of the Gothic love of things beautiful. Church sacristies and museums are filled with finely carved and inlaid works of Gothic art.

Throughout Europe, these largest economic enterprises of the Middle Ages represented an unprecedented technical accomplishment and tremendous spiritual dedication. The building of a Gothic church dominated the rich and poor alike of an entire area for generations. Paris' Notre-Dame took 200 years to complete.

Sculpture took a giant leap forward in Gothic times. No longer just pillars with faces, as Romanesque statues tended to be, Gothic sculpture was more natural and freestanding. Many classical techniques were used, especially in making clothing appear to drape naturally over the body. Sculpted faces reflected personality and emotions. But art was still considered to be a religious tool, and, like Gothic stained glass, every piece of sculpture had a symbolic message.

Notre Dame *(b. 1163–1345), Paris, France*

Duomo *(b. 1386–1809), Milan, Italy*

Dom *(b. 1248–1880), Köln, Germany*

Gothic Sculpture. *Romanesque sculpture is "low relief" (embedded deep in church walls and niches), cluttered, and tells a story. Gothic protrudes from the wall and shows a sense of calm, orderly composure. Still, Gothic carvings are symbolic rather than realistic, and sculpture remains supportive of the architecture, far from the bold freestanding works of the Renaissance.*

A Gothic church was carefully designed to be and usually still is a place of worship, not a museum. If you think of it as just a dead building to wander through and photograph, you'll see the nave but miss the boat. To best experience a Gothic church, see it in action. Attend a service.

Gothic cathedrals are especially exciting when filled with music. Attend a concert or enjoy an "evensong" service. Meditate, cup your hands behind your ears, and catch every echo as the music rinses the medieval magic into your head. Follow with your eyes the praying hands of the arches; the fingers point upward to heaven. Be dazzled by the warm light of the sun shining through the glistening treasure chest that

Altar *built to house the Crown of Thorns, Sainte Chapelle. Relics were an important focus of worship in the medieval church. The king of France paid more for this crown than he paid for the Sainte Chapelle, which was built to house the relic. Many great altarpieces are ornate relic-holders.*

Favorite Gothic Cathedrals

France
- Ste. Chapelle (best pure Gothic and glass), Paris
- Notre Dame (fine carving, view from top, gargoyles), Paris
- Reims (medieval and Chagall stained glass)
- Chartres (fine glass and carvings, great tours by Malcolm Miller or his associate)
- Mont St. Michel (worthwhile evening sound and light show)

Germany
- Köln (best in Germany, great early art, worth a tour)

Britain
- King's College Chapel (best glass in Britain; bright, boxy perpendicular style; Rubens masterpiece), Cambridge
- Salisbury (fine setting, copy of Magna Carta)
- York Minster, York (Britain's best)

Spain
- Toledo (best in Spain, sacristy has one of Europe's top collections of paintings, especially El Greco)

Italy
- Orvieto (ornate facade, great Signorelli paintings)
- Milan (a forest of Sequoia pillars and a fantasy rooftop open to the public)

was melted down and painted onto the timeless windows. A Gothic church can be as alive as you are.

Pre-Renaissance Troubles: The Black Death

"When was such a disaster ever seen? Even heard of? Houses were emptied, cities abandoned, countrysides untilled, fields heaped with corpses, and a vast, dreadful silence settled over all the world."
　　　　　　　　　　　　　　—Petrarch, 14th-century Italian writer

The medieval equivalent of a nuclear holocaust, the bubonic plague—or "Black Death"—killed as much as one-third of Europe's people in three long years (1347–1350). The disease spread quickly, killed horribly, and then moved on, leaving whole cities devastated in its wake. The economic, physical, and emotional shock is unsurpassed in European history. Most saw the plague as not just a disease but a heavenly curse "sent down upon mankind for our correction by the just wrath of God." Whatever the cause, it killed with such power and swiftness that "the living could scarcely bury the dead."

The Bubonic Plague: Origin and Symptoms

The plague came out of Central Asia. In 1347, Mongols, who were sieging a Genoese trading town on the Black Sea, had the plague. The clever commander catapulted diseased corpses into town and it spread. One ship escaped, bringing its terrible cargo to Sicily. By 1348, this plague had spread through Italy, France, and all of Europe. An estimated 30 million—one-third of the entire European population—died. The disease is caused by a bacteria carried by fleas (which travel on rats). Humans get it when bitten by the fleas, and then spread it by coughing. The unsanitary conditions in medieval Europe allowed the disease to move rapidly northward. London, Vienna, Florence, and Avignon (the papal city at the time) were particularly hard-hit. In Florence alone, 100,000 died within four months. In some cities, 90 percent of the population was wiped out.

The symptoms were quick and harsh. The first sign was sneezing (hence, "bless you"), followed by the appearance of lumps or "buboes" (hence, "bubonic") in the groin or armpits, fever, constant vomiting (often blood), diarrhea, pneumonia, and, almost inevitably, death within three days.

So many died so quickly that there was no place to bury them. The survivors resorted to mass graves. After the churchyards were full, they made vast trenches where bodies were heaped. The disease was so infectious that it seemed impossible to avoid. The most frightening part was that nothing could be done to help the afflicted, and they were abandoned by the healthy to avoid contagion.

Convinced the plague was a punishment from God, certain fanatics thought worldwide repentance was necessary. The "Brotherhood of the Flatulence" tried to take the sins of Europe upon themselves. They marched through the cities, calling on the citizens to join them as they scourged themselves with whips. They became more popular in some areas than the priests, whose rituals had been powerless before the plague.

The Danse Macabre. *Fourteenth-century Europeans believed everything was going to Hell—which was an eternity of people dancing the chicken.*

Europe Recovers: The Black Plague's Silver Lining

The plague eventually became just a lingering memory in Europe's collective subconscious. Petrarch, who witnessed the horror of the plague years, correctly prophesied: "Posterity, will you believe what we who lived through it can hardly accept? . . . Oh how happy will be future times, unacquainted with such miseries, perhaps counting our testimony as a mere fable!"

Strange as it may sound, some good came out of all the loss of life, creating the economy that would support the Renaissance more than a century later. With fewer people, labor was scarce, and the common worker could demand a better wage. Technology itself had not been affected by the plague, and there were now fewer people to divide the fruits of that technology.

The survivors went on a materialistic and hedonistic buying spree, trying to forget the horrors they'd seen. Luxury goods—fancy clothes, good food and drink, lavish houses, entertainment—were in high demand. For the first time, the lower classes enjoyed such "luxury items" as chairs, dishes, and fireplaces.

With so many people dead, there was a surplus of clothes and cloth. This was used to make "rag paper" and for the first time, books became affordable. Later, when Constantinople fell to the Turks and the rich Byzantine culture fled west, a hunger for classical learning was stoked. Gutenberg's printing press and the success of the vernacular languages over Latin made knowledge even more accessible.

Now any educated person could read and afford books. And books were a powerful agent for change.

The Hundred Years' War

England and France fought each other on and off from 1337 through 1453. The war had more than enough causes. At the start, England controlled southwest France (Gascony). The French tried to take that area back. Fueling the fire, the French supported the Scots in their fight with England. The French even tried to control the English wool trade in Flanders. English and French fishermen bickered over rights in the English Channel. Finally, in 1337, when King Edward III of England claimed the French throne (because his mother was the sister of three French kings), war broke out.

Since France was three times as rich and populous as England, it managed to lose most of the battles and still win the war. Peasant rebellions, pillaging by unemployed soldiers, and an outbreak of the black plague all made this period even more of a mess.

The war sped the decline of feudalism, boosted the formation of a strong French state, and established England as a sea power.

The most famous figure of the war, a charismatic teenager named Joan of Arc, inspired the French to victory (even though she was captured by the English and burned as a witch). In the end, England lost all its holdings in France (except the port of Calais, which it lost a hundred years later).

More Pre-Renaissance Troubles

Europe suffered other labor pains in the century before the Renaissance. Besides the plague, Europe was rocked by wars: Germany ripped itself to shreds in a lengthy civil war, while England and France fought the bloody "Hundred Years' War."

The monopoly of the papacy led to corruption and extravagance within the church. Its giant bureaucracy had become flabby and self-perpetuating, and the popes lived in a grander style than any king. When there were two popes (one in Avignon and one in Rome), they excommunicated each other. No one knew whose ring to kiss. Reform was badly needed.

It was a strange and troubled time, and social neurosis swept across Europe. People figured it had to be the wrath of God. The popularity of witchcraft soared; devil appeasement and death cults had much of Europe doing the *danse macabre*. Some figured, "What the heck, the end is near" and dove headlong into one last hedonistic fling.

The wars, like the plague earlier, thinned out and vitalized society. The dead were mostly Europe's poor. For the first time, demand for laborers exceeded the supply. The European ship of state had to treat its bilge rats with a little more respect. A lean Europe was primed and ready to ride the waves of the future. Serfs up.

Relax . . .

You've just covered 1,000 medieval years. Before you leave the Dark Ages and enter the bright glow of the Renaissance, let your eyes adjust and take a break.

The Middle Ages—the bridge between the ancient and modern worlds—are often misunderstood. Review the timeline. Overlay your travel dreams on the map of medieval and Renaissance Europe.

Timeline of the Medieval World

After the fall of Rome, civilization stumbled through the Dark Ages, buoyed by the Christian church and, later, by contact with the Byzantine empire and Islamic nations. At first, Europe had little connection with the Byzantines and Moslems and little cultural activity, as shown by the blank lower half of the chart.

Then, in the pivotal year 1000, great changes began. The Crusades sparked cultural exchange between East and West and a new spiritual awakening. Increased agricultural production, industry, and trade brought new prosperity.

Looking vertically at history, we see the fruits of these High Middle Ages in the rise in building and art. The spiritual awakening and prosperity inspired the construction of many churches in Romanesque and, later, Gothic style. France, then Italy, England, and Germany, each developed its own type of Gothic, becoming increasingly more decorative. The Crusaders brought back Eastern knowledge of castle-building, and soon every feudal lord had his own stone home.

As the European economy became more productive, centered in towns and relying more on trade and industry than on subsistence farming, feudalism was replaced by larger political and economic units. With two popes, the Catholic Church lost its political power. The Black Plague and costly wars further destroyed the old order. But all that blood and chaos fertilized the fallow soils of European civilization. The modern world was about to blossom.

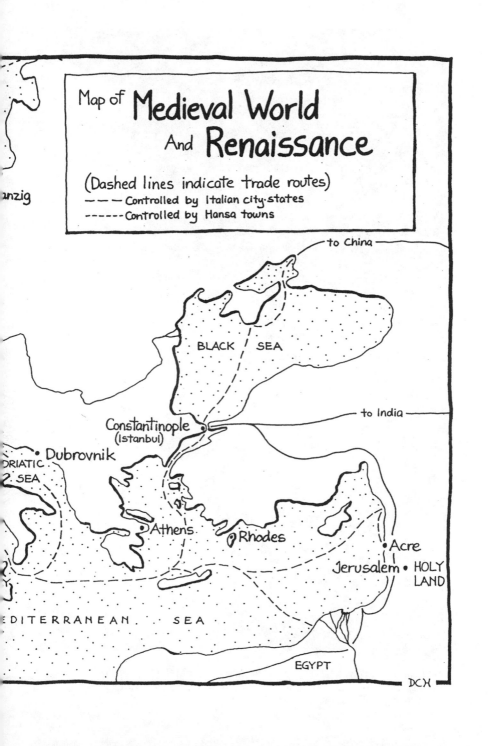

Map of **Medieval World** And **Renaissance**

(Dashed lines indicate trade routes)
———— Controlled by Italian city-states
------ Controlled by Hansa towns

anzig

to China

BLACK / SEA

to India

Constantinople
(Istanbul)

• Dubrovnik

DRIATIC
SEA

Athens

Rhodes

• Acre
Jerusalem • HOLY
LAND

EDITERRANEAN . SEA

EGYPT

DCH

Michelangelo, **David,** *1504 (Accademia, Florence). The face of the Renaissance. Man was the shaper of his destiny, no longer merely a plaything of the supernatural.*

The Renaissance
A.D. 1400–1600

"Renaissance" means rebirth. The Renaissance was the rebirth of the classical values of ancient Greece and Rome. Northern Italians, taking a fresh, new, secular view of life, considered themselves citizens of a new Rome.

The new Renaissance man was the shaper of his destiny and no longer a mere plaything of the supernatural. Individualism and humanism skyrocketed, and life became much more than a preparation for the hereafter. People were optimistic and confident in their basic goodness and in their power to solve problems. This new attitude freed an avalanche of original thinking and creativity that gave our civilization its most exciting and fertile period of art since that great Greek streak 2,000 years earlier.

The Renaissance also did more for tourism than any other period in history. All over Europe, but especially in Italy, today's visitors set their touristic sights on the accomplishments of the creative geniuses of the Renaissance.

The Renaissance was a period of new birth, as well as rebirth, which laid the foundation of the modern world. Politically, the modern nation-state was born. Economically, as capitalism replaced feudalism, the middle class was born. Intellectually, this period spawned the Protestant Reformation, humanism, modern science, and an age of secular thought.

Italy was the perfect launch pad for this cultural explosion. As the natural trading centers and intermediaries between the East with its luxury goods and the West with its merchants, Italy's cities were rich. Venice alone was bustling with 100,000 people and 3,000 ships in 1400. The East–West trade shuttled many classical ideas, which had fled eastward with the fall of Rome a thousand years earlier, back to Italy. Italy never completely forgot her classical heritage, and she welcomed its return.

The Renaissance followed the money: born in the trading and banking capital of Florence, it migrated to Rome (as the pope gave the Vatican a face-lift) and then settled in Venice.

Northern Italy was the most urban corner of Europe. In 1400, 26 percent of its people were city-dwellers, compared with the mere 10 percent of the English who lived in cities. Italian cities were generally independent, not having to cope with a pope or worry about a king. They did their own thing, and that required participation in government, more literacy, and better communication. This urban metabolism stimulated commerce and industry. The cities actively recruited skilled craftsmen, and the social structure became more flexible, offering the working class hope for improvement.

New ways of thinking brought prosperity. The most talented and ambitious men of the Middle Ages had served in the church. Now an active life of business and politics was considered just as meaningful and respectable as the passive, contemplative life of the monastery. Chasing money was no longer considered shameful, as long as the wealth was used properly. Secular schools based on Roman models became popular. Throughout Europe, educated upper-class people had a common culture based on a common secular morality and a common language (Latin). There was a new international network besides the church to cut across borders and spread new ideas.

The Renaissance was not the repudiation of God; it was the assertion of humankind. In 1450, a Florentine author summed it up: "The world was created not for God, who had no need of it, but for man. Man is the most perfect work of God, the true marvel of His genius. Man has his end not in God, but in a knowledge of himself and his own creativity."

Renaissance Florence: Cradle of the Modern World

There was something dynamic about the Florentines. Pope Boniface VIII said there were five elements: earth, air, fire, water . . . and Florentines. For 200 years, starting in the early 1300s, their city was a cultural hive. Art historians refer to the great Florentine centuries as the Florentines did, by dropping a thousand years. The Trecento (300s), the Quattrocento (400s), and the Cinquecento (500s) were the 1300s, 1400s, and 1500s.

Florence's contributions to Western culture are immense: the whole revival of the arts, humanism, and science; the seeds of democracy; the modern Italian language (which grew out of the popular Florentine dialect); the art of Michelangelo, Leonardo, and Botticelli;

the writings of Machiavelli, Boccaccio, and Dante; and Amerigo Vespucci, who gave his name to a fledgling continent. Florentines considered themselves descendants of the highly cultured people of the Roman Empire. But Florence, even in its Golden Age, was always a mixture of lustiness and refinement. The streets were filled with tough-talking, hardened, illiterate merchants who strode about singing verses from Dante's *Divine Comedy*.

Florentine culture came from money, and that money came from the wool trade, silk factories, and banking. It had a large middle class and strong guilds (labor unions for skilled craftsmen). Their success was a matter of civic pride, and Florentines showed that pride in the mountains of money they spent to rebuild and beautify the city.

Technically, Florence was a republic, ruled by elected citizens rather than a nobility. While there was a relatively large middle class and some opportunity for upward mobility, power lay in the hands of a few wealthy banking families. The most powerful was the Medici family. The Medici bank had branches in ten sites in Europe, including London, Bruges (Belgium), and Lyon (France). The pope kept his checking account in the Rome branch. The Florentine *florin* was the monetary standard of the Continent.

Florence dominated Italy economically and culturally, but not militarily. The independent Italian city-states squabbled and remained scattered until the nationalist movement four centuries later. (When someone suggested to the Renaissance Florentine Niccolo Machiavelli that the Italian city-states might unite against their common enemy, France, he wrote back, "Don't make me laugh.")

Lorenzo de Medici (1449–1492), inheritor of the family's wealth and power and his grandfather Cosimo's love of art, was a central figure of the Golden Age. He was young (20 when he took power), athletic and intelligent, a poet, horseman, musician, and leader. He wrote love songs and humorous dirty songs to be sung loudly and badly at carnival time. His marathon drinking bouts and illicit love affairs were legendary. He learned Greek and Latin and read the classics, yet his great passion was hunting. He was the Renaissance Man—the man of knowledge and action, the scholar and man of the world, the patron of the arts, and the shrewd businessman. He was Lorenzo the Magnificent.

Lorenzo epitomized the Florentine spirit of optimism. Born on New Year's Day and raised in the lap of luxury (Donatello's *David* stood in the family courtyard) by loving parents, he grew up feeling that there was nothing he couldn't do. Florentines saw themselves as part of a "new age," a great undertaking of discovery and progress in man's history. They boasted that within the city walls there were more "nobly gifted souls than the world has seen in the entire thousand years before." These people invented the term "Dark Ages" for the era that preceded theirs.

Lorenzo surrounded himself with Florence's best and brightest. They formed an informal "Platonic Academy," based on that of ancient Greece, to meet over a glass of wine under the stars at the Medici villa and discuss literature, art, music, and politics—witty conversation was considered an art in itself.

Their "neo-Platonic" philosophy stressed the goodness of man and the created world; they believed in a common truth behind all religion. The Academy was more than just an excuse to go out with the guys: the members were convinced that their discussions were changing the world and improving their souls.

Arts and Artists in the Renaissance

Botticelli was a member of the Platonic Academy. He painted scenes from the classical myths that the group read, weaving contemporary figures and events into the ancient subjects. He gloried in the nude body, which he considered God's greatest creation. In Botticelli's art we see the lightness, gaiety, and optimism of Lorenzo's court.

Another of Lorenzo's protégés was the young Michelangelo. Impressed with his work, Lorenzo took the poor, unlearned 14-year-old boy into the Medici household and treated him like a son.

Michelangelo's playmates were the Medici children, later to become Popes Leo X and Clement VII, who would give him important commissions. For all the encouragement, education, and contacts Michelangelo received, the most important gift from Lorenzo was simply a place at the dinner table, where Michelangelo could absorb the words of the great men of the time and their love of art for art's sake.

Lorenzo the Magnificent

Artists thrived on the patronage of wealthy individuals, government, church groups, and guilds. Botticelli commanded as much as 100 florins for one work, enough to live for a year in high style, which he did for many years. During the High Renaissance, artists mingled with scholars and people of wealth—a far cry from earlier generations, when artists were anonymous craftsmen.

Although artists were sought after in high society, some were rather odd ducks. Leonardo da Vinci, though very learned and witty, was considered something of a flake who never finished his projects. His claim to fame as a youth was his fine lute-playing. Michelangelo put people off by acting superior.

The great masters were friends and rivals. When the established Leonardo and the young genius Michelangelo competed for the commission to paint a battle mural in the town hall, all eyes were on them. (Raphael even interrupted his studies to visit Florence for the event.) Both submitted much-admired rough sketches or "cartoons." Competition between their fans was fierce. Michelangelo's cartoon was ripped up in jealousy by one of Leonardo's pupils, but the artists treated one another with respect.

Botticelli, **The Birth of Venus,** *after 1482 (Uffizi, Florence). More graceful, thinner, and more flowing than the massive figures of Masaccio and Michelangelo. Her long neck and smooth skin appear almost medieval.*

Competition and jealousy showed itself in other ways, however. Vasari, the painter and biographer, insulted Leonardo's slow working pace and bragged that he himself had done the painting in the entire Roman chancellor's palace in 100 days. (Michelangelo responded, "It's obvious.")

Savonarola: A Return to the Middle Ages

Even with all the art and philosophy of the Renaissance, violence, disease, and warfare were present in medieval proportions. For the lower classes, life was as harsh as it had always been. Many artists and scholars wore swords and daggers as part of everyday dress. This was the time of the ruthless tactics of the Borgias (known for murdering their political enemies) and of other families battling for power. Once, Lorenzo himself barely escaped assassination during Mass.

Fifteenth-century Florence was decaying. The Medici banks began to fold due to mismanagement and political troubles. The city's wealth had brought decadence and corruption. Even Lorenzo got caught with his hand in the till. Many longed for a "renaissance" of good old-fashioned medieval values.

Into Florence rode a Dominican monk named Savonarola, preaching fire and brimstone and the sinfulness of wealth, worldly art, and secular humanism. He was a magnetic speaker, drawing huge crowds, whipping them into a frenzy with sharp images of the corruption of the world and the horror of hell it promised. "Down, down with all gold and decoration," he roared, "down where the body is food for the worms." He presided over huge bonfires where his believers burned "vanities" such as fancy clothes, cosmetics, jewelry, and wigs, as well as classical books and paintings.

When Lorenzo died the worldly Medicis were thrown out, replaced by a theocracy with Jesus Christ at its head and

Savonarola

Savonarola ruling in His absence. The theocracy (1494–1498) was a grim part of the Renaissance. Many leading scholars and artists followed Savonarola's call and gave up their worldly pursuits. Vice squads of boys and girls roamed the streets chastising drinkers, gamblers, and over-dressed women. Even so, governmental and church reforms promised by Savonarola were never accomplished.

As the atmosphere of general fanaticism faded, so did Savonarola's popularity. In April 1498, to prove his saintliness and regain public support, he offered to undergo the "ordeal by fire"—to be burned at the stake and escape unharmed. At the last minute he got cold feet, backed out, and was arrested. Then he had no choice. He was hanged and burned at the stake in the town square. (A plaque on Florence's main square marks the spot.) The Medicis returned.

Florence in 1500 was a more somber place than it had been during the heady days of Lorenzo. Botticelli, under Savonarola's spell, had given up painting his nudes and pagan scenes, letting the melancholy side of his personality come out.

The center of the Renaissance gradually shifted to Rome, but her artists were mostly Florentine. In the 15th century, the Holy City of Rome was a dirty, decaying, crime-infested place, unfit for the hordes of pilgrims

*Botticelli, **Slander**, 1495 (Uffizi, Florence). The Florentine Renaissance passed. Savonarola turned the city into a theocracy. High thinking is clubbed and dragged ingloriously past Renaissance statues that look down from their perfectly proportioned world with shock and disbelief. Ideal Venus looks up at God and seems to say, "Not the Dark Ages again!"*

that visited each year. The once-glorious Forum was a cow pasture. Then a series of popes, including Lorenzo's son and nephew, launched a building and beautification campaign. They used fat commissions (and outright orders) to lure Michelangelo, Raphael, and others to Rome. The Florentine Renaissance, far from over, moved southward.

Renaissance Art

The Renaissance accomplishments most obvious to the tourist are those in art and architecture. The art of the 15th and 16th centuries is a triumph of order, harmony, and the technical remastery of the secrets of the classical artists which had been lost during the Middle Ages. This period also saw the discovery and exploration of many new artistic techniques.

Like Greece's Golden Age, the Renaissance was a time of balance between stiff formality and wild naturalism. Later, in the Baroque period (as in Greece's Hellenistic era), the artists went overboard in their naturalism, losing the sense of order in their works.

Renaissance art has many classical characteristics: realism, glorification of the human body, nonreligious themes, and an appreciation of beauty for its own sake. As in Greece and Rome, the focus was earthly and humanist. As in classical times, balance—between emotion and calm, between motion and rest, and among the various figures in the composition—was very important. Medieval art showed God's viewpoint. Space and time didn't matter. Now, perspective attached the viewer to the scene.

Acquiring beautiful art was a rich man's hobby. The new secular patronage stimulated art, giving it more pizzazz. The artist was hired to please the viewer sensually and to satisfy the patron. Youth, the good life, and wealth were sexy. Rich merchants of the Italian city-states commissioned art for their personal collections and for public display as a show of civic pride. They wanted art to reflect the power, dignity, and vitality of humankind.

The medieval church's monopoly on art was broken. Secular patronage opened new realms for artists previously confined to religious subjects. Pagan themes were very popular.

Many Renaissance artists were devout, however, and created works more emotional and moving than anything produced during the Middle Ages. They glorified God by glorifying humanity, His greatest creation. Religious themes were portrayed more realistically, emphasizing the human aspect. In Michelangelo's *Pietà*, the suffering of

Jesus and his grieving mother are shown not symbolically, but graphically. Michelangelo intentionally elongated Jesus' dead body to exaggerate its weight and the burden of sadness borne by Mary.

In the past, like anonymous laborers, artists had groveled for a prince's commission. During the High Renaissance, when every town and court was competing for a famous artist's work, the tables turned—the artist could almost dictate his terms and create what he wanted for whichever lucky prince landed him. Even though he still had a patron to keep happy, the artist could create more freely than ever before.

Raphael and Leonardo were both wealthy and famous. Their presence at a party made the evening. Artists of the Renais-

*Michelangelo, **Pietà**, 1500 (St. Peter's Cathedral, Rome). Sculpted when Michelangelo was 22. The dead Christ is held by the eternally youthful Virgin Mary.*

sance deserved the respect they got. They merged art and science; their apprenticeship required mastery of the mathematical laws of perspective. They studied nature as a biologist would. They studied human anatomy as avidly as a doctor, learning not just how the body looks but also how it works, so they could catch it in motion. They were well-rounded Renaissance men.

Technical expertise, secular patronage, and the classical love of sheer beauty raised Europe to an unprecedented level of artistic excellence.

Renaissance Architecture

The proud people of the Renaissance looked down on the "Middle Ages" that separated the glorious ancient world from their own glorious time. They labeled the art "Gothic" after the barbarians who looted Rome. To them, Gothic cathedrals looked tense, strained, and unstable. The Renaissance architect turned to his ancient Roman forefathers and developed, or rediscovered, a style that was round, geometrical, stout, symmetrical, domed, and balanced.

*Brunelleschi, **Cathedral Dome,** 1420–1436, Florence. Inspired by the ancient Pantheon, this dome in turn inspired later ones, from Michelangelo's to the present.*

Filippo Brunelleschi fathered Renaissance architecture, traveling to Rome to carefully measure and study the classical buildings and monuments. Back in his hometown of Florence, he conscientiously copied Roman styles, building with columns, arches, pediments, and domes.

Courtyard of a Medici Palace *by Michelozzo, 1450, Florence. Typical Renaissance architecture: balance, symmetry, arches, Corinthian columns, track lighting, circles, and squares.*

Top Renaissance Architecture

Italy
- San Miniato al Monte (church on a hill), Florence
- Cathedral dome, Florence
- Hospital of the Innocents (Brunelleschi), Florence
- Uffizi Gallery (the building), Florence
- Pazzi Chapel, Florence
- St. Peter's dome, Rome
- Tempietto, Rome
- Campidoglio square (Michelangelo), Rome
- Urbino Palace, Urbino
- Many palaces in Venice
- Palmanova, a planned town (north of Venice)

France
- Chambord, Chenonceaux, and other châteaus in the Loire Valley

Palmanova, 1593, near Udine, northeast of Venice. In the Renaissance, every snowflake's the same.

Brunelleschi's masterpiece was the huge dome of Florence's cathedral, a triumph of beauty and science, demonstrating that Renaissance architects were the equals of the great builders of Rome. It was the model for many domes to follow. The classical order and the harmony of his design caused great excitement, inspiring other artists to mix Roman forms with original designs.

Italian architects and artists, in demand throughout Europe, had no shortage of commissions to build secular palaces, homes, and public buildings in the Renaissance style. The pope hired Michelangelo to travel to Rome and design the dome of St. Peter's, Christendom's greatest cathedral. French kings built Renaissance châteaus on the Loire, and even the Russian tsar imported Italian expertise to remodel Moscow's Kremlin in the new style.

Renaissance church design echoed the upbeat optimism and confidence of the time by trading the medieval Latin cross floor plan (symbolic of the Crucifixion) for the Greek cross floor plan (four equal arms symbolizing the perfection of God and the goodness of man, who was made in His image).

Early Renaissance Sculpture: Donatello

Like the ancients, Renaissance sculptors concentrated on portraying realistic, three-dimensional, natural, and preferably naked human bodies. They posed their statues classically, catching their subjects balanced between motion and rest.

Donatello (1386–1466) was the first true Renaissance sculptor, combining the skill of creating classical sculpture and the personality of the Renaissance artist. His statues show his classical attitude toward the human body.

Sculpture gradually emerged from the shadows of church architecture. At Chartres, the stiff column-like figures are embedded in the Gothic wall, entirely supportive of the architecture. Nanni's *Four Saints* has Renaissance solidity, but is still niched deep within the wall. Nanni sat on the cusp of the revolution. Donatello's confident *St. George* steps right up to the edge of his niche and looks boldly into the future. Renaissance Man is stepping out. A few years later, Donatello's *David* stood on his own in the light of day: proud, naked, and ready to do a little fencing.

To see how far Donatello had progressed from Gothic sculpture, compare it with Nanni di Banco's *Four Saints*, done at the same time for the same church. Donatello's *St. George* stands boldly on the edge of his niche, but just around the corner, Nanni's saints hide within a deep Gothic niche, attached to half-columns, afraid to step from the safe support of the church into the light of day. Donatello freed sculpture from its thousand-year subservience to architecture.

These works were commissioned by the church and civic organizations. But another Donatello work, *David,* funded by a private citizen for private display, is an example of how secular patronage freed the artist from medieval constraints.

Donatello's *David* was the first freestanding male nude sculpted since ancient times. During the Middle Ages, it would have been condemned as a pagan idol. Although the subject matter comes from the Bible (the boy David killing the giant Goliath), it's just an excuse for a classical study of a male nude. The focus is on the curves of the body (no longer a "dirty" thing), not the action or the

Di Banco, **Four Saints,** *1413 (Orsanmichele Church, Florence)*

Cathedral sculpture, *1140, Chartres, France. "Going up."*

Donatello, **St. George,** *1416 (Orsanmichele, Florence). He stands like a symbol of the Renaissance man: alert yet relaxed, strong yet refined, aggressive yet Christian. The serene beauty of medieval art was being replaced by the defiant and determined new outlook.*

Donatello, **David,** *1430 (Bargello, Florence). The first freestanding male nude sculpted since Roman times, this boy David (looking like Boy George) is blatant art for art's sake.*

Sculpture gradually emerged from the shadows of church architecture. At Chartres, the stiff, columnlike figures are embedded in the Gothic wall. Nanni's Four Saints has Renaissance solidity but still sits deep in a niche. Nanni sat on the cusp of the revolution. Donatello's confident St. George steps right up to the edge of his niche and looks boldly into the future. Renaissance Man is stepping out. A few years later, Donatello's David stood on his own in the light of day: proud, naked, and ready to do a little fencing.

facial expression. The statue is a simple appreciation of beauty. Art for art's sake.

Renaissance Painting

The great Florentine painters were sculptors with brushes. They painted the same way the ancient Greeks had sculpted, making solid figures that had great weight, solemnity, and presence. Many of them, such as Michelangelo, were equally famous for sculpting and painting. During the Renaissance, both painting and sculpture evolved from the flat symbolism of medieval art to three-dimensionality and full realism.

Giotto (pronounced "ZHOTT-o," 1267–1337), who preceded the High Renaissance by 200 years, made the first radical break with the medieval past. He is the father of modern painting. Nothing like his astonishing paintings had been seen in a thousand years. Medieval artists painted stiff, two-dimensional figures with no sense of movement. Backgrounds didn't matter. No one cared about depth. Subjects were icons as seen from God's perspective. Painters told religious stories with symbols.

But Giotto takes us right to the scene of the action. He places his figures on a 3–D landscape, giving them depth, weight, and individuality. It's as though he has created small theater vignettes, designing the stage scenery and then peopling it with actors.

Much of his art was Gothic (pointed arches, gold-leaf backgrounds, halos, no visible light source, and unrealistic scale), but he was influenced by Byzantium and made great strides toward realism. The Byzantine influence

Giotto, **Ognissanti Madonna,** *1310 (Uffizi, Florence). Single-handedly, Giotto nearly started the Renaissance a century before its time. To give depth to this painting, he used shadows and an architectural framework.*

Giotto, **Return of Joachim to the Sheepfold,** *1305 (Arena Chapel, Padua, Italy). Working for the illusion of 3–D, he painted sculptural people in realistic settings. The background (the cliff) and foreground (the sheep) give the scene lifelike depth.*

gave Giotto the classical techniques of light and shading (which the Byzantine East had stored in an artistic time-capsule since the fall of Rome) and foreshortening, which gives the illusion of depth. His style excited the West and stimulated a renewed interest in the classics.

Giotto was famous and in demand throughout Italy. This popularity for a painter was as revolutionary as his work. Giotto made it into all the gossip columns. Anecdotes were told about his social wit as well as his skill as a painter.

A century later, Masaccio carried Giotto's techniques further by using light and shadow to depict depth and drama. Applying the mathematical laws of perspective that Brunelleschi developed, Masaccio portrayed objects receding into the distance (for example, a tree-lined road). Masaccio, another Florentine (who died at the age of 27), was more influential than he was famous. The anatomical realism and dramatic power of his paintings (such as *The Expulsion of Adam and Eve from the Garden of Eden*) inspired many masters who followed.

After Masaccio, lesser painters grappled with the new problems of perspective. Paolo Uccello's *Battle of San Romano* looks like a crowded, colorful, two-dimensional work in the medieval style. It's only when we look closer that we see it as a study in perspective: all the fallen weapons form a three-dimensional grid superimposed on

Three Expulsions:
Medieval, Early Renaissance, and High Renaissance

Medieval church of St. Michael,
1015, Hildesheim, Germany

Masaccio, **Brancacci Chapel,**
1425, Florence

Michelangelo, **Sistine Chapel,**
1508–1512 (Vatican Museum, Rome)

In these three looks at the expulsion of Adam and Eve from the garden of Eden, compare medieval, early Renaissance, and high Renaissance views of the same scene. Notice the artistic differences, as well as how man's view of himself in relation to God changes. In the medieval example, Adam and Eve are puny, bug-like creatures, ashamed of their nakedness and helpless before God. In Masaccio's painting, you feel the agony of a lifelike, suffering Adam and Eve. Michelangelo shows a strong Adam with a gesture that almost says, "All right, already, we're going!" While Adam knows he and Eve will survive, Eve wonders, "Shouldn't we be wearing our money belts?"

the background. The fallen soldier at left is scarcely larger than the fallen helmet at right in Uccello's awkward attempt at foreshortening. All in all, it's a fascinating but weak transition from two-dimensional Gothic to three-dimensional Renaissance realism.

Uccello, **Battle of San Romano,** *1455 (National Gallery, London). Panels from this early attempt at 3–D traveled from Lorenzo's study to the Uffizi, the Louvre, and London's National Gallery.*

Perspective was mastered by relief artists of the period, such as Donatello and Lorenzo Ghiberti. Donatello achieved the effect of infinite background in his low-relief of St. George and the Dragon, beneath his statue of St. George at Orsanmichele. In Ghiberti's famed bronze doors of Florence's Cathedral baptistery, we see Brunelleschi's influence. The Story of Jacob and Esau (one of ten Bible scenes on the door) includes imaginary Brunelleschian architectural forms in the background receding into the distance.

Botticelli (pronounced "bott-i-CHELL-ee," 1445–1510) excelled in his mastery of color, detail, and line. Not as sculptural as Masaccio, Michelangelo, and other Renaissance artists, Botticelli's figures have a pure, elegant, yet dreamlike quality. He mixed Gothic grace and fleshy classicism in his popular and wonderfully restored masterpieces *La Primavera* and *The Birth of Venus* (both in Florence's Uffizi Gallery). A master diplomat, Botticelli was able to do justice to the pagan classical scenes he loved while not offending the religious powers with too much flesh.

Ghiberti, **Story of Jacob and Esau**, *1430*
(Baptistery, Florence). The contest to decorate the
bronze doors of Florence's Baptistery encouraged
artists throughout the city. Here, the winning
artist shows mastery of depth and perspective.

Brunelleschi's entry and Ghiberti's entry. You be the judge. Here are the two
*finalists for the **Baptistery door** competition. Which do you like the best?*
The originals stand side by side in Florence's Bargello Museum.

(Ghiberti's, on the left, won.)

Botticelli, **Allegory of Spring,** *1482 (Uffizi, Florence). Pagan innocence. Botticelli was part of a youthful band of Florentines who saw beauty as an expression of the divine.*

The High Renaissance: Leonardo, Michelangelo, and Raphael

The art of the Low Renaissance concentrated mainly on religious themes, with subjects more lifelike than heroic. Artists were still craftspeople. The High Renaissance was humanist. Huge projects were undertaken. Artists explored sacred, secular, and even sexy themes. And subjects were sometimes larger than life (Michelangelo's *David*). Human attributes were glorified, and artists (such as Leonardo, Michelangelo, and Raphael) were revered as geniuses.

The art of Leonardo, Michelangelo, and Raphael was the culmination of the Renaissance. The tremendous output of "the big three" sprang from their personal genius, spurred on by a huge demand for quality art. Never before had artists been asked to do so much and been given so much money and freedom to do it. Cities wanted monuments and public buildings. Wealthy individuals wanted palaces and decorations. Popes wanted churches. And all of them wanted to hire Leonardo, Michelangelo, or Raphael.

Major Collections of Renaissance Painting

Italy
- Uffizi, Florence
- Pinacoteca Gallery, Vatican Museum, Rome
- Accademia, Venice

France
- Louvre, Paris

Britain
- National Gallery, London

Austria
- Kunsthistorisches, Vienna

Germany
- Alte Pinakothek, Munich

Spain
- Prado, Madrid

Leonardo da Vinci

Leonardo da Vinci (1452–1519) typified the well-rounded Renaissance man. He was a painter, sculptor, engineer, musician, and scientist. He learned from nature, not books, which made his observations often more accurate than those of contemporary scholars. From his notebooks—written in code (backward and inside out as if reflected in a mirror) in case some of his thoughts could be construed as heretical—we know that he dissected corpses, investigated the growth of fetuses in the womb, formulated laws of waves and currents, diagrammed the flight of birds and insects, and followed the growth

Leonardo da Vinci, **Self-Portrait**

Byzantine mosaic

Fra Angelico, **The Annunciation**
*(detail), 1435 (Prado, Madrid).
With no interest in anatomy,
you're washing dishes with
two left-hand rubber gloves.*

Botticelli's **Eve**

Botticelli's **Venus**

From the Middle Ages to the Renaissance, art progressed from flat-narrative
Byzantine to colorful, delicate Gothic to realistic Renaissance. Notice the two
Botticelli nudes. They are both ideal "tens" in the classical style. At first it
had to be labeled Biblical . . . "Eve." Later you could call a Venus a Venus.

of fetuses in the womb, formulated laws of waves and currents, diagrammed the flight of birds and insects, and followed the growth of
plants. He also designed military fortifications and sketched many
inventions, foreshadowing the development of the airplane and sub-
marine. Some claim he even envisioned a crude carry-on-the-plane-
sized convertible suitcase/rucksack.

Leonardo was best known for his painting and sculpting. In spite
of his popularity and the demand for his work, he was temperamental and often left works unfinished. He insisted on working at
his own pace. None of his sculptures and only about twenty of his
paintings survive.

Last Supper demonstrates Leonardo's mastery of balance, realism,
and drama. Depicting Christ and his 12 disciples, it's painted on the
wall of a church, positioned so it looks like just another chapel
extending off the aisle. The lines of the walls recede toward the
horizon (following the laws of perspective) and come together at
Christ's head. All the motion of the picture flows toward that serene
center, giving the masterpiece a subconscious cohesiveness.
Leonardo composed the Twelve in groups of three, each group con-
tributing a dramatic movement in a wavelike effect toward the central figure of Jesus. (Groups of three symbolize the Trinity; four, the
Gospels.)

Leonardo da Vinci, **Last Supper** *(with schematic lines), 1498 (Santa Maria delle
Grazie, Milan). The lines of perspective tell us Jesus is the target . . . whatever
the price. The fresco, in a terrible state of repair, is a disappointment to visit.*

Despite this complex composition, the picture is highly emotional, not forced or sterile. The Lord has just said that one of the disciples will betray him. Leonardo paints a psychological portrait of each of them at the very moment they ask, "Lord, is it I?"

It's said that Leonardo went whole days without painting a stroke, just staring at the work. Then he'd grab a brush, rush up, flick a dab of paint on . . . and go back to staring. (When you visit _Last Supper_ or any artistic sight in Italy, you can dial the neighboring tourist information box to English, put in a few coins, and listen to the story of the masterpiece. Many works of art can be brilliantly lit for another coin.)

Leonardo used a technique called _sfumato_. He blurred the outlines and mellowed the colors around the borders of his subject, making the edge blend with the background. This makes Lisa appear lifelike and her smile appear mysterious. Try as you will, you can't actually see the corners of her mouth.

When you finally see this most famous painting, you might wonder, "Why is she so famous?" _Mona Lisa_ was a people's favorite from the start because the woman portrayed is a noblewoman of very low rank. The painting was Leonardo's personal favorite, one he never sold, keeping it in his possession until he died. (Leonardo spent his last years living in Amboise on the Loire, in the service of French King Francis I. So _Mona Lisa_ wound up in the French collection.)

Leonardo da Vinci, **Virgin and Child with St. John the Baptist and St. Anne** _(National Gallery, London). Baby Jesus enjoys a pyramid of maternal security (while St. Anne whispers into Mary's ear, "It's just not fair when a kid's birthday falls on Christmas")._

Works of Leonardo da Vinci

France
- *Mona Lisa, Madonna of the Rocks, John the Baptist,* Louvre, Paris
- His home and models of inventions, Amboise, Loire

Italy
- *Last Supper,* Santa Maria delle Grazie, Milan
- *St. Jerome,* Pinacoteca Gallery, Vatican Museum
- *Annunciation* and *Adoration,* Uffizi Gallery, Florence

Britain
- *Virgin and Child* (cartoon) and *Madonna of the Rocks,* National Gallery, London

Germany
- *Madonna and Child,* Alte Pinakothek, Munich

Leonardo's **Mona Lisa,** *1505, found in tourist shops throughout Paris (and in the Louvre—just follow the crowds).*

The portrait of Mona was kidnapped early in the 20th century. Her safe recovery made headlines, boosting her fame even higher. Artistically, she epitomizes the art of the Renaissance: balanced, subtle, and true.

Michelangelo

Michelangelo Buonarroti (1475–1564), perhaps the greatest painter and sculptor of all time, mastered nature and strove to master himself. Michelangelo's art reflects the inner turmoil of his emotional and spiritual life. His biography is as important as his work; the two are intertwined.

At the age of 15 Michelangelo was a prodigy, a favorite of Florence's leading citizen, Lorenzo de Medici. After serving his apprenticeship, he became dissatisfied with book knowledge and set out to study nature firsthand.

He had the curiosity and quick mind of Leonardo, but he applied them to only one subject: the human body. Mastering the techniques of the ancient Greeks and Romans, he added to them by dissecting corpses to learn anatomy. Dissection, which was strictly illegal, was key to understanding the body and portraying it realistically.

Throughout his life, Michelangelo's talents were in great demand. He worked for nine popes. Even more than Leonardo, Michelangelo struggled to remain independent of his patrons' demands. And he succeeded.

Despite his great technical skill, Michelangelo thought that true creative genius came not from the rational planning of the artist, but from divine inspiration. He was one of the first "mad geniuses," working only when he felt inspired and then going at it with the intensity of a maniac. Michelangelo took Plato's words to heart: "If anyone tries to be an artist without the madness of the Muses, persuaded that skill alone will make him good, then both he and his works of sanity shall be brought to nothing."

*Michelangelo, **Campidoglio**, 1550, Capitol Hill, Rome. Michelangelo, typical of the Renaissance genius, was expected to sculpt, paint, and be a world-class architect on command.* No problema. *He designed this square above the Roman Forum.*

Michelangelo's statues show us this divine genius trapped within the body, struggling to get out. The works are outwardly calm, stable, and balanced, but seem to be charged with pent-up energy. They convey the inner restlessness and turmoil that marked Michelangelo's own life.

David, sculpted when Michelangelo was 26, displays this blend of vibrant energy and calm. David's posture is relaxed, but his alert, intense stare reminds us of Donatello's Christian warrior, St. George. Michelangelo's *David* became a symbol of the ready-for-anything confidence of the Florentine Renaissance.

When this monumental 13'5" tall David was unveiled, it was understood that a new era in art history had begun. He was designed to stand on top of the cathedral, but the city fathers elected to put him in a more visible spot outside the town hall (the Palazzo Vecchio) as a symbol of civic pride. Some interpret this act to symbolize the republic's overthrow of the Medici autocracy. Today a *David* copy stands in the square; the original is in the Accademia, a 15-minute walk away.

Donatello's *David* is young and graceful, coyly gloating over the head of Goliath, almost Gothic in its elegance and smooth lines. Michelangelo's *David* is pure Renaissance: more massive, heroic in size and superhuman in strength and power. The tensed right hand, which grips a stone in readiness to hurl at Goliath, is much larger and more powerful than any human hand; it's symbolic of divine strength. When you look into *David's* eyes you're looking into the eyes of Renaissance man.

*Michelangelo, **David**, 1504 (Accademia, Florence). Michelangelo's version of the giant-slayer shows the Renaissance Man in full bloom—alert, poised, cultured, ready to conquer his foe. Man has asserted himself. Donatello's boy-toy David now eats meat.*

Michelangelo's **David** *with* **Prisoners**, c. *1518 (Accademia, Florence)*

At times, Michelangelo must have felt cursed by the "divine genius" within him and its accompanying responsibility to create. His *Prisoners*, works that struggle to free themselves from the uncut stone around them, symbolize the neo-Platonic struggle of the divine soul to free itself from the prison of the body.

Many painters, including Leonardo, thought of themselves as almost divine creators who could take a blank canvas and make a beautiful picture. Michelangelo, the sculptor, disagreed. He thought of himself as a tool of God, gifted with an ability not to create, but to reveal what God had put into the stone.

Artists such as Leonardo and Raphael took great pride in their high-class profession. They painted while wearing fine clothes, nibbling fresh fruit, sipping wine, and maybe even being entertained with live music. They'd wash up before dinner and enjoy a high-society ball that evening. But Michelangelo worked in a frenzy. In his sweaty work clothes, covered with marble dust, he'd often work deep into the night wearing a candle on his cap.

For Michelangelo, history's greatest bodybuilder, sculpture was the noblest art form. Michelangelo said that the more a painting looked like a sculpture the better it was, and the more a sculpture looked like a painting the worse it was. He considered himself a sculptor, not a painter. Fortunately for us, his patrons thought otherwise.

Michelangelo, **Pietà del Duomo,** *1555 (Museum dell' Opera del Duomo, Florence)*

Pope Julius II, as part of a massive effort to return Rome and the papacy to its former splendor and prestige, bribed and pressured a hesitant Michelangelo into painting an enormous fresco ("painting" with wet plaster) on the ceiling of the Sistine Chapel. Michelangelo worked furiously for four years, producing a masterpiece of incredible proportion, unity, and emotional power.

The Sistine Chapel is the pictorial culmination of the Renaissance. It chronicles the Christian history of the world, from the Creation to the Coming of Christ to the Last Judgment. The several hundred figures not only tell the story, but add up to a unified, rhythmically pleasing composition. Their bodies are dramatic, expressive, and statuesque, in the tradition of Giotto and Masaccio.

The central scene shows the Creation of Man; Adam reaches out to receive the divine spark of life from God. We can see the tenderness between a fatherly God and his creation, but the most striking thing

Michelangelo, **Holy Family,** *1506 (Uffizi, Florence). Michelangelo insisted he was a sculptor, not a painter. This painting shows it with solid, statuesque people posed in sculpture groups. This is Michelangelo's only surviving easel painting.*

*Michelangelo, **Sistine Chapel**, 1508–1512 (Vatican Museum). The pictorial culmination of the Renaissance, Michelangelo's Sistine Ceiling tells the entire history of the Christian world, from Creation to Christ. Later he painted* The Last Judgment, *on the wall behind the altar. Today, this room is newly restored and sparkles like the day Michelangelo finished it.*

Michelangelo, **Study for Adam for the Sistine Chapel,**
*1510. The Florentines were sculptors at heart. Here
Michelangelo's sculptural orientation shows through.
Compare this with the finished product below.*

about the relationship is its equality. Man is not cowering before a terrible God. He is strong and confident. Michelangelo shows us the
essential goodness of man who was created in the image of God, one
Biblical idea that the Renaissance really liked.

Michelangelo, **Creation of Adam,** *c. 1510 (Sistine Chapel, Vatican
Museum)*

Michelangelo, **The Last Judgment,** *1534–1541 (Sistine Chapel, Vatican Museum).*

Michelangelo, **The Last Judgment** *(details, Sistine Chapel, Vatican Museum). Painted about 25 years after the original work on the ceiling, a disillusioned and self-doubting Michelangelo paints his own face in the flayed, wretched skin in St. Bartholomew's hand. To the right, Michelangelo portrays Christ as a powerful, wrathful, and terrifying deity posed to strike down the wicked. With the Reformation, the Vatican is on the defensive. Renaissance optimism has ended.*

Michelangelo, ***Apse and Dome of St. Peter's Cathedral***, *begun 1547, Rome. When asked to build the dome of St. Peter's, Michelangelo said, "I can build one bigger but not more beautiful than the dome of my hometown, Florence."*

Climb to the top, 100 winding, sweaty yards up, and judge for yourself. Matching (but not outdoing) the grandeur of ancient Rome, the builders of St. Peter's respectfully "put the dome of the Pantheon atop the Basilica Maxentius."

Works of Michelangelo

Italy
- *Pietà* (the famous one), St. Peter's, Vatican, Rome
- Dome of St. Peter's, Vatican
- Sistine Chapel and *The Last Judgment*, Vatican Museum
- *Moses*, St. Peter in Chains church, Rome
- *Christ Bearing Cross*, Santa Maria Sopra Minerva church, Rome
- Campidoglio square, Rome
- *David, Pietà,* and *Prisoners*, Accademia, Florence
- *Pietà del Duomo*, Museo del Duomo, Florence
- *Night, Day,* and others, Medici Chapel, Florence
- *Bacchus, Bruto,* and a minor *David*, Bargello, Florence
- *Holy Family* easel painting, Uffizi, Florence
- Rondanini *Pietà*, Milan

Belgium
- *Madonna and Child*, Bruges

France
- *Slaves*, Louvre, Paris

Britain
- *Entombment* (unfinished painting), National Gallery, London

Michelangelo was also a great architect. He designed the dome of St. Peter's in Rome, influenced by Brunelleschi's dome in Florence.

Whether he died satisfied with his life's work, we don't know. But he lived almost 90 years and was productive until the end. As a final show of independence and artistic devotion, when he designed the great dome of St. Peter's, he refused payment for his services.

Raphael

Raphael (1483–1520) is the best single embodiment of the harmony and pure beauty of the Renaissance style—a synthesis of the grace of Leonardo and the power of Michelangelo. He managed to achieve what had eluded painters before him: the realistic and harmonious composition of freely moving figures.

Raphael's fresco *The School of Athens* embodies the spirit of the High Renaissance. Its subject is classical—Plato and Aristotle surrounded by other Greek philosophers (modeled by Raphael's contemporaries), all engaged in highbrow jawing. The pure Renaissance architecture of the school is actually a look at the new St. Peter's basilica, which was under construction at the time.

The composition, like Leonardo's *Last Supper*, has figures grouped rhythmically around a center of calm. The lines of sight meet at the "haloed" figures of the two "saints" of knowledge, just as they did at Leonardo's Jesus. Plato points up, reminding us that mathematics and pure ideas are the source of truth, while Aristotle points down, showing his preference for scientific study of the material world. The bearded figure of Plato is none other than Leonardo—Raphael's tribute to the aging master. Michelangelo is shown meditating, sitting with his head in his hand in the foreground.

The fresco shows Michelangelo's influence in the solid, sculptural bodies and the dramatic power reminiscent of the Sistine Chapel. In fact, Raphael was working on this in the Vatican Palace while Michelangelo was climbing the walls of the Sistine Chapel next door. *The School of Athens* is one of many Raphael masterpieces that adorn the rooms through which you walk immediately before you enter the Sistine Chapel.

Raphael, **School of Athens**, *1510 (Raphael Rooms, Vatican Museum, Rome). Renaissance thought united the church and the great classical philosophers. Notice how the Renaissance architecture provides a halo for the pre-Christian saints of knowledge (and gives us a sneak preview of the unfinished St. Peter's church). As in Leonardo's* **Last Supper**, *the receding lines of perspective meet at the heads of the central figures, Plato and Aristotle.*

Raphael's fame was equal to Michelangelo's, and his influence on subsequent generations was perhaps even greater. Periodically through the centuries, artists returned to the vision of ideal beauty depicted by Raphael, the "Master of Grace." However, these imitators often ignored the realism and power of Raphael, turning out pretty pictures with little substance.

Raphael was the most beloved Renaissance painter until this century. Only in our generation have Michelangelo and Leonardo surpassed him in postcards and calendars sold. When Raphael died in 1520, the center of Renaissance painting shifted once again—this time northward, to Venice.

Raphael, **La Belle Jardiniere,** *1507 (Louvre, Paris). A typical pyramid composition by the "Master of Grace." Most tourists burn out on the very common Madonna-and-child scene long before they get to Raphael. Save yourself for Raphael.*

Raphael, **The Transfiguration** *(detail), 1520 (Pinacoteca, Vatican Museum, Rome). As he was dying, Raphael set his sights on heaven and painted possibly his most beautiful work, this heavenly face of Jesus.*

Raphael's Works

Italy
  • *School of Athens, Deliverance of St. Peter,* and others, Raphael Rooms, Vatican Museum
  • *Transfiguration,* Pinacoteca Gallery, Vatican Museum
Most major art galleries, including Florence's Uffizi, Madrid's Prado, Paris' Louvre, Munich's Alte Pinakothek, and Vienna's Kunsthistorisches.

Renaissance Venice: Europe's Rich Middleman

In Venice, Renaissance art and architecture were financed by trade. For 500 years, Venice was known as "the Bride of the Sea" and the envy of all of Europe. The economy, glorious buildings, art, and elegant way of life all depended on sea-trading. Every year the leader of Venice, after renewing a kind of wedding vow, tossed a ring into the Adriatic. This act symbolized the marriage between the sea and its bride.

Doge's Palace, 1340, Venice. The multinational corporation known as the Venetian Empire was ruled from this palace, the home of its C.E.O., the Doge. Today, this Venetian Gothic building is packed with art masterpieces, history, and tourists.

Doge's Palace, today, Venice. A 1995 photograph proves that the town has changed (and sunk) little in 655 years, though the tower is clearly sliding to the right.

Venice had been founded as a kind of refugee camp around the year 400 by Italian mainlanders. After suffering one too many barbarian rape-pillage-and-plunders, the Venetians got together and decided to move out into the lagoon, hoping the barbarians didn't like water. They built on muddy islands, pounding in literally millions of tree trunks for support. Rather than trying to build solid roads, they dredged canals for passageways.

Farming was impossible in the mud, so the Venetians quickly learned to trade fish and salt (for preserving meat) for agricultural products. Gradually, their trading took them to more and more distant lands. They were situated perfectly to link Europe with the wealthy Byzantine Empire and the treasures of the East. When the Crusades created a demand in Europe for Eastern luxury goods, Venice became the go-between.

Venice went between so well that by the year 1200, she was Europe's economic superpower. Products from as far away as Scotland and India passed through Venetian warehouses. The Rialto Bridge area became the world's busiest trading center: iron, copper, and woven textiles from Northern Europe and raisins, pepper, wines, lemons, silk, Persian rugs, leathers, precious stones, perfumes, and spices from the East.

Venetians traded by ship using a chain of ports and friendly cities in the eastern Mediterranean. Goods arrived (sometimes by camel caravan) and the Venetians shipped them westward where European land traders picked them up.

Venice, with 150,000 citizens, was the most populous city in Europe in 1500. (Paris had 100,000.) The ducat, because of its stability and high gold content, became the monetary standard for the Eastern world. (The Florentine florin was the West's.) The gross "national" product of this city was 50 percent greater than that of the entire country of France.

Her sea-trading spawned other industries, including shipbuilding, warehousing, insurance, and accounting. The Arsenal, the largest single factory in Europe, employed 16,000 people at its peak and could crank out a warship a day.

Besides expanding its commercial empire, Venice hired generals to conquer many of the cities in northern Italy. And Venice profited greatly from the Crusades.

All this wealth did not go to waste. The 15th century was a time of massive building and rebuilding. The earliest structures of this century show a Byzantine influence. The most distinctive, however, are "Venetian Gothic" in style, such as the Doge's Palace. They have Gothic pointed arches, but they're much lighter and more fanciful than the Gothic churches of Northern Europe. Later structures are Renaissance style, with rounded Roman arches.

St. Mark's, one of the world's most famous cathedrals, is the best example of "Venetian Byzantine" architecture with its onion-shaped Eastern domes, Greek-cross floor plan, and interior mosaics. But the style might better be called "Early Ransack." The cathedral is a treasure chest of artifacts looted from other cities during Venice's heyday.

Even the bones of Venice's patron saint, Mark, which rest under the altar, were booty. Middle Age Europe was into relic worship. In A.D. 829,

*St. Mark's Cathedral, 1063–1073, Venice. Mark Twain called
St. Mark's "a great warty bug taking a walk."*

the young but powerful city-state of Venice was really nothing on the religious map. It needed relics to give it some clout. A band of merchants trading in Alexandria, Egypt, stole the bones of the Evangelist (a writer of one of the New Testament Gospels) from Alexandria's Moslem rulers, put them in their church, and, presto! Venice became an important religious destination. St. Mark's symbol, the winged lion, replaced Theodore and his dragon as the symbol of the Venetian Republic.

With its newfound sanctity, Venice grew rapidly. The Rialto Bridge that spans the Grand Canal, originally a covered wooden drawbridge, was rebuilt as a grand stone arch. The straight, wooden planks of Venice's drawbridges had allowed horses and mules to cross. When builders installed the new arched bridges, horses were banned from the city—just as cars are today.

The Venetian empire was controlled by an oligarchy of wealthy families. This top 5 percent of the population elected a council of rulers led by a duke who served for life, known as the Doge (pronounced "dozh," not "doggie").

The rest of the population had no political rights, but they were treated well and did prosper. Until 1423, the people had final veto

Tintoretto, **Paradise** *(Doge's Palace, Venice). Tintoretto's monsterpiece, with more square footage than my apartment, includes over 500 figures.*

power over election of the Doge. The council would present him in St. Mark's Square, saying, "This is your Doge, if it please you." They invariably approved the election by cheering, until one Doge-elect, an unpopular man, feared he might not please them. From then on, the council said only, "This is your Doge." Throughout history, democracy has been a bonsai tree in the house of the powerful—it looks nice, and when it grows too big you simply cut it back.

Venetian society, while rigidly structured, was quite tolerant. It was a cosmopolitan city where traders from all over the world rubbed elbows. Some foreigners (Turks, Arabs, and others) were even allowed to settle there. (The bell at St. Mark's is rung by two statues of Moors.) There was a Jewish community, giving us our word "ghetto" to identify a neighborhood set aside for minorities. The largest foreign group was the Greek population, especially after the disastrous sack of Constantinople by the European Crusaders (in 1204) and the city's fall to the Turks (in 1453). One of the 5,000 Venetian Greeks was Domenico Theotocopoulis, who became a famous painter in Spain . . . El Greco.

The Catholic Church was often at odds with Venice, partly because of the city's close ties with the rival Greek Orthodox Christians. The proud Venetians thought of themselves as Catholics—but not Roman Catholics.

Elegant Decay: Venice's Cinquecento

Venice peaked economically in the year 1450. Then, a series of world events set in motion three centuries of slow decline. In 1453, the Moslem Turks captured and looted Constantinople. Uninterested in trading with the West, they began attacking Venice's foreign ports. Venice not only lost its link with the East but was also forced to fight costly wars with the Turks.

The next blows came from the West, when explorers from Spain and Portugal discovered America and new sea-trade routes to the East. By 1500, Portugal was using Vasco da Gama's route around South Africa to trade with India. Venice's Eastern monopoly was broken. Her trade plummeted.

Venice's decline was a glorious one. Like so many cultures past their peak of economic expansion, Venice turned from business to the arts, from war to diplomacy, from sternness to partying, from buying gold to selling tacky souvenirs. The "Cinquecento" (pronounced "CHINK-kwa-CHEN-to"), as the Italians call the century of the 1500s, was a time for merrymaking and festivity that was legendary in Europe.

Venice's economic decline went hand in hand with political corruption and repression. Local rule grew more and more autocratic. Venice had some of Europe's most convincing torture chambers.

The renowned rogue Casanova spent time in a Venetian prison, which he described as follows: "Those subterranean prisons are precisely like tombs, but they call them 'Wells' because they contain about two feet of filthy water which penetrates from the sea. Condemned to live in these sewers, they are given every morning some thin soup and a ration of bread which they have to eat immediately or it becomes the prey of enormous rats. A villain who died while I was there had spent 37 years in the Wells."

The famous Bridge of Sighs (rebuilt in 1600 and open today to visitors) connected the lawyers' offices in the Doge's Palace with the prisons. Prisoners could be brought from the prisons, tried in closed court, and sentenced without the public knowing about it. As they passed over the bridge to their deaths, they got one last look at their beloved city—hence the name, "Bridge of Sighs."

Venice's long decline was hastened by two brutal plagues that devastated the population. By Napoleon's arrival in 1797, the city was defenseless. He ended the Republic, throwing the city into even worse chaos. It became a possession of various European powers until 1866, when it joined the newly united Italian nation.

The city today is older, crumbling and sinking, but it looks much the same as it did during the grand days of the Renaissance. For that we can thank Venice's economic decline: the inhabitants were simply too poor to rebuild. Venice is Europe's best-preserved big city. It is the toast of the High Middle Ages and Renaissance in an elegant state of decay.

Many people actually avoid Venice because of its famously smelly canals. So that you'll know how serious this problem is, we've recreated the Venetian stench here so you can scratch 'n' sniff and decide for yourself.

Scratch 'n' sniff—Venice

Art of the Venetian Renaissance

The Cinquecento produced some of the greatest Renaissance art. Bellini, Titian, Giorgione, Tintoretto, and Veronese, whose works embellish churches, palaces, and museums throughout the city, forged a distinct Venetian style that emphasized color over outline. While Florentine painters drew massive sculptural figures with a strong outline, Venetians used gradations of color to blend figures into the background. The result was a lighter, more

Giorgione, **The Tempest,** *1505 (Accademia, Venice). Florentine art tended to be sculptural with strong outlines; Venice's Renaissance art, like the city, was colorful and romantically atmospheric.*

refined, and more graceful look understandable in an elegant city of lavish palaces and glittering canals.

The same delicate, atmospheric haze that often hangs over the city of Venice also characterizes Venetian art. It's like a picture taken with a soft-focus lens on the camera, making everything glow and blend together, bathing it in light. This is Leonardo's *sfumato* taken one step farther.

Giorgione's *The Tempest*, with bright colors and a hazy quality, marks a trend new to Italian painting—the landscape. Like painters from the North, Venetians enjoyed painting pleasantly detailed scenes that show a love of the natural world.

Titian the Venetian was one of the most prolific painters ever, cranking out a painting a month for almost 80 years. His canvases have a richness of color and brilliance of light burning through the night. He used color and light rather than the drawn line to balance his work and direct the viewer's eyes. (When Michelangelo met the great Titian, whose fame rivaled his own, he praised his work and then said, "But it's a pity you Venetians cannot draw.")

When Raphael died in 1520, Venice became Italy's art capital. Titian (about 1490–1576) became the most sought-after portrait artist. A famous example of Titian's prestige: once, when he dropped a brush during a sitting, his subject, Emperor Charles V of Spain, picked it up for him. Whether this actually happened is unimportant. This often-repeated anecdote represented to future generations the triumph of artistic genius.

The happy-go-lucky Venetian love of the good life can be seen in Paolo Veronese's huge, colorful scenes of Venetian high-life. He once painted the Last Supper scene as if it were a typical Venetian dinner party. We see drunks, buffoons, dwarfs, a German mercenary soldier, dogs, a cat, and a parrot. The authorities were so shocked that they

Titian, **Venus and the Organ Player,** *1550 (Prado, Madrid). Rich Venetians dealt with the conflict between sacred artistic pursuits (for example, music) and worldly, sensual pursuits (for example, the naked lady). Here, the torn musician leers at Venus while keeping both hands on his organ.*

Veronese, **Feast of the House of Levi,** *1564 (Accademia, Venice). Veronese was hauled before the Inquisition for painting the Last Supper of Christ and His holy apostles looking like a Venetian orgy. Veronese didn't change a thing, except the title.*

demanded he repaint it to reflect a more somber mood. Instead, he simply retitled it. We know the work as *Feast of the House of Levi* (see it in Venice's Accademia).

The bright colors of the Venetian style take on an almost surrealistic tint with Tintoretto (1518–1594). His works glow like black-velvet paintings. He also experimented with new techniques of composition, showing his main subjects at odd angles and in twisted poses, whipping up the excitement. Tintoretto's dramatic style went beyond serene Renaissance balance, pointing toward the next phase in art—Baroque.

Venetian Art

Italy
- Accademia, Doge's Palace, Chiesa dei Frari, and Scuola San Rocco (Tintoretto), Venice
- The city of Venice herself, including many churches

Spain
- Prado, Madrid

Austria
- Kunsthistorisches Museum, Vienna

Croatia
- City of Dubrovnik

The Northern Renaissance

In northern Europe, the Renaissance was more an improvement on medieval art than a return to classical forms. Northern artists used Italian discoveries of perspective, anatomy, and knowledge of classical forms, but kept their style distinctly Northern.

Riemenschneider woodcarving, 1504 (St. Jacob's Church, Rothenburg, Germany). Riemenschneider was the Michelangelo of German wood-carvers. His greatest altarpiece is in Rothenburg. Museums in Würzburg and Munich show off more of his work.

In the north, late Gothic art is characterized by grace and lightness, delicate flowing lines, and an appreciation for things that are just plain beautiful. Human bodies are slender and gently curved, with smooth, unmuscled skin. Colors are bright and pleasant.

Northern artists loved detail. Like craftsmen working on a fine Swiss watch or German cuckoo clock, they thought nothing of spending hours on end slaving over, say, the hairs on a dog's head to get them just right, even when the dog was just a minor figure in a large canvas. Their appreciation of the many wonders of nature shows in their work.

Van Eyck, **Arnolfini Wedding,** *1434 (National Gallery, London). This early Northern Renaissance masterpiece shows the characteristic medieval attention to detail and the down-to-earth personal style typical of Belgian and Dutch art. You can even see the couple's reflection in the round mirror in the rear. "Wedding?" Women used to wear pillows to their weddings thinking that would improve their chances of becoming pregnant.*

Dürer, **Adam and Eve** *(engraving), 1504 (Museum of Fine Arts, Boston)*

Medieval paintings often look crowded. Details abound—the more, the better. Crammed with objects and minute details, Northern Renaissance works are best viewed as they were painted, slowly and carefully.

Albrecht Dürer (1471–1528), a German working at about the same time as Michelangelo, finished his apprenticeship and traveled to Venice to learn the techniques he'd heard so much about. When he returned home and achieved fame, he helped "Italianize" his world. He has been called the "Leonardo of the North."

Dürer combined the Italian painters' laws of perspective and human anatomy with the Germans' attention to detail. Although he never mastered Michelangelo's ability to make a solid, statuelike body, his paintings are astonishingly realistic. With the patience formed from his mastery of the grueling process of woodcuts and engraving, he painted with incredible detail. Dürer was Europe's first top-selling artist. His popular woodcuts and engravings were reproduced and sold in large quantities.

A woodcut is made by sketching black lines on a white-painted block, then chipping off the white so that only the desired lines protrude. This woodcut is then dipped into ink and used the way we use a rubber stamp

Dürer, **Four Horsemen of the Apocalypse,** *1498 (British Museum, London). Dürer's woodcuts were the first mass-produced art Europe had seen. His mastery of line and detail went well with this painstaking medium. Notice his famous D-inside-A monogram at the bottom.*

Dürer, **Self-Portrait***, 1498 (Prado, Madrid). In this first full self-portrait by an artist, the German Dürer declares that—even in a goofy hat— artists deserve and will get respect.*

today. An engraving, the opposite of a woodcut, cuts the "lines" into the plate and, when mastered, allows for even more detail than a woodcut. An etching, which is an improved version of engraving and was used by later artists such as Rembrandt, is made by coating a copperplate with wax and scratching an image into the wax, which is then burned with acid. Prints are then made from the plate in the same manner as engravings.

Dürer was impressed by the respect Italian artists enjoyed. Northern artists had always been anonymous craftsmen, laboring in guilds. Dürer helped change that. Convinced that his personal life and thoughts were as important as his handiwork, he kept journals and wrote books. His famous self-portraits (a first) portray him as an elegant, confident, even arrogant man of the world.

Matthias Grünewald (pronounced "GROON-uh-vald," 1470–1528) was a great but mysterious Northern Renaissance artist. (We're not even sure that's his real name.) Like Northern Renaissance art in general, his style grew out of the Gothic stage. His anonymity is medieval, as is his gripping religious devotion. Grünewald often ignored realism (so important to Dürer and the Italians) to make a religious point.

Grünewald's famous *Isenheim Altarpiece* in Colmar, France, is one of Europe's most exciting and powerful masterpieces. In this set of scenes from Jesus' life, Grünewald uses distorted shapes and dazzling, unreal colors to grab the emotions. You feel the agony of Christ twisted stiffly and heavily on the cross, the humility of Mary, and the exuberance of the resurrected Christ springing psychedelically from the tomb as if shot out of a Roman candle.

Hieronymous Bosch (rhymes with "gosh," 1450–1516) was another interesting artist of this era. We know almost nothing about him except

Grünewald, **Isenheim Altarpiece,** *1515 (Colmar, France). The mysterious, late-Gothic master painted one of the most gripping crucifixions ever. Notice the weight of Christ's body bending the cross bar, his mashed feet, dislocated elbows, the grief on Mary's face (kneeling), and Jesus' stiff fingers praising God in spite of it all. Though Renaissance in technique, it includes medieval symbolism: the lamb with a cross and cup, and John the Baptist holding a book.*

Northern Renaissance Art

Austria
  • Kunsthistorisches Museum, Vienna
Spain
  • Prado, Madrid
France
  • Isenheim Altarpiece, Unterlinden Museum, Colmar
  • *The Last Judgment,* Hôtel Dieu, Beaune
Netherlands
  • Rijksmuseum, Amsterdam
Belgium
  • Ancient Art Museum, Brussels
  • *Adoration of the Mystic Lamb,* St. Bavo's Church, Ghent
Germany
  • Dahlem Museum, Berlin
  • Alte Pinakothek, Munich

Bosch, **Garden of Delights,** *1510 (Prado, Madrid). This three-paneled altar-piece takes you from the Creation to the gnashing torments of Hell via the fleeting "delights" of earthly life.*

Bosch, **Garden of Delights** *(detail from Hell), 1510 (Prado, Madrid). In just a tiny bit of this monumental work we see a self-portrait of Bosch with a broken-eggshell body and tree trunk legs crashing through wooden dinghies in a frozen lake with giant birds leading naked people around the brim of his hat. Gosch.*

what we learn through his fantastic paintings. "Hieronymous the Anonymous" painted medieval fears with modern skill. His huge symbolism-packed canvases are crowded with grotesque, humorous, and all-around bizarre people and creatures.

Bosch's intriguing themes probably made complete sense to the medieval mind. He painted strange-looking plants and animals in many of his works. Doing so was common among artists who painted during the years when Columbus and other explorers were bringing fascinating creatures back from the New World. Today, although much of the meaning of his art is lost, the intrigue remains.

After the Renaissance: Mannerism

Looking at the ceiling of the Sistine Chapel might make you think, "How could there be anything more beautiful?" Well, that's what artists after Michelangelo thought and worried about, too. How could art advance beyond the works of the great Renaissance masters? They had explored and conquered every facet of painting and sculpture. It seemed as though the future of art would be little more than copying the forms and techniques of Michelangelo, Leonardo, Raphael, and Titian.

The Renaissance was a hard act to follow, and for a while many artists were stuck in the beautiful rut of Raphael's style. We call the style of this period (1530–1600) Mannerism because the art seemed to follow only the "manner" of the Renaissance masters, often neglecting the spirit of their work.

Many artists made bold, occasionally ridiculous, attempts to be original, to do something new. Using Renaissance techniques of portraying nature, they experimented with more complex composition, more striking colors, the contrast of light and shadow, and a heightened display of emotions. This led to the Baroque style. Elongated bodies are the easiest way to identify a Mannerist painting.

Parmigiano, **The Madonna with the Long Neck,** *1535 (Uffizi, Florence). "I'm melting!"*

Timeline of the Renaissance

The Renaissance spread as countries reached an economic affluence that could support the arts. It began in Florence and then took over Rome, Venice, Spain, Portugal, and finally the northern countries, Flanders, France, and England.

The earliest Renaissance artists—Brunelleschi, Masaccio, Donatello, and Botticelli—lived in Florence at the time the powerful Medici banking family ruled the city. The High Renaissance shifted to Rome (Michelangelo and Raphael) and then to Venice (Titian).

Meanwhile, the rest of Europe was discovering new lands and trading opportunities. Spain and Portugal broke Venice's monopoly on Eastern trade by finding new routes to the East. England, Holland, and France built large merchant fleets and banking houses to expand their trade with the rest of Europe and the New World. With the invention of the printing press, ideas were exchanged as quickly as goods.

Each of these countries was touched by its own Renaissance. Portugal flowered with the Manueline architectural style; Spain inspired the art of El Greco (he arrived via Venice); and the northern countries spawned the masterpieces of Dürer, Bosch, and Grünewald.

THE RENAISSANCE

The Absolute Monarch—*ruling like a god in Heaven. The 1600s and 1700s were a time of "divine" kings and absolutism. Many a king convinced his people that he had been deputized by God to rule with complete, unquestioned power.*

The Early Modern World
A.D. 1500-1815

In the early 1500s, Europe was entering the modern world. You could now get to Asia without a camel. You could get to heaven without a pope. Royal families established huge empires, but as cities thrived, the Old Regime gradually became more and more of a dinosaur. From the Reformation to the age of divine monarchs to the age of revolution, the ultimate power shifted from the pope to the king to the people.

The Reformation

Before the Renaissance, the church was the richest, most powerful, and best-organized institution in Europe. Like a monastic mafia, it was Europe's greatest landowner, collected taxes through tithes, patronized great art, and influenced political decisions. Kings and princes needed papal support to maintain their political power. Average Europeans identified themselves by their bishopric, not by citizenship in a particular country. A crime was a sin, and a sin was a crime.

But the church's rich and worldly position led to corruption, and a reforming spirit grew. When political rivalries and jealousies were added, reforming changed to splitting. New churches were formed, and because religion and politics were intertwined, Europe experienced a chaotic period of political upheaval and war. This tumultuous period is called the Reformation. Much of the Europe you see today was shaped to some extent by this period.

Church Corruption

The church certainly needed reform. Many priests were illiterate and immoral. Bishops meddled in politics, governing like petty tyrants. The clergy sold important church offices and dispensations (exemptions from church laws) to the highest bidder. The medieval church showed not a hint of the voluntary poverty of the early Christians. In addition, the church had lost touch with ordinary folk. Mass was celebrated in Latin, a language spoken only by the educated.

To pay for Rome's face-lift, the pope sold indulgences. (Renaissance artists such as Michelangelo didn't come cheap.) To anyone who paid the price, the pope promised "forgiveness for all thy sins, transgressions and excesses, how enormous so ever they may be, so that when you die the gates of Hell shall be shut and the gates of Paradise shall open with delight" . . . a bargain at twice the price.

"I'd like two adulteries and a small order of lies to go."

Tickets to heaven: *the sale of indulgences. In this German woodcut, people buy letters of forgiveness in the marketplace. This peddling of pardons bothered Martin Luther.*

Church corruption was one reason for the Reformation, and the sale of indulgences might have been the final straw. But there were deeper causes: the decline of papal power, a new secularism, and stronger, more assertive national governments.

The pope had lost prestige among both kings and commoners. During their medieval heyday, popes could make or break kings. But after the popes moved to Avignon, France (where they resided from 1309 through 1377) to enjoy the protection of the strong French kings, they were seen as French popes and their international influence suffered. When a second pope popped up back in Rome and each pope excommunicated the other, papal prestige sank to mud-wrestling depths. Even after the reunited papacy returned to Rome, it never quite recovered from what was called the "Babylonian Captivity."

Secular Forces

Europe's new secularism was bolstered by the rise of capitalism and many new Renaissance ideas. The newly invented printing press sped the spread of new scientific discoveries and secular ideas. Reformers risked death to print local-language versions of one especially radical book: the Bible. After Copernicus (in 1543) and Galileo (in 1632) disproved the church's traditional explanation of the earth-centered universe, nothing was accepted blindly. A new, more independent, scientific, economic, and political world confronted the church.

Kings jumped on the reforming bandwagon out of political greed. They saw the church as a rival power within their borders. Tithes sent to Rome were taxes lost. The church was Europe's number-one landowner. The clergy was exempt from taxes and could ignore local laws. Many kings wanted not only to reform the church, but also to break with it for good. The political rewards were obvious. Kings and princes encouraged people to challenge church authority.

Martin Luther

At first, Martin Luther (1483–1546) was merely an ordinary German monk trying to reform church abuses from within. He never meant to create a new church. He simply believed that the word of God lay not in the doctrine of the church but in the Bible. The Bible talked of salvation by faith in God. Salvation was a free gift to believers, not something anyone could earn or buy. To him, elaborate church rituals made no sense. And the granting of dispensations and indulgences by church authorities cheapened, and even denied, the grace of God.

A typical sales pitch used by the German archbishop Tetzel was: "Listen to the voices of your dear dead relatives and friends beseeching you and saying 'Pity us, pity us. We are in dire torment from which you can redeem us for a pittance.' Remember that you are able to release them, for as soon as the coin in the coffer rings, the soul from Purgatory springs."

Martin Luther, 1483–1546

In 1517, Luther nailed to the door of the Wittenberg cathedral a list of 95 ideas for debate. In Thesis #82 Luther wrote: "If he redeems a number of souls for the sake of miserable money with which to buy a church, why doesn't the pope empty Purgatory for the sake of holy love and of the dire need of the souls that are there?" Not interested in debating, the church called Luther a heretic and sent him a papal bull of excommunication. Not cowed, Luther burned the pope's letter—the Renaissance equivalent to burning your draft card, only much more serious.

Now a criminal as well as a heretic, Luther took refuge in a German prince's castle. From behind those walls he established the German church, translated the Bible into German (giving birth to the modern German language), and led the rebellion against the pope. Printing presses churned out Luther's ideas, which spread quickly and widely to an audience weary of the Church's insatiable need for funds. Within two weeks all of Germany knew of the renegade monk. Within a month all of Europe had heard. Local kings confiscated church lands, established their own "protestant" (protesting) state churches, and geared up to face the armies of the nations loyal to the church.

Catholic and Protestant Differences

The differences between Protestant and Catholic doctrines have divided Christians for centuries. Protestants emphasize a more direct relationship between the individual and God, rejecting church rituals and the necessity of ordained clergy for salvation. Bible study and personal prayer are seen as more valuable than sacraments presided over by a priest. Some Catholic practices rejected by Protestants are: celibate priests, veneration of saints and the Virgin Mary, and holy orders of monks and nuns. The differences between Catholics and Protestants are not so great today, and a spirit of unity is growing.

Reformation and Religious Wars

And the religious wars began. Luckily for the German Protestants, the pope's strongest defenders (the southern countries that remained Catholic) were preoccupied with internal problems and with fighting the Turks who were invading Eastern Europe. The Treaty of Augsburg (1555), which allowed each German prince to choose the religion of his territory, caused a lull in the fighting, but the religious wars continued into the next century.

The Reformation spawned more than one new religion. In Switzerland, around 1550, Geneva was ruled by a theocratic government under the direction of John Calvin. Calvinism, which stresses belief in salvation by God's grace rather than by rituals and good deeds, spread from Switzerland through France, the Netherlands, and beyond to Scotland.

England's break with the church had political roots. King Henry VIII wanted the pope's permission to divorce Catherine of Aragon so he could marry Anne Boleyn. The pope refused to grant a divorce and so, to break all ties with Catherine, Henry broke all ties with Rome (1534). He confiscated church lands, formed the Church of England, and married Anne. The Church of England, or Anglican church, was largely an English Catholic church without a pope. For the next hundred years, England struggled as her kings and queens tried to impose their various personal religions on the people.

The religious wars between Catholics and Protestants lasted for more than 100 years (1527–1648) and were some of the bloodiest in

The Religious Wars, 1527–1648. Europe fought bloody religious wars for over a hundred years after the Reformation. Often called "the First World War," Europe's biggest war yet involved nearly every nation.

European history. Kings generally fought for purely political reasons, but the soldiers were fueled by religious fervor, convinced that God was on their side.

The grand finale was the Thirty Years' War, Europe's first world war, with mercenary warriors from just about every country taking part. When the war ended in 1648, Europe was devastated, a third of Germany was dead, and Western civilization realized what it should have known from the start—that Catholics and Protestants would have to live together.

The Peace of Westphalia (1648) ended the wars, decreeing that the leader of each country would decide the religion of his nation. Generally, the northern countries (Scandinavia, the Low Countries, northern Germany, and England) went Protestant and the southern ones (Spain, Portugal, Italy, France, and southern Germany) remained loyal to Rome. The line dividing Protestant from Catholic Europe was (and remains) almost the same line that separated barbarian Europe from Roman Europe way back when the Christians were still hiding out. Hmmm.

Counter-Reformation

The Vatican countered the Protestant revolution with the Counter-Reformation—an attempt to put the universal Catholic Church back together by means of internal reform, missionary work, propaganda (including the effective use of art), and the Inquisition.

From 1545 to 1563, the Catholic Church held the Council of Trent, a series of conferences that addressed each of the Protestant concerns, defined Church doctrine, and encouraged more careful training and oversight of the clergy. The pope approved the formation of the Society of Jesus, a Jesuit order that became known for its fine teaching and missionary work. At the same time the Church was losing members in Europe, it was gaining recruits in the Americas.

A powerful church weapon was the Inquisition, a network of church courts for trying and punishing heretics and sinners. The medieval Inquisition was used to punish witches, devil worshipers, and adulterers as well as Jews, Moslems, and unorthodox Christians. In 1542, its Counter-Reformation reincarnation was used to haul Protestants and heretic Catholics before the courts on the slightest evidence of guilt or nonconformity.

Torture, terror, imprisonment, and confiscation of property were often used to extract confessions. It was the standard judicial practice

Heretics, Protestants, Jews, and others could be punished quite thoroughly by the church.

of the day. Once the accused confessed, they were really punished. Punishments ranged from recitation of a certain number of prayers, fasting, and alms-giving to imprisonment and death.

Reformation Art

The period of the religious wars took its toll on European culture. In Spain, the only major building of a generation was the palace of the Inquisition, El Escorial, just outside of Madrid. Henry VIII left the English countryside littered with the ruins of Catholic abbeys. The great York Minster was spared so Henry's church would have a northern capital. Rothenburg, Germany, has a museum devoted to medieval crime and punishment. People in trouble with whichever church was in power were the victims of much of this creativity.

Museums throughout the north show early Bibles and books printed by Gutenberg's revolutionary printing press. With the vernacular languages established and the printing of books affordable, common people had access to ideas—a powerful mix.

While Catholic art was royal art, well-funded and dazzling, Protestant communities preferred a simpler art. Music became more important (Bach and the greatest organs came out of Protestant Europe).

Absolutism and Divine Monarchs

The Thirty Years' War reshuffled Europe's political cards. The old-style baronies and dukedoms were replaced by new, more modern governments headed by strong kings. In the Middle Ages, the nation had been a weak entity. Popes, nobles, and petty kings bickered for power while the common people went about their business, ignoring the affairs of state.

Now government functions were specialized, bureaucrats ran things, and the state took over many jobs that had been carried out by the church. A strong "divine" monarch was all-powerful, claiming that his right to rule came directly from God. More than ever, the government was mothering its people. And after 100 years of war, most Europeans didn't mind.

Growing Economy

The growing merchant class welcomed this strong central government. Traders needed stable governments, common currency, standard measures, and fewer tariffs. Early medieval trade had been stifled by the chaos of rural, feudal kingdoms. The trend toward unification, begun in the High Middle Ages, was paying off. Centralized governments and the wealthy urban middle class were natural allies.

Overseas trade gave these new governments wealth and strength. The newly discovered Americas and routes to the Far East opened a floodgate, bringing in waves of raw materials and luxury goods. The sale of captured Africans as slaves in the New World brought unprecedented wealth. Spain, England, France, and the Netherlands built large merchant fleets to exploit this wealth, which required naval protection, which required more taxes to maintain, which required more efficient governments to collect and administer the taxes. The state grew.

Louis XIV: Controlling Nature, Controlling Nobles

France's Louis XIV (who reigned from 1643 to 1715) was Europe's king of kings—the absolute example of an absolute monarch. Louis ruled for seventy years, making France the political and cultural heartbeat of Europe. He strengthened the military, expanded France's borders, stimulated trade, and built a large and effective government.

The France Louis inherited was the strongest nation in Europe, with 18 million people. (England at this time had about 5 million.) The economy, directed by Minister Colbert (the first man to take a balance sheet seriously), was healthy at home and spreading, thanks to a large

Rigaud, **Louis XIV,** *1701 (Louvre, Paris). Louis XIV, the premier monarch of Europe, was every king's role model. He ruled the "Oz" and "Hollywood" of Europe for more than five decades and, even as an old man, looked good in tights.*

merchant marine and to trade with the luxurious East and West Indies. Louis organized an efficient bureaucracy for gathering taxes, yet he himself remained at the helm. He was no scholar—in fact, he was "extraordinarily unlearned," but as a ruler he was top-notch.

Although he was neither tall (5'5") nor handsome, he seemed to strike people as both. He was charming, a great conversationalist, and an excellent horseman. He played the harpsichord and guitar (acoustic) and loved ballroom dancing. He was perhaps the most polite king ever, listening closely to his courtiers and tipping his hat to everyone on the street. Most of all he loved the outdoors, and that made him want his palace in the countryside, not in stuffy Paris.

Louis called himself the "Sun King." State medallions showed the light and warmth of the sun bouncing off his chest onto the people of France. To make their "divine authority" more believable, divine monarchs such as Louis

Louis XIV, the Sun King. *"If Louis XIV had not existed, it would have been necessary to invent him." – Voltaire*

went to great lengths to control nature. Louis had an orange grove on wheels that he had his servants roll out of his greenhouse on sunny days. His people would stroll through the finely manicured gardens of Versailles, proud to be ruled by such a wonderful king—a king deputized by God, and the only one who could sip an Orange Julius in the dead of winter.

Louis "domesticated" his nobles by reducing them to petty socialites more concerned with their position at court than with political issues. It worked so well that Louis had the high-and-mighty dukes and earls of France bickering over who would get to hold the candle while he slipped into his royal jammies. The tremendous expenses of court life weakened the nobility economically. Louis had them in a state of loyal servitude.

As Louis said, *"L'etat, c'est moi!"* ("The state, it's me!")

Versailles: Europe's Palace of Palaces

A divine monarch needs a big house. Louis moved his court to Versailles, 12 miles outside Paris. There he built Europe's greatest palace, at the cost of six months' worth of the entire income of France. Swamps were filled in, hills were moved, and a river was rerouted to give Louis a palace fit for a divine king. He established a magnificent court (the Oz and Hollywood of Europe) that attracted

Europe's Palace of Palaces, **Versailles**

the leading artists, thinkers, and nobles of the day. Though it was France's capital for only a century (1682–1789), Versailles was the social, cultural, and intellectual capital of Europe.

The enormous palace was dwarfed by endless gardens. Great halls decorated in the "Grand Style" with chandeliers and mirrored walls. Tapestries, gold leaf, and silver plating. Fountains, pools, and manicured shrubs. We can marvel at these today at Versailles, but they hardly give a full picture of the glory and decadence of everyday life under the Sun King, Louis XIV.

What we don't see: those thousand orange trees planted in silver tubs; the zoo with exotic animals in cages; the sedan-chair taxis shuttling nobles from château to château; the 1,500 fountains (only 300 remain); the Leonardos, Raphaels, Titians, Rubenses, and Caravaggios (now in the Louvre) that hung in halls and bedrooms; the gondolas from Venice poling along the canals at night, accompanied by barges with musicians; the grand halls lit by thousands of candles for a ball. Most of all, we don't see the thousands of finely dressed nobles and their servants and the center of all the gaiety, Louis himself.

Louis lived his life as though it was a work of art to be admired by all. He rose late and was dressed not by servants, but by nobles and barons. Around noon he ate breakfast, and then he attended Mass. In

The Hall of Mirrors, *Versailles. This is where France's beautiful people partied. Pass the Fromage-Whiz.*

the afternoon Louis worked, and worked hard, meeting advisers, generals, and bishops. At 5:00 p.m. he ate dinner, either alone or with the queen, though he wasn't ever really alone. Every action was a public ritual attended by nobles of the court.

Louis had an enormous appetite. His typical dinner might have included four different soups, two whole fowl stuffed with truffles, a huge salad, mutton, ham slices, fruit, pastry, compotes, and preserves.

Nighttime was spent playing royal games, gambling, or socializing. Louis then had a late supper (near midnight) and retired.

Louis' life of leisure was nothing compared with that of the nobility, who had absolutely nothing to do day after day except play. They had no government function in France's modern bureaucracy except to attend to Louis' daily rituals. They survived on favors from the king: pensions, military and church appointments, and arranged marriages with wealthy nobles. It was essential to be liked by the king or you were lost. If Louis didn't look at you for weeks on end, you knew you had to seek an audience with him and apologize with many tears and much hugging of the royal knees. Compare the position of France's weakened nobility with that of England's at the same time: the lords in Parliament had just beheaded their king.

Versailles in its heyday had 5,000 of these domesticated nobles (with at least as many dependents) buzzing about the grounds seeking favors. Business was conducted at the billiards tables, dances, concerts, and receptions, and—the most common pastime—while gambling. (They usually played a version of 21.) Large gambling debts made many nobles still more dependent on Louis.

Dressing properly was part of the favor-seeking game. Men shaved their rough beards and put on stockings and silk clothes. Big, curly wigs became the rage when Louis started to go bald. A contemporary wrote, "It was possible to tell the women from the men only when it was time to go to bed."

One of the "fashions" was adultery, an accepted, almost obligatory social ritual. Louis' succession of mistresses was legendary. Still, he remained faithful to the institution of marriage itself and fulfilled his obligation to the queen, Marie-Therese of Spain, by sleeping with her every night (after a rendezvous with one of his lovers).

Versailles allowed the perfect escape from life's harsh realities. Even in his choice of art, Louis preferred grandeur and idealized beauty to simplicity and realism. He detested the naturalism of the Dutch and Flemish masters and encouraged Baroque opulence.

Still, on his deathbed, he advised his 5-year-old great-grandson Louis XV, "Don't imitate my extravagance. Alleviate the suffering of your people and do all the things I was unfortunate enough not to do." Perhaps little Louis was too young to understand, for he, too, succumbed to the lure of wealth. The Sun King's words went unheeded, and his successors in the Old Regime at Versailles continued in their gambling, fashion shows, and canoodling, oblivious to the world changing around them, right up until the French Revolution literally knocked on the palace doors.

Le Nain, **Peasant Family in an Interior** _(detail), 1642 (Louvre, Paris). And when their stomachs grumbled, the queen said, "Let them eat cake."_

The grounds surrounding Versailles are a sculptured forest, a king's playground. Explore the backyard. Marie Antoinette's little Hamlet (_le Hameau_) gives any historian or romantic goosebumps. This is where the queen (who eventually laid her neck under the "national razor" during the Revolution) escaped the rigors of palace life by pretending she was a peasant girl, tending her manicured garden and perfumed sheep.

Other Absolute Monarchs

Louis was every king's role model. Every nation in Europe had its "Louis" and its own "Versailles." As you travel, you'll notice that most palaces, from La Granja in Spain to Peter the Great's Summer Palace outside St. Petersburg, are modeled after Versailles with sculpted gardens and Halls of Mirrors—all trying, but none succeeding, to match the splendor of Louis' place.

In Vienna, the Hapsburg King Leopold built the impressive Schönbrunn Palace. A musician at heart, he established Vienna as the

Palaces of the Divine and Absolute Monarchs

France
- Versailles (near Paris)

Austria
- Schönbrunn, Vienna
- Hofburg (Imperial Palace), Vienna

Spain
- Royal Palace, Madrid
- La Granja, outside Madrid

Germany
- Residenz of the Prince Bishop, Würzburg
- Residenz, Munich

Denmark
- Frederiksborg Slot (north of Copenhagen)

Sweden
- Drottingholm, Stockholm

music capital of Europe. Vienna later produced Haydn, Mozart, Beethoven, and many of the classical superstars, who lived, worked, taught, and occasionally jammed together in the city.

King Frederick William of Prussia (eastern Germany) copied France's centralized government and turned his loose collection of baronies into a monolithic European power. The "goose step" and Germany's strong military tradition came from Prussia.

England also had strong monarchs, but her people insisted on constitutional limits. Henry VIII's daughter, Elizabeth I, made England the world's top naval power and enjoyed the loyalty and support of nobles and commoners alike. However, her successors, the Scottish Stuart family, alienated the English with their divine-right style. The English Parliament rebelled against King Charles (Stuart), and a Civil War broke out in the mid-1600s. In the end, the king was beheaded and a member of Parliament, Oliver Cromwell, took power. When Cromwell died the monarchy was restored, but the ruler's power came from Parliament, not from God. (You'll find much more about England's bloody and glorious history in the Appendix.)

Spain and Portugal: A Capsule History

Louis XIV's great rivals for European superiority were his neighbors to the southwest, Spain and Portugal. During their Golden Age (1500–1650), Spain and Portugal dominated the economy of Europe. Gold and raw materials poured in from their colonial possessions in the New World, Asia, and Africa, making the Iberian Peninsula the most powerful corner of Europe.

The story of Spain and Portugal's rise as Europe's first colonial powers is a fascinating one, weaving strands from different cultures. To explain it, we'll need to backtrack a bit in time. Switch your orientation from chronological to geographical and prepare yourself for a slight jolt. Here goes.

The Moors (711–1492)

The Moors, North African Moslems who occupied Spain, had a great cultural influence on Spanish and Portuguese history. They arrived on the Rock of Gibraltar in 711 and moved north. In just seven years, the Moors conquered virtually the entire peninsula, leaving only small pockets of Christian culture.

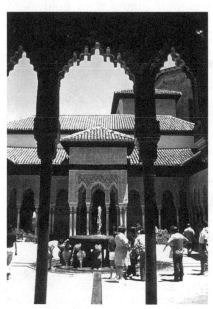

Court of the Lions, Alhambra, Granada, Spain

They established their power and Moslem culture, but in a subtle way. Non-Moslems (both Christians and Jews) were tolerated and often rose to positions of wealth and power. Instead of blindly suppressing the natives by force, the Moors used their superior power and knowledge to develop whatever they found. They encouraged the growing of grapes for wine even though, for religious reasons, they themselves weren't allowed to drink alcohol.

Throughout the seven-century reign of the Moors, feisty enclaves of Christianity remained. Local Christian kings fought against the Moors whenever they could, whittling away at the Moslem empire, gaining more and more land. After a sustained push, the last Moorish stronghold, Granada, fell to the Christians in 1492.

The slow process of the Reconquista (reconquest) resulted in the formation of the two independent states of Portugal and Spain. In 1139, Alfonso Henriques conquered the Moors near present-day Beja in southern Portugal and proclaimed himself the king of the region. In 1200, the state of Portugal had the same borders it has today (making it the oldest unchanged state in Europe). The rest of the peninsula was a loosely-knit collection of smaller kingdoms until 1469, when Ferdinand II of Aragon married Isabella of Castile. Known as the "Catholic Monarchs," they united what is essentially modern Spain under their rule.

The Golden Age (1500–1650)

The expulsion of the Moors set the stage for the rise of Portugal and Spain as naval powers and colonial superpowers. This was Spain's "Golden Age."

It was Ferdinand and Isabella who financed Columbus' expedition to seek a new western trade route to Asia. Through exploration (and exploitation) of the colonies, tremendous amounts of gold were stockpiled in Portugal and Spain. The aristocracy and the clergy swam in money. Art and courtly life were well funded.

Monument to the Discoverers, *1960, Belem, near Lisbon. With Henry the Navigator at the lead, these explorers expanded Europe's horizons and made Portugal a superpower 500 years ago.*

The Spaniards, fueled by the religious fervor of their Reconquista of the Moslems, were interested in spreading Christianity to the New World. Wherever they landed, they "Christianized" the natives—by persuasion when possible, by sword when necessary.

The Portuguese expansion was motivated more by economic concerns. Their excursions overseas were planned, cool, and rational. They colonized the nearby coasts of Africa first, progressing slowly to Asia and South America.

When Vasco da Gama sailed around the southern tip of Africa to India in 1498, he opened a profitable new trade route with the East, breaking Italy's monopoly on trade with the Orient. The states on the Atlantic seaboard—Portugal, Spain, Holland, and England—emerged as the superpowers of trade.

From that point on, Italy stagnated, becoming an economic backwater and a political pawn of the stronger nations that took the lead economically as well as culturally. The Prado collection, chock-full of Italian masterpieces bought with New World gold, testifies to Spain's wealth. The focus of European civilization shifted further west.

Iberian Art and Architecture

The two most fertile periods of architectural innovation in Spain and Portugal were the Moorish occupation and the Golden Age. Otherwise, Spanish architecture followed many of the same trends as the rest of Europe.

The Moors brought with them many Middle Eastern design elements, such as the horseshoe arch, minarets, and floor plans designed for mosques. The Islamic religion forbids the sculpting or painting of human or animal figures ("graven images"), so artists expressed their creativity with elaborate geometric patterns. The ornate stucco of the Alhambra in Granada, the striped arches of Cordoba's mosque, and decorative colored tiles are evidence of the Moorish sense of beauty. Mozarabic (Christians under Moslem rule) and Mudejar (Moslem) styles blended Eastern and Western elements.

As Christians slowly reconquered the peninsula, they turned their fervor into stone, building huge churches in the heavy, fortress-of-God Romanesque style (as seen at Santiago de Compostela) and in the lighter, heaven-reaching, stained-glass Gothic style (as seen in Barcelona, Toledo, and Sevilla). Gothic was an import from France, trickling into conservative Spain long after it swept through Europe.

The money reaped and raped from Spain's colonies in the Golden Age (1500–1650) spurred new construction. Churches and palaces were built in both the solid, geometric style of the Italian Renaissance (such as the severe El Escorial palace) and the more ornamental Baroque. Ornamentation reached unprecedented heights of frilliness in Spain, culminating in the Plateresque style of stonework, so called because it resembles intricate silver filigree work.

Portugal's economic boom also triggered a cultural boom. The 16th-century Manueline style in art and architecture is an exuberant combination of Gothic and Renaissance forms decorated with shells, anchors, and ropes. These nautical motifs are a tribute to the source of the money that made this art possible: the lucrative sea-trade. You can see fine examples of this Portuguese Renaissance style in the Lisbon suburb of Belem. The cloisters of the Jeronimos Monastery are the most impressive in Iberia.

After the Golden Age, innovation in Spain and Portugal died out, and most buildings from the 18th and 19th centuries follow predictable European trends.

In painting during the Golden Age, Italian Renaissance style was the rage. The Prado's vast collection of Titians makes this clear. Local Spanish painters, caught in the grip of the medieval Inquisition and the holy war against the Moors, concentrated on religious scenes. Secular art had to be imported.

El Greco

El Greco (1541–1614) fused Italian Renaissance technique with the Spanish religious passion. Born in Greece (his nickname means "The Greek"), trained in Venice, and caught up in the devout fervor of Spanish mysticism, El Greco combined Greek iconography, Venetian color, and Spanish Catholicism to create an individual style.

El Greco's people have unnaturally elongated, slightly curved bodies, like flickering flames. The serene faces look like those of saints on a Byzantine icon. Yet it is obvious from the natural, personal details of his portraits that El Greco learned Renaissance realism.

El Greco is often called the first "modern" painter because he deliberately chose to tamper with realism to emotionalize a painting. By now, nature and realism had been mastered. Artists set about busily exploring new realms.

If you fall in love with El Greco at the Prado, then you must visit his hometown, Toledo, which is dotted with his works. The histori-

El Greco, **Pentecost** *(detail), 1604 (Prado, Madrid). From El Greco's time on, artists were free to go beyond naturalism.*

cal and cultural capital of Spain, Toledo is a great place to gain an appreciation of the Spanish Renaissance. A tour of Toledo's cathedral, with masterpieces from the greatest Spanish artists of each era from Gothic to Baroque, will open your eyes to the fact that Italy didn't have a monopoly on artistic genius. Local pride shines through as your guide shows you what was going on in Spain while Michelangelo was busy painting the Sistine Chapel.

Slow Decline

The dazzling, fast money from the colonies blinded Portugal and Spain to the dangers at home. Great Britain and the Netherlands, which had become strong naval powers, defeated the Spanish Armada in 1588.

During the centuries when science and technology in all other European countries developed as never before, Spain and Portugal were occupied with their failed colonial politics. The Portuguese imported everything, stopped growing their own wheat, and neglected their fields.

Endless battles, wars of succession, revolutions, and counter-revolutions weakened Spain and Portugal.

In the 18th century, Spain was ruled by the French Bourbon family. Major sights of the era, such as Madrid's Royal Palace and the nearby La Granja Palace, are French in style. In the chaos, there was no chance to develop democratic forms of government. Dictators in both countries made the rich richer and stifled the underprivileged masses.

Democracy is a recent phenomenon in Spain and Portugal. In the 1930s, Spain suffered a bloody and bitter civil war between fascist and democratic forces. The fascist dictator Franco won, ruling the country until his death in the 1970s, when democratic elections were finally held. Portugal, following an unbloody revolution, also held democratic elections in 1975. Today, moderate Socialists are in power in both countries, trying (with moderate success) to fight the problems of unemployment and foreign debts. Spain, a latecomer to the European Union, is now enjoying a boomtime. Since the events of 1992 (the World's Fair, Olympic Games, and 500th anniversary of Columbus' "discovery" of America), *Viva España* is sung *con gusto*.

Baroque Art

After 100 years of religious wars and squabbles over who would rule whom and who would worship which way, Europe chose religious toleration, stability, strong absolute monarchs, and a pro-status-quo art called Baroque. Baroque contrasts with the simplicity and balance of Renaissance art.

Baroque is propaganda art. It was meant to wow the masses into compliance with authority. Artists promoted respect for their patrons, the church, and the king by using the most complex, dazzling, and moving effects ever. Ornamentation abounds. Abundance abounds.

With the Renaissance, the viewer entered the world of art. In the Baroque era, art enters the world of the viewer. While Renaissance art appealed to a small elite corps of humanists (through classics, logic, and intellect), Baroque appeals to the masses with emotion. This was pop art with super-dramatic interpretations. If Renaissance art was meditation, Baroque art was theater.

Church decoration became a cooperative adventure, with painters, sculptors, stucco workers, and metalworkers all teaming up to portray Heaven itself. The average person could step into a world of glittering gold, precious stones, and a ceiling painted as if it opened up to the sky, with angels, saints, babies that looked like clouds, and

St. Peter's Basilica, *Vatican City, Rome. The Baroque movement was born here, in the grandest church in Christendom.*

clouds that looked like babies—everything (in better Baroque) balanced into a unified whole.

Baroque architecture uses Renaissance symmetry decorated with lots of ornamental curlicues, stucco work, ovals, and elliptical shapes. The interiors are bright, with clear windows, whitewashed walls, colored marble, and gold leaf. Many darker medieval buildings were given an update as centuries-old frescoes were whitewashed and fine old sets of stained glass were replaced by clear windows. Subtlety was out, as straight lines were interrupted whenever possible with medallions and statues.

Bernini, **St. Theresa in Ecstasy** *(detail), 1652 (Santa Maria della Vittoria, Rome)*

Bernini, **Apollo and Daphne,** *1624 (Borghese Museum, Rome). Bernini, the father of the Baroque movement, captures the exciting moment when Apollo thinks he's caught the nymph Daphne. But just as he's ready to pounce, she turns into a tree—her fingers sprout leaves, her feet sprout roots, and Apollo is in for one rude surprise.*

Bernini: Father of Baroque

Baroque was born in Rome. Its father was Lorenzo Bernini (1598–1680), its mother the wealthy Catholic Church. Rome bubbles with Bernini fountains and sculpture. Bernini spent 40 years working on his masterpiece, St. Peter's church. St. Peter's Square and the church's interior are also his. Bernini was a master of all the Renaissance techniques, but wasn't chained by its classical rules of simplicity.

His art maximizes emotion in the subject as well as the viewer. His famous statue of the mystic nun, St. Theresa, is a perfect example of

Michelangelo, **David**, 1504 (Accademia, Florence)

Bernini, **David**, 1623 (Borghese Museum, Rome)

Michelangelo's _David_ and Bernini's _David_

Michelangelo's David (1504) is textbook Renaissance, while Bernini's David (1623) is the epitome of Baroque. Compare the two styles: Michelangelo's David is a thinker—rational, cool, restrained. Bernini's is a doer—passionate, engaged, dramatic. Renaissance David is simple and unadorned, carrying only a sling. Baroque Dave is "cluttered" with a braided sling, a hairy pouch, flowing cloth, and discarded armor. A model of perfection, Michelangelo's David is far larger and grander than we mere mortals. We know he'll win. Bernini's David, with his tousled hair and set mouth, is one of us; the contest is less certain. Winding up for the pitch, Bernini's David threatens to break out of the very stone. Michelangelo's David will throw the rock when he's good and ready.

a complex but unified composition, expressive portraiture, and details suggesting movement and passion, all adding up to a very theatrical and emotional work. Bernini shows her with a heart pierced by an angel's arrow. Theresa described the feeling as "a pain so great that I screamed aloud; but simultaneously I felt such infinite sweetness that I wished the pain would last forever." As we gaze at the statue, Bernini makes us feel the same ecstasy, the same "sweet pain."

Rubens' Fury of the Brush

In painting, Baroque meant big canvases of bright colors, classical subjects, optical illusions, and swirling action.

Bernini's painting counterpart was Peter Paul Rubens (1577–1640) from Catholic Flanders (Belgium). Rubens studied in Rome, where he picked up the Italian fad of painting giant compositions on huge canvases.

He could arrange a pigpile of many figures into a harmonious unit. Each painting was powered with an energy and gaiety that people called his "fury of the brush."

Rubens' work, while colorful, intricate, and lively, was always robust, strong, and solid. Like Bernini, Rubens draped clothing on his subjects in a manner that suggested rippling motion and energy—a popular trick.

A famous scholar and diplomat, Rubens was welcomed at every royal court in Catholic Europe. His Antwerp house (now a fine museum) was an art factory, designed to mass-produce masterpieces. After he laid out a painting, his apprentices painted the background and filled in the minor details. Rubens orchestrated the production

from a balcony, and before a painting was carried outside his tall, narrow door, he would put on the finishing touches, whipping each figure to life with a flick of his furious brush.

Rubens' typically robust, energetic style: fleshy women and the "fury of the brush" were his trademarks. Compare this Baroque vibrancy to the Renaissance composure of a Raphael Madonna and Child or Leonardo's Mona Lisa.

Caravaggio

Caravaggio (carra-VAW-jee-o, 1573–1610) set out to shock people with his paintings. He depicted subjects realistically, no matter how ugly or unpleasant. He set sacred Bible scenes in the context of the seedy, seamy side of his Roman neighborhood. Caravaggio lived much of his life on the edge of society. Quick-tempered and very opinionated, he killed a man over a dispute in a tennis match and spent years as an outlaw. Twelve years after he first picked up a brush, he died of a knife wound.

Caravaggio painted with a profound psychological realism that captures the inner feelings of the common people he used as subjects. It brings to mind the style of his contemporary, Shakespeare, who acquainted himself with English low-life and incorporated it into his plays.

You'll recognize Caravaggio's works by the strong contrast between light and dark. Whole sections of canvas are in shadow, with details obscured. If light does shine on a subject, it's a harsh, unflattering, "third-degree interrogation" light that pierces through anything glorified or idealized, exposing the real person underneath.

As Caravaggio's art shows, the Bible happened to real people and miracles transform the commonplace. His saints have dirty feet. Caravaggio paints Doubting Thomas as an old common laborer. To depict the scene when Jesus said, "Reach hither thy hand and thrust it into my side," Caravaggio would paint Thomas with his grubby finger actually sticking inside Jesus' wound.

Caravaggio, **Entombment of Christ,** *1604 (Pinacoteca, Vatican Museum, Rome). Not only does this thrilling composition draw you into the action, the action threatens to come to you.*

Caravaggio, **David with the Head of Goliath,** *1605 (Kunsthistorisches Museum, Vienna). Using harsh, exaggerated light/dark contrasts, Caravaggio powers his early Baroque paintings with emotion. The severed head is his self-portrait.*

Royal Art Court Painters

You'll see plenty of royal portraits in European museums. The court painter was the official "photographer" of the day. To keep the royal egos happy, most court paintings were unrealistic, melodramatic, and flattering. One royal portraitist, Velázquez, was unusually realistic, offering a rare, real look at royal Europe.

Diego Velázquez (vel-LOSS-kess, 1599–1660), the Spanish royal court painter, was ahead of his time. Influenced by Caravaggio's hypernaturalism, he painted without showy emotion or unnecessary ornamentation. His work appears intricately detailed, but if you look closely,

Velázquez, **Prince Balthasar Carlos on Horseback,** *1635 (Prado, Madrid). To keep his boss—the king—happy, even "realistic" Velázquez had to make the prince look really good on a horse.*

Velázquez, **The Maids of Honor,** *1656 (Prado, Madrid), shows the Spanish court and the painter himself (at left) in a realistic way, without emotion. In this unusual court portrait, the artist captures the royal couple's view as they sit for a portrait. Their reflection appears in the mirror at the back of the room. More art historians consider this the greatest single painting than any other.*

you see a new technique in brushwork. Velázquez suggested details with a quick stroke of the brush, a bit like Rubens but also with a peek at a future style, Impressionism.

His *Prince Balthasar* is typical of most court portraits of the time (unnatural, grandiose, focused on royalty), but his *Maids of Honor* is a stunning departure. The artist himself is the largest figure in the piece. In the relaxed setting of his studio, the royal child is on equal footing with the maids; the king and queen are just a reflection in the background.

Christopher Wren

England's chance to make a radical break with the medieval past came when London burned in the Great Fire of 1666. Almost before the ashes had cooled, a young architect named Christopher Wren was in the mayor's office with exciting plans to rebuild the city. He got the job and set out to decorate the new downtown with more than fifty of his churches.

Wren's style shows Baroque and Gothic influences (Gothic remained popular in England long after the Middle Ages) as well as many classical features.

Wren, **St. Paul's Cathedral,** *1675–1708, London. Wren's tomb inside the church bears the epitaph: "If you seek a monument . . . look around you."*

Although better examples of Wren's architectural genius are found in smaller churches nearby, his most famous work is St. Paul's Cathedral. In studying St. Paul's, you'll notice a central Baroque cupola lined with classical columns and flanked by Gothic towers. The overall effect, however, is one not of Baroque movement, tension, or exuberance, but of classical restraint and stability.

Rococo: Uncontrolled Exuberance

The Baroque movement spread from Rome throughout Catholic Europe by way of the court of Louis XIV at Versailles. Louis' great-grandson, Louis XV, championed a new style called Rococo (pronounced "ro-KO-ko").

Rococo was an early 19th-century celebration of happiness and love. Rococo is lighter and daintier, without the Renaissance-like robustness and classical balance of Baroque. Light pastel colors, ivory, gold, mirrors, and slender columns with curvy frills characterize Rococo interior decoration. This giddy style, using decoration almost to the obliteration of form, spread quickly from Paris to Germany and Austria during the 1700s. Rococo survives today only on the stage sets of TV evangelists.

Boucher: Textbook Rococo

Wieskirche, 1746–1754, near Oberammergau, Germany. A breathless example of Bavarian Rococo, the Wieskirche (or church of the meadow) sits peacefully in the countryside of southern Germany. Built to enshrine a wooden crucifix (believed to have miraculously wept in 1738), this church has long been a popular destination for pilgrims and tourists.

Baroque and Rococo Art and Architecture

France
- Versailles

Italy
- St. Peter's church (including Bernini's altar canopy, dove window, and statues), Vatican City, Rome
- Il Gesu church (its scroll-shaped facade was the model for Jesuit churches throughout Latin America), Rome
- *St. Theresa in Ecstasy*, Church of Santa Maria della Vittoria, Rome
- Piazzas of Rome, especially St. Peter's Square
- Bernini fountains, Rome

Germany
- Residenz and Chapel of the Prince Bishop, Würzburg
- Bavarian churches (Wieskirche, Oberammergau, Ettal, Asam in Munich)

Austria
- Schönbrunn, Vienna
- Benedictine monastery, Melk on Danube
- Salzburg's Old Town

Britain
- St. Paul's, London

Czech Republic
- Charles Bridge and most of old Prague

Belgium
- Rubens' home, Antwerp. Also, paintings by Rubens in the Prado (Madrid), Louvre (Paris), National Gallery (London), and most major museums

Music
- Bach, Vivaldi, Scarlatti

Fake dome, 1684, Church of St. Ignazio (near the Pantheon), Rome. Baroque artists (like late 20th-century Republican economists) were masters of illusion. This flat ceiling was painted to look like a dome from the pews.

Northern Protestant Art

There's not a single great Protestant building or statue. The art in Protestant Northern Europe is entirely different from the flashy art that filled the churches and palaces of the Catholic world. Protestant artists had to manage without the rich and powerful Catholic Church's patronage. Depiction of elaborate ritual and anything with even a hint of idolatry was out. Religious art fell out of favor, and Protestant artists specialized in subjects that had nothing to do with the church.

During this period, many northern European churches channeled their artistic energy into music, with orchestras and elaborate church organs. Choirmaster/composer/organists (such as J. S. Bach) enjoyed a new, loftier status.

New Patronage, New Art

The wealthy merchants of the prosperous middle class became the new patrons of northern art. These city burghers were playing catch-up with the ruling class, and a great way to rise above society's small-fries was to commission a distinguished portrait of yourself.

The commissioned portrait was the artist's bread and butter. Northern artists made portraits come alive without employing the artificial or flattering poses of Baroque portraiture. From Hans Holbein to Frans Hals to Rembrandt, portraitists got better and better at capturing the real character of their subjects in relaxed, "unposed" poses.

Sadly, many of those who paid and posed were tight-fisted, more interested in value for their money than in encouraging good art. Great artists often wasted their talents on unimaginative works simply to earn a meager living from the fickle patronage of a nouveau riche whose taste was mostly in its mouth.

Rembrandt, **De Staalmeesters** (a.k.a. The Dutch Masters), 1662 (Rijksmuseum, Amsterdam). Even in his later years, Rembrandt could paint better portraits than anyone. He shows us not just faces but personalities as well. These men were members of a textile guild (clothes, but no cigars).

Jan Steen, **Die Verkehrte Welt** *(The Topsy-turvy World) (Kunsthistorisches Museum, Vienna). Without a king or the Catholic Church to buy their art, Dutch artists painted fun, unpreachy, and affordable art for the urban middle class.*

The only alternative for artists was to sell their work on the open market—an art-history first. Art was sold in marketplaces and fairs as well as through art dealers.

This new patronage pointed art in new directions. Along with portraits, artists painted scenes the average person would like and buy, such as landscapes, seascapes, slices of daily life, and fun looks at human folly. Paintings were generally small and affordable.

Slice-of-Life Art

Peter Brueghel (1564–1638) used Italian techniques to depict Flemish peasant life. A townsman himself, painting for fellow townspeople, he depicted peasants as peasants, simple and happy, but also as hicks

Brueghel, **Peasant Wedding,** *1565 (Kunsthistorisches, Vienna). Crowded, colorful, detailed look at everyday peasant life. These scenes were popular with the urban middle class.*

worth laughing at. His crowded and brightly colored scenes of people are fun and entertaining. At the same time, we can sympathize with his characters, seeing a bit of ourselves in their actions. Brueghel's paintings were very popular and often imitated. They give travelers a great glimpse of old peasant lifestyles. (The Museum of Ancient Art in Brussels and the Kunsthistorisches Museum in Vienna have two of Europe's best collections of Brueghels and Brueghel-style art.)

In a more serious style, Jan Vermeer (1632–1675) perfected the art of showing the natural beauty of common people and simple, everyday objects. His tiny domestic scenes and tranquil landscapes are a far cry from the huge, colorful, fleshy, and exciting Baroque scenes of Greek gods.

Vermeer, **Kitchen Maid**, *1658 (Rijksmuseum, Amsterdam). Vermeer creates a quiet little world where we can see the beauty in everyday things.*

Rembrandt

The plight of the creative artist at the mercy of unenlightened patrons is epitomized by the life of Dutch genius Rembrandt van Rijn (1606–1669). Young, successful, and famous as a portrait painter for wealthy merchants, he fell out of favor, probably because he had a mind of his own and refused to compromise in his portraits. If his painting's composition required it (or if he didn't like someone), he might depict his patron in a shadow or even with an arm in front of his face. Few would invest in a wonderful but risky Rembrandt portrait. He spent his last years

Rembrandt, **Self-Portrait**, *1669 (National Gallery, London)*

Northern Art Museums

Netherlands:
- Rijksmuseum (Dutch art, especially Rembrandt and Vermeer), Amsterdam

Belgium:
- Museum of Ancient Art, Brussels

Germany:
- Alte Pinakothek (German art), Munich

Austria:
- Kunsthistorisches Museum, Vienna

painting portraits of himself and poor street people. He died in poverty.

The silver lining to this story is that by failing to get commissions, Rembrandt was free to paint subjects he found interesting and challenging. His Bible scenes come to life before your eyes. Like Caravaggio, he refused to idealize or beautify his subjects. His religious scenes are portraits of the common people of Amsterdam.

Also like Caravaggio, Rembrandt can be recognized by his experimentation with contrasting light and shade. He played around with the source of light and the illumination of his figures. When he shines a light on his subject, the effect is powerful and dramatic.

Rembrandt, **The Supper at Emmaus** *(detail), 1648 (Louvre, Paris). Christ's face shines brightly out of the dark-brown surroundings. Rembrandt often chose Amsterdam commoners as models for religious subjects.*

Rembrandt, **The Night Watch**, *1642 (detail, Rijksmuseum, Amsterdam). Rembrandt makes this much more than a group portrait. It's an action scene, capturing the can-do spirit of the Dutch Golden Age.*

Van Der Helst, **Schuttersmaaltijd** *(Rijksmuseum, Amsterdam). Everyone got his money's worth in this colorful group portrait—every face is flashbulb perfect. Compare it with Rembrandt's rowdy* Night Watch.

The Age of Enlightenment

The scientific experimentation begun in the Middle Ages and the Renaissance finally bloomed in the 1600s. Copernicus (born 1473), Galileo (b. 1564), Kepler (b. 1571), and Newton (b. 1642) explained the solar system, disproving the church's view that the earth was the center of the universe.

The "scientific method" was seen as a way to solve all problems: if science enabled humanity to figure out the motion of the planets and explain the circulation of blood through the body, this enlightened thinking should be useful in answering moral and political questions as well.

The philosophers of the Enlightenment (1700s) thought that nature obeyed laws and that all of those laws could be understood by reason. Every institution and every established school of thought was given the "test of reason." Superstition and ignorance were attacked. The "Old Regime" (the era of divine monarchs, feudalism, serfdom, and so on) was picked to pieces. Thinkers and writers proposed a complete reorganization of society determined by reason, not by accident of birth.

England and France produced the social philosophies that laid the foundation of modern thought. Adam Smith established the basis for laissez-faire, the free economy of capitalism. Rousseau wrote about the "Social Contract," saying that the government is the servant of the people and that a people's revolution is justified when their government screws up. A kind of "religion of reason" was created, and for the first time, many people—respected people—said, "Christianity is stupid."

John Locke and Voltaire wrote of "natural laws" and "self-evident truths" in human relationships that make necessary a more democratic form of government. Many of Locke's phrases are used in the U.S. Declaration of Independence, a document based on the ideals of the Enlightenment. Thomas Jefferson prided himself on being a part of this enlightened movement.

The kings of this period are called "enlightened despots." They ruled efficient, modern states and supported many ideas of the Enlightenment. But while royal parlor talk might have been enlightened, royalty still refused to share power with the lower classes. The growing urban middle class, often as wealthy and educated as the nobility, wanted a bigger slice of the governmental pie. But the Old Regime lived on, and people were divided by birth, not by ability or wealth, into the rulers and the ruled.

In the Enlightenment, a new world was conceived. Europe was fast outgrowing its archaic shell. Enlightened thoughts turned to violent actions.

The French Revolution

In France, the decay of the Old Regime made especially fertile conditions for the seeds planted by the Enlightenment to blossom.

With the rise of the cities and strong monarchs, the Old Regime became the dying regime. While the three-part feudal order of nobility, clergy, and peasantry survived legally, it no longer fit the European reality. Two new social forces—the merchant class and Europe's national monarchs—would forcibly re-slice Europe's political and economic pie.

Nationalism

Basic loyalties had shifted, over the centuries, from tribe to church to monarch to nation. Nationalism was the "ism" of the 19th century.

Nationalism and the democratic ideas of the Enlightenment were tested and proven practical and possible by the American Revolution. The United States was the first truly modern nation to have a constitution based on the protection of individual rights, freedom of religion, and democracy. In 1776, Europe's eager revolutionaries were taking careful notes.

France, the home of the Enlightenment, ruled by a very unenlightened government, was ripe for revolt. Two percent of the country—the nobles and clergy—owned one-third of the land and paid no taxes. The ambitious middle class, or *bourgeoisie,* was economically

Dubbed **"The Marseillaise in Stone,"** *1836, decorating the Arc d'Triomphe, Paris*

strong but politically weak. They were unhappy with a society based on a divinely ordained division of people into rulers and ruled.

France's National Assembly, the First Step to Revolution

The restless middle class got its chance in 1789 when King Louis XVI (the Sun King's great-great-great-grandson) called an assembly of representatives to raise taxes.

The parliament met as three "estates," or classes: nobility, clergy, and peasants. The merchant class, newcomers to the social scene, were lumped in with the peasants as part of the "Third Estate." Historically, the estates voted as a unit, and the nobility and the clergy always outvoted the peasantry two to one. The middle class demanded that the assembly be restructured so that the vote would be general rather than by estate. Because the peasant estate had more representatives, this would break the Old Regime's monopoly on power. After a six-week deadlock on this issue, the Third Estate declared itself the National Assembly whether the other two liked it or not, and vowed not to go home until a modern constitution had been created.

This was a revolutionary step. In an act commoners perceived as a show of loyalty to the nobles, the king called out 18,000 troops. Traditionally, the king was anti-feudal and pro-people. The masses felt betrayed. Sides were drawn and royal orders were boldly defied.

The National Assembly became a forum for all kinds of democratic ideas. The privileged classes protested feebly as the common people shouted, "*Liberté, Egalité, Fraternité.*" Liberty, Equality, Brotherhood would now be fought for.

Mass Revolution

Like most revolutions, the French one started moderately and then took off. The masses had been awakened, and before they knew it the rich and liberal middle-class leaders of the Third Estate were riding out of control on a lower-class revolutionary stallion.

The masses were hungry and restless, having suffered several bad harvests. By allowing the price of bread to climb to record heights, the rulers had ignored the first rule in keeping the people docile. (Even today, authoritarian governments subsidize the price of bread to pacify the masses.) When the mad mobs of Paris demanded cheaper bread, Queen Marie Antoinette enraged them with her famous solution, "Let them eat cake." ("Cake" being the burnt crusts from the oven normally fed to the cattle.)

On July 14, 1789, angry Parisians stormed the Bastille, a prison that symbolized the Old Regime. The revolution escalated when prisoners were released. The mayor of Paris was beheaded with a dagger, and the mob paraded through the streets with his head on a pole. Bastille Day, the French "Fourth of July," is celebrated today with comparable pageantry but fewer deaths. (All that's left of the actual Bastille is a mark on the pavement.)

Angered by a lavish and well-publicized party at Versailles, the hungry women of Paris marched on the palace. They returned the king to Paris, where the government had come under the control of the radical city elements.

Throughout the countryside that summer, the peasants went on a mysteriously spontaneous rampage, sacking châteaus, rousting the nobility, and burning the feudal documents that tied them to the land. Overnight, the manorial system (serfdom) was physically destroyed. The National Assembly followed by legally abolishing serfdom, manorialism, tithes, and so on.

Feudalism was dead in France and shock waves rippled through Europe. Royalty quivered, nobility shivered, and the middle classes and peasantry drooled with excitement as the French created the "Declaration of the Rights of Man and of the Citizen."

Much of France's ruling class took refuge in foreign palaces. They pushed for war, telling their European counterparts that they would be the next to go if they didn't do something quickly.

The revolutionaries running France also wanted a war, both to establish and solidify their new republic by banding against a common enemy and to spread their enlightened revolutionary gospel.

Revolutionary government of France at work, accusing each other of insufficient revolutionary zeal.

By 1793, it was France against the rest of Europe. France declared war on Britain, Spain, and the Netherlands. Then Austria, Piedmont, and Prussia joined the battle against France. A *levée en masse*, or complete mobilization of the society, fueled by tremendous national patriotism and led by brash young risk-taking generals, powered France to victory.

Reign of Terror

On the home front, pressures of the war and economic problems drove the revolution to wild extremes. During this "Reign of Terror" (1793–1794), the king and queen were beheaded and wave after wave of people went to the guillotine. Political factions accused each other of halting the progress of the revolution. Enemies of the current ruling party were executed in public demonstrations in Paris' Place de la Concorde. People were sent to the "national razor" if they were even suspected of insufficient patriotism. Flags waved furiously as the blade dropped on over 17,000 necks.

The revolution snowballed until even the raging fanatic liberal Robespierre was made a foot shorter at the top by the blade of the guillotine. Paris cooled off when it realized that the revolution was out of control and actually eating itself up. Some people even considered reinstating the monarchy.

The revolution struggled along for five years. At the same time, from his Italian refuge, the French heir to the throne was calling for revenge. To keep the revolution alive, the revolutionary leaders decided to give the army control rather than lose everything to an Old Regime king. They needed a revolutionary hero . . . an enlightened, charismatic, dashing general . . . a short guy who

*The head (right) of **King Louis XVI** (left). Thousands of heads rolled in the early 1790s. The guillotine was set up on Paris' Place de la Concorde.*

kept his feet on the ground, his eyes on the horizon, and his hand in his shirt. In 1799, a 30-year-old general named Napoleon took power. He promised to govern according to the principles of the revolution.

Napoleon

Although Napoleon was basically a dictator (who later proclaimed himself emperor) and many civil liberties were suspended during his reign, he was true to his promise to carry out what the revolution was all about. Church lands were confiscated and sold and privileged classes were abolished. Feudalism was finally buried.

During his rule (1799– 1814), Napoleon carried the revolution by war to the rest of Europe. His arsenal was France—Europe's richest, most populous, and best-educated state. With the barriers of class and privilege smashed, he opened positions to talent. The French army had grown strong and tough during the wars of the revolution, and Napoleon had no trouble conquering Europe. A grand Napoleonic Empire covering the entire Continent was created, and many people spoke of Paris as the "New Rome."

Napoleon Bonaparte

Britain was one of the few countries to frustrate Napoleon. By winning the Battle of Trafalgar (off the coast of southwest Spain) in 1805, Britain successfully established control of the seas, thwarting Napoleon's hope of a French takeover. The British hero Admiral Horatio Nelson died in the Battle of Trafalgar. Today, London's main square is named after this battle. The square is decorated by a huge column with Nelson at its top, looking out in the direction of the battle that saved Britain from Napoleon.

To some Europeans, Napoleon was a genius, a hero, a friend of the common people, and an enemy of oppression. (Beethoven had originally planned to dedicate his Third "Heroic" Symphony to him.) To others, he was the tyrant of his century—pompous, vain, and egotistical, suppressing a desire to be like the royalty he opposed.

The Complex Corsican

Born on the Mediterranean isle of Corsica (the year after it became French) of Italian parents, Napoleon was educated in French military schools. Originally an outsider, he quickly lost his accent and rose through the ranks of the army during the chaotic French Revolution.

Napoleon's personality was as complex as his place in history. He was actually of average height and thin (until age and high living put on the pounds), with a classic, intense profile. He was well read, a good writer, and a charming conversationalist who could win friends and influence people with ease. He had few of the vices that plague world conquerors: he cared little for good food and drink or fancy clothes, and he worked himself as hard as he worked others. Nevertheless, he could be cold, distant, and ruthless with his enemies.

Above all else, he was egotistical and power hungry, convinced of his inherent right to rule others. Yet he was a genius of military and political administration. Although he was easily flattered, he never let flattery cloud his judgment.

Ingres, **Napoleon I on the Imperial Throne** *(detail), 1806 (Museum of the Army, Paris). "We must not leave this world without leaving traces which remind posterity of us."* – *Napoleon, Emperor of France*

Russia, Waterloo, and a New King

Napoleon's empire didn't last long. In 1812, he led half a million soldiers into Russia. The vastness of Russia, Russia's "scorched earth" policy, and its special ally, the horribly cold winter, spelled disaster for Napoleon's Grand Army. Only 10,000 Frenchmen returned to France. The nightmares of that ill-fated invasion haunted soldiers' minds for generations. (Europe's best military museum, Les Invalides, is in Paris, next to Napoleon's tomb.)

With Napoleon reeling, all of Europe called for a pigpile on France, vowing to fight for twenty years, if necessary, until France was defeated. The French people took the hint, toppled Napoleon's government and sent him on a permanent vacation to the island of Elba, off the Italian coast.

As evidence of Napoleon's personal charisma, he soon returned from his exile-in-disgrace, bared his breast to the French people, and said, "Strike me down or follow me." They followed him into one last military fling. It was only after the crushing defeat at Waterloo in 1815 that Napoleon was finished. (The battle site is in Belgium, south of Brussels, but not worth a detour except to true Bonapartisans.)

Bonaparte was exiled again, this time to a tiny island in the south Atlantic, and France was ruled by a modern king. Napoleon was the last of the enlightened despots of the Old Regime and the first of the modern popular dictators. He was a rationalist, an agnostic of the passing age of Voltaire and the Enlightenment, and the model heroic individual of the future Romantic world.

After swinging from Louis XIV to the Revolution to Napoleon, France finally settled down with another king. But French kings after Napoleon were limited by a constitution. Knowing they'd better keep their wigs and leotards out of sight, they went to work every day like any businessmen: wearing suits, carrying briefcases.

Neoclassicism

Baroque had been the art of the Old Regime—of divine-right monarchs, powerful clergy, and landed aristocracy. The French Revolution killed that regime and its art, replacing it with a style more in tune with the Enlightenment. This new art was "Neoclassical," modeled not on the aristocratic extravagance of Versailles or the Rococo excess of the Wieskirche, but on the "democratic" simplicity of ancient Greece and Rome.

Archaeological discoveries had roused France's interest in the classical world. Pompeii, the Roman city buried by a volcano in A.D. 79, was rediscovered in 1748, giving Europe its best look ever at Roman daily life, dress, customs, art, and architecture. Books on Roman and Greek life came into vogue. Parisian women wore Pompeiian hairdos. Artists studied ancient art; they found that the art of the Renaissance was not truly classical, and they tried to capture the true Greek and Roman style. Ancient became modern, and classical was in.

Throughout Europe, but especially in Paris, tourists are fooled by classical-looking buildings that are actually Neoclassical—only 200 years old.

Boucher's Rococo **Madame Pompadour** *(left, from 1756) and David's Neoclassical* **Madame Hamelin** *(right, from 1800) could well have been mother and daughter. But in the age of revolution, Europe dumped its curls and ribbons for pure classical truth. Talk about a generation gap.*

French Art of the "New Rome"

In France, the official style of the Revolution and the Napoleonic era was Neoclassical. The French thought of themselves as citizens of a new Rome and wanted art to match. In Paris, the Pantheon and the Arc de Triomphe were built to look like grand Roman monuments. Funded by the spoils of Napoleon's conquests in Europe, Paris was rebuilt and ornamented with gas lamps and new bridges.

Napoleon had himself crowned emperor in an elaborate ceremony in the style of the Caesars. Classical backdrops masked the Gothic columns of Notre Dame cathedral so the emperor could be crowned as "Romanly" as possible. Paris was the new Rome. Napoleon was the new Caesar.

The great painter Jacques-Louis David (pronounced "dah-VEED," 1748–1825) was France's virtual dictator of fashion during this period. Marriage ceremonies, clothing styles, hairdos, and giant government propaganda spectacles were designed according to David's interpretation of Neoclassicism. David's painting style was realistic, dignified, and simple, like a classical statue.

Napoleon's armies spread Neoclassicism throughout Europe. Then, like the Enlightenment, Neoclassicism spread throughout the world. Thomas Jefferson, a child of the Age of Reason, designed his residence,

David, **The Coronation of Napoleon,** *1807 (Louvre, Paris). There's Napoleon with his wife Josephine (kneeling) and his proud mom, not actually in attendance but painted (looking on from the balcony). The pope (seated behind Napoleon) came all the way from Rome to crown him. But no ordinary mortal was good enough for that job, so Napoleon crowned himself.*

Monticello (of nickel fame), in the Neoclassical style. The Capitol of the United States and many state capitols have similar Neoclassical architecture. "Enlightened" people everywhere rejected the gaudy ornamentation of Baroque in favor of austere arches and pure columns.

New Patronage: The Academy

The French Revolution and the rise of democracy in Europe changed the economics of art just as the Reformation had changed the economics of art in the Protestant countries of the North. As art became

David, **Death of Socrates,** *1787 (Louvre, Paris). Classical scenes were in vogue in Neoclassical Paris.*

less and less the domain of the elite class and the church, it became more the domain of the middle class. As commissions became rare, artists had less money, but more freedom.

Previously, artists had studied as apprentices under a master who was employed by a wealthy patron. Now they went to "Academies" (pompously named after Plato's Academy of Philosophy in Athens) to study art history, theory, and technique. Here, artists were free to pursue and paint their own ideas of beauty, not those of whomever was paying them. Art became an expression of individuality—not merely a craft, but Art with a capital "A."

Neoclassical Art, Architecture, and Music
France
   • Neoclassical room (Ingres, David), Louvre, Paris
   • Arc de Triomphe, Pantheon, and La Madeleine, Paris
Britain
   • Royal Crescent and Circus, Bath
   • Georgian mansions in Bath, England,
     and Edinburgh, Scotland
Finland
   • Lutheran Cathedral and Senate Square, Helsinki
Music
   • Mozart, Haydn, Beethoven

Pantheon, *Paris. Built during France's bold experiment in democracy and free-thinking, this was like a Greek Temple of Reason.*

Musical Vienna

While France dealt with revolution and Napoleon, Vienna enjoyed Europe's greatest age of music. Vienna was to music what ancient Athens and Renaissance Florence were to painting and sculpting. Never before or since have so many great composers and musicians worked and competed side by side. Haydn, Mozart, Beethoven, and Schubert all worked in Vienna at roughly the same time (1775–1825). Their works changed music forever, raising it from simple entertainment to High Art.

Why Vienna? A walk through the city explains part of it. The peaceful gardens, the architecture, and the surrounding countryside inspired the composers, many of whom wrote tunes in their head as they strolled through the streets. Beethoven was a familiar sight, striding quickly, his hands behind his back, staring straight ahead with a brooding look on his face. He claimed he did his best writing away from the piano.

Money Makes Music

But the true root of all musical inspiration in Vienna was (as is the case with most art) money. The aristocracy found music more interesting than politics. Concerts were the social hub of high society. Many leading families employed their own orchestras to play at their parties. Some nobles were excellent amateur musicians: Emperor Joseph II played both violin and cello; Empress Maria Theresa was a noted soprano.

Professionals were needed to perform, conduct, compose, and give lessons. Musicians from all over Europe flocked to Vienna, where their talents were rewarded with money and honor.

Before 1750, music had been considered a common craft, like shoemaking, and musicians were treated accordingly. Composers wrote music to order, expecting it to be played once and thrown away (like Kleenex). Beginning with Haydn, however, the new breed of composers saw music as a lasting art on par with painting and sculpture.

They demanded respect from their employers. Beethoven, it is said, considered himself to be superior to his employers: he was an artist; they were merely royalty. When Mozart became composer-in-residence for a Viennese prince, he was paid a princely sum and then told to eat his meals with the servants. Mozart turned on his heel and walked out, refusing from then on to accept an "official" position.

Unappreciated Geniuses

Vienna fawned over its composers but only as long as they cranked out pleasant tunes. The minute they tried something new, daring, or difficult, the public turned on them.

Mozart was adored as a cute, clever 6-year-old who could play the harpsichord as well as anyone in Europe. He won the hearts of the nobility by declaring that he wanted to marry the Princess Marie Antoinette.

But as a grown man writing mature and difficult works, he was neglected and often maligned. When he died, broke, at 35, his body was buried in an unmarked grave. Only later was his genius fully appreciated and a statue erected to honor him. As the saying goes, "To be popular in Vienna, it helps to be dead."

Beethoven, like Michelangelo before him, played the role of the temperamental genius to the hilt. His music and personality were uncompromising. A bachelor, he lived in rented rooms all his life— 69 different ones at last count. He had some bad habits that explain his migratory existence, such as playing the piano at 2:00 a.m. and pouring buckets of water on himself to cool off. His rooms were

*Portrait of the child prodigy, **Mozart**. It's said Wolfgang had his cheeks kissed by more queens than anyone in history.*

always a mess, with music, uneaten meals, and atonal chamber pots strewn about.

While late 20th-century America will be known for bringing together the best basketball players of the age, Vienna assembled a musical "dream team" of its own. Beethoven, Mozart, and Haydn might have jammed together in Vienna. "Papa" Haydn (so called because of his fatherly way with younger musicians) encouraged Mozart and gave lessons to Beethoven. Beethoven also learned from Antonio Salieri, Mozart's composing rival. Music in Vienna flourished with so many talented people rubbing elbows and engaging in healthy competition.

Strauss Waltzes

And then there was Strauss. And then there was Strauss, Jr. The waltz craze swept through Vienna in the early 19th century and has continued in three-quarter time to the present. The two leading composers and conductors of the waltz were father and son: Johann Strauss, Sr., and Johann Strauss, Jr.

The waltz was the Beatlemania of its time. Many considered it decadent because of the close contact of the partners and the passionate sound of the music. Dances lasted from dusk to dawn, night after night. Johann the Elder played the violin and simultaneously conducted with wild gestures, whipping the crowd to "bewildering heights of frenzy till they were frantic with delight and emitting groans of ecstasy," according to composer Richard Wagner.

Young Johann took the baton when his father died and raised the waltz to respectability. His "Tales from the Vienna Woods" and "Blue Danube" immortalized his beloved hometown.

Imagine the lavish balls and mirrored halls where this music was played during the Golden Age of Emperor Franz Joseph. Chandeliers, carriages, sumptuous costumes, ceremony, and white-gloved ritual were the heart and soul of the conservative aristocracy. Franz Joseph of the royal Hapsburg house was not merely a king, but also the emperor of the Holy Roman Empire, namely, Austria and Hungary.

The Vienna of today clings to the elegance of its past and maintains much of that musical tradition. The Ministry of Culture and Education is the new patron. The State Opera, the Philharmonic Orchestra, the Vienna Boys' Choir, and the Society of Friends of Music still thrive as they did in Beethoven's time. There are statues of all the famous composers who were neglected in their day. And if you dial 1509 on a telephone in Vienna, you will hear a perfect A-note (440 Hz) for tuning your instrument.

Congratulations . . .

You've survived the wars, despots, and revolutions of Europe's Early Modern Age. Next come the wars, despots, and revolutions of the Modern World. But first, see if you can make some sense of this timeline.

Timeline of Early Modern Europe

The Reformation and religious wars split Europe into two camps: the Protestant North (northern Germany, the Netherlands, England, Scandinavia) and the Catholic South (Italy, France, Spain, southern Germany). The northern countries, relying on a strong middle (merchant) class, were generally democratic. The South tended toward rule by absolute (and occasionally Enlightened) despots. In succeeding centuries, the democratic ideals of the Enlightenment sank in and old regimes gave way to more modern governments.

This historical journey from religious division to absolute monarchy to democracy is also apparent in art styles. The rich Baroque style, associated with the Catholic Church and absolute monarchs such as France's Louis XIV, was centered in Italy and France. At the same time, the middle-class Northern Protestant countries (Holland and England) developed a less grand style, as exemplified by the works of Rembrandt. As both North and South moved toward democracy, a new style appeared that reflected the ideals of the ancient world—Neoclassicism. This was the dominant style of the French Revolution and the reign of Napoleon, the emperor of the "New Rome."

EARLY MODERN EUROPE

Delacroix, **Liberty Leading the People,** *1830 (Louvre, Paris). This dramatic scene captures the spirit of patriotism. Liberty, in the form of a woman, carries a gun in one hand and a flag in the other—the winning combination for 19th-century nationalist movements.*

The Modern World
A.D. 1815–Today

The Age of Nationalism

In spite of the brief conservative backlash which followed the French Revolution and Napoleon, the rights of individuals and nations had forever replaced the world of feudalism and the Old Regime.

Nationalism, a patriotic desire for national unity, was the dream and the political drive of the 1800s. When you travel in Europe, keep in mind that 140 years ago Germany and Italy did not exist. They were patchwork quilts of feudal baronies, dukedoms, and small kingdoms. As you tour castles, treasuries, and palaces scattered across these nations, you're seeing the White Houses and crown jewels of such "countries" as Piedmont, Saxony, and Bavaria.

In the 1800s, as democratic ideals became popular among the middle class and intellectuals, the people were no longer satisfied to be ruled by a royal family that was usually from another country. In the previous century, most of Europe had been ruled by the Bourbon, Hapsburg, and Hohenzollern families. The king often spoke a language different from that of his subjects.

Now people insisted on a government that reflected their language, ethnic heritage, culture, and religion. People now identified themselves as citizens of a particular ethnic heritage, even if their nation was not yet a political reality. The stove setting switched from "simmer" to "high" and Europe's nationalistic stew was ready to boil over.

Unification of Italy

In the mid-1800s, the petty kingdoms and city-states of the Italian peninsula began a move toward unity. The governments were content but the people weren't, and talk of the *"Risorgimento"* (resurgence) of national pride was everywhere. As national revolts were crushed by

ITALIAN UNIFICATION

Four Italian leaders welded the Italian States into the Kingdom of Italy. Dates indicate year of annexation to the Kingdom of Sardinia (after 1861, the Kingdom of Italy).

Garibaldi

Cavour

Mazzini

Victor Emmanuel

DCH

local governments, patriotism grew. The liberals of Europe supported the Italian cause, and a local writer, Mazzini, made unification almost a holy crusade. Several shrewd patriots organized a campaign for unification, channeling nationalistic fervor into the formation of Italy.

The logical first king of Italy was the only native monarch of the region, Victor Emmanuel II, King of Sardinia. His prime minister, Cavour, a cunning, liberal, yet realistic politician, orchestrated the unification of Italy. Guided by Cavour, Sardinia joined the Crimean War in order to get allies who would support Sardinia in a war with Austria (a war Sardinia needed but couldn't win without allies). Sure enough, Cavour wrested Italian Lombardy (North Italy) from Austria. His clever statesmanship, combined with many local revolutions that were legitimized by plebiscites (local votes of popular support), brought most of northern Italy together by 1860.

Meanwhile, the powerful revolutionary general Garibaldi sailed with his motley army of a thousand "red shirts" to Sicily, where his forces were joined by local revolutionaries in annexing the Kingdom of Two Sicilies into the New Italian State.

Remember the names of these Italian patriots. Throughout Italy you'll find squares and streets named after the "Washingtons" and "Jeffersons" of the Italian resurgence—Via Cavours, Piazza Garibaldis, and monuments to Victor Emmanuel. (The most famous of these is the giant Victor Emmanuel monument near the Roman Forum.)

National pride was fueled by the romantic movement in art. Artists returned to their ethnic roots, incorporating folklore into their novels and folk music into their symphonies. In Italy, Giuseppe Verdi used the opera to champion the unification movement. In a time when flying the Italian colors was still dangerous, opera houses rang with the sound of patriots singing along with anthem-like choruses. The letters in Verdi's name were used as a nationalistic slogan: Victor Emmanuel *Roi* (king) *di Italia*.

Unification of Germany

In 1850, Germany was 39 little countries. Twenty years later it was united, and it was Europe's number one power.

During that period of growth, German iron and coal output multiplied sixfold, surpassing that of France. Cities, industries, and trade boomed. The stage was set for one of the German states, Prussia (a militaristic eastern German state), under Prime Minister Bismarck, to assert itself as the goose-stepping force behind German unity.

Otto von Bismarck, the original master of "realpolitik," was one of the greatest political geniuses of all time. He said, "Not by speeches and majority votes are the great questions of the day decided, but by blood and iron." For him, the great issue was German unification under Prussia.

Otto von Bismarck, 1815–1898. The great realistic politician of the 1800s, Bismarck created a united Germany.

Bismarck united Germany as if reading from a great political recipe book. With a logical, calculated, step-by-step approach, he created the dish nobody in Europe wanted—a united Germany.

German unification seemed inevitable. The big question was: would Germany be united under Prussia or Austria? Bismarck accomplished his objective of a united Germany under Prussia by starting and winning three wars after carefully isolating each opponent.

Bismarck got into a war with Denmark over the disputed territory of Schleswig-Holstein. He won easily, with the unnecessary help of Austria. But dividing the spoils gave Bismarck the excuse he needed to fight Austria. His goal in defeating Austria was only to knock her out of the lead, which he did. The last step necessary for German unification was to get the small German states between Prussia and France in his fold. The only thing these states hated more than Prussia was France. So, Bismarck got into a war with France and these states were forced to choose. The Franco-Prussian War lasted only a few weeks and the Sparta of modern Europe emerged as the leader of a united Germany.

Bismarck made alliances simply to break them, thereby creating a handy excuse to fight. After wiping out his opponent, he would make a fast and generous peace so he could work with that country in the future. He made concessions to the liberals of his parliament to win their support. He levied and collected unconstitutional taxes to build up his armies. He winked at Europe's great leaders, gained their confidence, and proceeded to make them history's fools. He leaked inflammatory comments to the press to twist public opinion into just the political pretzel he needed.

He did whatever he had to, and in the end he got exactly what he set out to get. In 1871, the fragmented Germany that Europe had enjoyed for centuries as a tromping ground became a Prussian-dominated conservative and militaristic German Empire. The leaders of Europe were concerned. The balance of power had been disturbed. They hoped the unification of Germany would not lead to a large war or two.

Romanticism and Romantic Art

Nationalism and the artistic movement known as "Romanticism" went well together. Romantics and nationalists each threw rules and authority out the window to assert their right of personal expression. And just as national groups could not be suppressed by Old Regime

Turner, **Buttermere Lake**, *1798 (Tate Gallery, London). Nature stirred the hearts of romantic artists as well as poets. "My heart leaps up when I behold a rainbow in the sky / So it was when my life began, so is it now I am a man / So be it when I shall grow old, or let me die!" – William Wordsworth, "The Rainbow," 1807*

aristocratic rulers, Romantic artists refused to conform their powerful inner feelings to society's code.

Romanticism, which has little to do with roses and chocolate hearts, was a reaction to the stern logic and reason of the Neoclassical movement. While Neoclassicism was a return to Europe's Greco-Roman roots, Romanticism was a return to a country's indigenous roots, folklore, and nature. Like Neoclassicism (which carried on through much of the romantic period), Romanticism went beyond art—it was a way of living. It meant placing feeling over intellect and passion over restrained judgment. The rules of Neoclassicism were replaced by a spirit that encouraged artists to be emotional and create not merely what the eyes saw, but also what the heart felt.

Romantics made a religion of nature. They believed that taking a walk in the woods and communing with nature taught man about his true self—the primitive, "noble savage" beneath the intellectual crust. A nostalgic reassessment of the medieval age and an awareness of the sublime also contributed to the Romantic movement. While many abandoned Christianity in the 18th century, those who did still needed to find the divine. They found it in nature.

The cultural heartbeat of this movement came not from the rich Medici palace in Florence or the elegant salons of Paris but from a humble log cabin in England's Windermere Lake District, the poet William Wordsworth's "Dove Cottage." English poets Blake, Coleridge, and Wordsworth rejected the urban, intellectual, scientific world for "simple living and high thinking." They nourished their souls in nature.

At Oxford and Cambridge, a walk in the woods was a part of every scholar's daily academic diet. Even today, the Lake District in northern England is a popular retreat for nature-lovers. Its youth hostels (more per square mile than any place on earth) are filled with rucksack romantics worshiping the wonders of nature—walking.

Until the Romantic era, mountains were seen only as troublesome obstacles. Now they attracted crowds of admirers drawn to their rugged power. High-class resorts, such as Interlaken in the Swiss Alps, were born. Why did people climb these mountains? Because they were there. Romanticism.

Gericault, **Raft of the Medusa,** *1819 (Louvre, Paris).Gericault goes to great lengths to portray the death and despair on this raft. At the same time, a powerful pyramid of hope reaches up to flag down a distant ship.*

Constable, Delacroix, Gericault, and Ludwig II

Romantic artists glorified nature. Landscapes illustrated nature's power. Englishman John Constable (1776–1837) painted honest, un-idealized scenes. He let nature be natural. His contemporary, J. M. W. Turner, differed by charging his landscapes with emotions, using bright supernatural colors and swirling brushwork. Peopling his paintings with clouds, Turner personified nature. He gave it the feelings and emotions of a romantic human being. (The Tate Gallery has the best collection of Turner landscapes.)

Eugene Delacroix (1798–1863) is a classic example of a Romantic painter. Solitary, moody, emotional, and endlessly imaginative, he broke all the Neoclassical rules. His exotic and emotional scenes, wild color schemes, and complex, unrestrained compositions bubble with enough movement and excitement to ring any viewer's emotional bells. (See *Liberty Leading the People*, facing this chapter's title page.)

Theodore Gericault (1791–1824), in preparing to paint his gripping masterpiece *Raft of the Medusa,* visited an insane asylum and slept in a morgue so that he could better portray death and terror on the faces of his subjects. Nature was awesome, emotions were truth, and the Romantic artists were the prophets of this new religion.

The fairy-tale castle of Neuschwanstein is textbook Romanticism. King Ludwig II of Bavaria put it on a hilltop not for defensive purposes . . .

Ludwig dashing through the snow

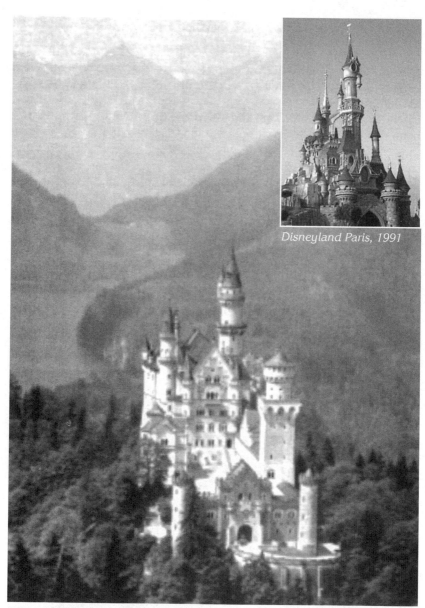

Disneyland Paris, 1991

Neuschwanstein Castle, *1869–1886, near Füssen, Germany. The fairy-tale castle of Bavaria's "Mad King" Ludwig II is typical of the Romantic period. It was built on a hilltop in medieval style long after castles had lost their function as fortresses. Ludwig put it here for the view. The only knights in shining armor you'll find in this castle are on the wallpaper.*

but for the view. The king was a romantic. His architect was a designer of theater sets. His best friends were artists, poets, and musicians. Scenes from Wagner's Romantic operas decorate the castle. His dreams were not of empires and big armies, but of fairy-tale castles and candlelit concerts.

Ludwig II is known as "Mad" King Ludwig because of his romantic excesses. He drowned mysteriously before Neuschwanstein castle, his dream about to come true, was completed.

Ludwig almost bankrupted Bavaria building his Disneyesque castles, but Germany is recouping its investment a hundredfold as huge crowds of tourists from all over the world pay to see Europe's most popular castle. Get there early or late or you might spend more time in line than in the castle.

Goya

Francisco de Goya (1746–1828) was a portraitist for the Spanish royal court. A Romantic painter, he's been described as the first painter with a social conscience. His *Third of May–1808* is a gripping combination of nationalism and Romanticism, showing a faceless government execution squad systematically gunning down patriots with all the compassion of a lawn mower.

Goya, **The Third of May–1808** *(Prado, Madrid). Romanticism expresses itself here in a powerful social statement against war and repression by faceless foreign invaders. The victims are Spaniards gunned down by Napoleon's troops for resisting French occupation.*

Goya, **Saturn Devouring His Son,**
*1823 (Prado, Madrid). While this
gives "child's portion" a new meaning, Goya's intended message is that
"Time devours us all."*

Artistically, Goya went through several stages. His last, after he lost
his hearing and became bitter and disillusioned with life, was one of
nightmarish fantasy. It's as if his innermost emotions finger-painted in
blood the grotesque figures that mirrored the turmoil that racked his
soul. (Romantic, huh?)

The Prado Museum in Madrid has a room dedicated entirely to the
bizarre visions of Goya's "Dark Stage." One of the most gripping is
the painting, *Saturn Devouring His Son,* detailing in ghastly, twisted
lines and vivid, garish colors how time eventually "eats" us all.
"Romantic" isn't only "mushy-kissy." This is Romanticism at its emotional best. No matter how cheery you are when you enter, you'll
leave Goya's Dark Stage in a gloomy funk.

Blake

William Blake of England was another master at putting inner
visions on canvas. A mystic, nonconformist poet, he refused
to paint posies for his supper. He made a living only through the
charity of fellow artists who recognized his genius. Blake's water-

Blake, **Elohim Creating Adam,** *1795 (Tate Gallery, London). Blake, who hobnobbed with the heavenly hosts, painted God creating Man.*

colors (in London's Tate Gallery), with their bizarre, unearthly subjects and composition, reveal how unschooled he was in classical technique. But his art grabs the viewer by the emotional lapel, and that's what Romanticism is all about.

Romantic Art Highlights

France
- Paintings in the Louvre's Romantic art room (Delacroix and Gericault), Paris
- Chopin's grave, Pére Lachaise Cemetery, Paris

Britain
- Tate Gallery (Blake and Turner), London
- Neo-Gothic Halls of Parliament, London

Germany
- Neuschwanstein and Linderhof castles, Bavaria
- The Rhine and the Lorelei poem

Switzerland
- The Alps

Poetry
- Shelley, Keats, Byron, and Blake

Music
- Liszt, Chopin, Beethoven, Wagner, Schumann

Delacroix, **Frédéric Chopin,** *1838 (Louvre, Paris). One romantic artist's tribute to another.*

The riches of England's Industrial Revolution came with its problems. This 19th-century engraving shows poor, dirty, overcrowded slums housing masses of industrial workers under roaring smokestacks.

The Industrial Revolution

The Industrial Revolution, along with the rise of nationalism and democratic governments, powered Europe into the modern world. While the scientific achievements of the Enlightenment broadened human knowledge, practical inventions and applications (such as the steam engine and telegraph) didn't crank into motion until the 1800s.

This century of exciting technological advancement shifted nations from dependence on agriculture to dependence on industry. Britain's textile industry led the way as new, steam-powered factories lured people from the countryside to the cities.

The invention of the train shifted the revolution into high gear. As more products could be shipped more quickly to more people, huge new trade markets opened up. Rails laced European nations together. A person could travel across a country in a day's journey or less. From 1830 through 1860, one-sixth of all the world's track was laid (and then came the Eurailpass).

Europe's business boom stoked its colonial appetite. The world was Europe's buffet line and it was "all you can eat." Europe divided up the underdeveloped world, harvested its raw materials, processed them, and sold the resulting products at great profits. Although every European nation grabbed a slice of the world economic quiche, Britain's empire included nearly a quarter of the world's land and people. England boasted, "The sun never sets on the British Empire."

Technological progress gave Europe a false optimism. Seeing how quickly technology changed nature and lifestyles, people figured it was the answer to the world's problems. Unfortunately, it lead to many new difficulties: slums, polluted and overcrowded cities, child labor, unemployment, overwork, and the alienation of workers from the fruits of their labor. As we step out of this Industrial Age and into the Information Age, these problems persist. While we have become ace producers/consumers, quality of life is a different story.

Socialism and Communism

The Socialist movement tried to solve the social ills brought on by the industrial age. Socialists challenged the laissez-faire policy of governmental non-intervention in business affairs. Socialists and trade unions worked to restrict the power of factory owners and distribute wealth more fairly.

Karl Marx (1818–1883) and Friedrich Engels (1820–1895), both from Germany, co-wrote the influential *Communist Manifesto* (1848), developing the fantasy that workers, not factory owners, should benefit most from industry. They predicted that a worker (proletarian) revolution would overthrow the capitalist (bourgeois) establishment. In the 19th century, Communist and Socialist organizations gained power throughout Europe. Though there was never a classic "workers' revolution," Marx' and Engels' ideas spurred reforms to benefit the working class.

Vladimir Lenin (1870–1924), a Russian, used Marxist ideas to plan the Bolshevik Revolution and overthrow Russia's monarchy (1917), giving birth to the Soviet Union. He had to adapt industrial Marxism to a country still mired in medieval feudalism. Josef Stalin (1879–1953) succeeded Lenin as ruler of the Soviet Union, instituting the iron rule we associate with Russian totalitarianism.

Soviet Marxism's Fab Four keep watch over a meeting of the Communist International, 1935. **Marx, Engels, Lenin, and Stalin** *(left to right) were the propaganda poster-boys of communism. Their faces decorated factories throughout Eastern Europe and the USSR until the revolutions of 1989 and 1990.*

One way or another, those denied their fair slice of the pie revolt to get it. The French Revolution re-sliced things to accommodate the merchant class. Now the urban peasantry was messing up the pie.

Social Realism

The USSR (and after World War II, its client states in Eastern Europe) attempted to control everyone and everything. They used whatever they could to achieve that end, including the media and art.

Soviet art was propaganda. Called "social realism," the style draws repeatedly on a few Socialist or Marxist-Leninist themes. (For example, the noble, muscular worker is depicted bashing the chains of capitalism and overcoming the evils of the bourgeois world.) The art portrays family ideals, Socialist morality, flags blowing heroically in the wind, and undying respect for the fathers of the ideology (and, of course, the imperial power behind the ideological cloak, Russia). Russia is featured as the liberator from the Turks, from the Nazis, and from the evil Western world.

Although art as propaganda is nothing new, only in the sphere of the Soviet Union was creativity channeled so effectively into one purpose. Art was justified only if it promoted the system. Abstract art, which

Soviet propaganda poster.
"Social realism" art was intended to rouse nationalist and class feelings against the threat of the capitalist West. Here the workers are shown victorious through passionate dedication to their state, industry, and military. Soviet art was a broken record of worker-triumph propaganda.

serves no purpose in inspiring the masses, was discouraged. Even artistic mediums as nebulous as music were censored for what they did not promote.

The Industrial Revolution and Art

The Industrial Revolution put new tools and materials in artists' hands. Concrete, iron, and glass opened new architectural doors. People were proud of their modernity and their ability to build like never before. More buildings were raised in the 19th century than in all previous centuries put together. It was the day after Christmas and Europe was a child with a colossal erector set.

At world's fairs and exhibitions, giant structures of iron ribs and glass walls were proudly assembled and promptly disassembled on rigid time schedules just to prove it could be done. People traveled from all over Europe to marvel at London's short-lived Crystal Palace. Paris, also feeling its industrial oats, built the Eiffel Tower to celebrate the centennial of the French Revolution. The French planned to take down the tower, which they considered ugly, but it became a symbol for Paris and so it stands today. As you travel around Europe, you'll see huge iron-and-glass train stations—more products of Europe's early industrial muscle.

But the Industrial Revolution also threatened art. New building techniques and materials made previous architectural styles obsolete, except as decoration. Like the ancient Romans who used Greek facades on buildings, architects would build modern buildings (such as the neo-Gothic British Houses of Parliament), then adorn them with fake Gothic arches or Renaissance columns.

Painters were threatened by the newly invented camera (developed around 1830), which could make portraits faster, cheaper, and sometimes better than they could. The challenge and incentive to portray nature was gone. With the camera, the artist's traditional role as the preserver of a particular moment, person, or scene had become obsolete.

Eiffel Tower, 1889, Paris. The Industrial Revolution made life one big erector set. This was built to celebrate the 100th anniversary of the French Revolution.

Technology widened the gulf between the artist and the public. Modern people could get homes, arts, crafts, and furnishings from

Halls of Parliament, 1836–1860, London

Industrial Revolution Sights

Britain
- Iron Bridge Gorge open-air museum (birthplace of Industrial Revolution), Coalport
- Covent Garden, London
- National Railway Museum, York
- Blackpool Tower, Blackpool

France
- Eiffel Tower, Paris
- Iron-and-glass train stations (Orsay Museum building)

Italy
- Gallerias (grand iron-and-glass shopping arcades) in Milan and Naples

Belgium
- Galleria, Brussels

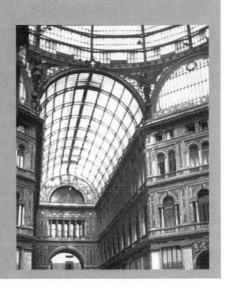

Galleria Vittorio Emanuele, 1877, Milan. In the age of iron and glass, fancy gallerias decorated European cities.

engineers, technicians, and mass production. Artists grew to disdain those who put a price on art the same way they priced pork, kerosene, or a day's work in the factory.

Struggling to come to terms with the modern industrial world, art left technology behind, focusing the artistic lens of the Western world on hazy frontiers of the future.

Art Nouveau

The Art Nouveau ("new-VOH") style was a reaction to the mechanization and mass production of the Industrial Revolution. Longing for the beauty of the pre-industrial age, artists rebelled against mass-produced goods. Their art emphasized uniqueness and included the artists' personal touch.

Gaudi, **Casa Mila apartment house,** *1905, Barcelona, Spain. This ice-cream castle of a building does everything possible to disrupt the rigid angles of the industrial world.*

Whereas industrial art and architecture were geometrical, with rigid squares and rectangles, Art Nouveau ("new art") used delicate, flowing lines, like the curvy stems of plants. Iron grillwork became a new art form.

Art Nouveau influenced architecture, painting, ironwork, furniture, graphic design, and even women's fashions. In America, Louis Tiffany's natural-looking "flower-petal" lamps were the rage.

Antonio Gaudi, born near Barcelona, employed the Art Nouveau style (called *"Modernista"* in Spain) in his distinctive architecture. Many architecture students make pilgrimages to Barcelona to see his famous "melted ice cream" works. He's considered a pioneer, a prophet, and a dreamer who was lucky enough to see his dreams become concrete.

Art Nouveau's intentional curviness eventually gave way to the straight lines and rigidity we see in modern "International Style" skyscrapers, but its influence has been seen throughout the 20th century.

Paris, Vienna, Barcelona, Brussels, Munich, Glasgow, Helsinki, and Alesund in Norway are all famous for their Art Nouveau, or *"Jugendstil,"* as the style is called in German.

Art Nouveau Sights

France
- Green iron grillwork at old Métro stops, Paris
- Orsay Museum (exhibits on mezzanine level), Paris

Austria
- Jugendstil facades through out Vienna

Spain
- Gaudi architecture (especially Sagrada Familia cathedral), Barcelona

Beardsley, **Salome,** *1892 (Princeton University Library). Art Nouveau's flowing lines in graphic design.*

Impressionism

Impressionism was the greatest revolution in European art since the Renaissance and the first real "modern" style of art. While the Renaissance found realism, Impressionism threw it out. The artist was interested only in the fleeting "impression" made by the light, shadows, and atmosphere of a scene.

Although its name was originally coined as an insult (like "Gothic"), Impressionism is actually one of the few appropriate art labels. Claude Monet (1840–1926), the movement's father, called the style "instantaneity." The artist, with a few quick brush-strokes, captures a candid, momentary "impression" of a subject.

The realistic and the Impressionist styles can be illustrated by comparing what Leonardo da Vinci and Monet each see as they drive across the Nevada desert on a hot summer day. Ahead of his Ferrari, realist Leonardo sees heat rising from the asphalt, making the black road look like a bright, shimmering patch of silver. In spite of the way it appears, he knows the road is really black and so he will paint it that way, disregarding the momentary impression of silver.

Monet's Garden at Giverny (an easy side trip from Paris) inspired much of Monsieur Lily Pad's art. Impressionists cried, "Out of the studio and into nature!"

Monet, an Impressionist, excitedly stops his Peugeot, sets up his easel, and captures the impression of the shimmering heat waves cutting a silver slice through the yellows and browns of the desert.

We don't actually see objects or people, but rather the light that bounces off them. The realist paints what his mind knows is there; the Impressionist paints what his eye sees.

Light and Color

Light plays endless games on the same subject and, to the Impressionist, that same subject is different with each time of day and atmospheric condition. Monet, the most famous Impressionist, often did a series of paintings of a single subject (for example, Rouen Cathedral) at different times of day.

The physical object has become just the rack upon which hangs the real subject: the light and colors. Paint often is laid on thickly, with heavy, textured brush-strokes.

Sometimes the painter, not even bothering to mix the colors on the palette, dabs bits of blue and red side by side to make a purple that shimmers in the viewer's eye. This brush technique was taken to extremes in Georges Seurat's "pointillism," a mosaic of colored dots with no lines at all. (If you look carefully at a newspaper photo, you'll see that it is a mechanical form of pointillism.)

From Ridicule to Acceptance

Impressionism was born in the "Salon of the Rejected," sort of the "off-off Broadway" of struggling Parisian artists. Initially, people were outraged by this rough, messy style. A newspaper reported

Compare the **photo** _of the_ **Rouen Cathedral** _with the Impressionist_ **painting** _by Monet (1893, Orsay Museum, Paris). We can see the artist's fascination with the play of light on the building. Detail fades away and we are left with a blurry, yet recognizable, impression of the cathedral._

Seurat, **Bathers at Asnieres,** _1883 (Tate Gallery, London). Here Seurat uses a technique called "pointillism," a mosaic consisting entirely of colored dots._

that after seeing an early Monet painting, one visitor went mad, rushed out into the street, and started biting innocent passersby. (Although it's much safer today, caution is still advised near Parisian modern-art galleries.)

Even though many Impressionist artists (Manet, Degas, Renoir, and Rodin) had first-class classical backgrounds, the stuffy board of the Louvre Museum refused to display the new art—even after the public accepted it. The nearby Jeu de Paume, a former indoor tennis court, was used to store the masterpieces of the movement. Today, Impressionism, far from radical, hangs in living rooms and corporate boardrooms and fills some of Europe's most popular galleries. The Jeu de Paume collection is now the major attraction in Paris' wildly popular Orsay Gallery.

Auguste Rodin ("ro-DAN," 1840–1917) blended Impressionist ideas with his classical training to become the greatest sculptor since Michelangelo. He had the uncanny ability to capture the essence of a subject with his powerful yet sensitive technique. The rough "unfinished" surfaces, particularly of his bronze works, reflect light the same way the thick brushwork of an Impressionist painting does. Check out the Rodin Museum in Paris, filled with the work of this great artist.

Renoir, **Moulin de la Galette***, 1876 (Orsay Museum, Paris)*

Post-Impressionism

After Impressionism, the modern art world splintered, never again to be contained by any one style. Within twenty years, Impressionism had branched into two Post-Impressionist movements. One stressed form and order (led by Cézanne, a forerunner of the Cubists) and the other demonstrated emotion and sensuousness (Gauguin and van Gogh, who inspired the Expressionists and Fauves).

Rodin, **The Kiss,** *1901 (Tate Gallery, London)*

Paul Cézanne ("say-ZAWN," 1839–1906) a man of independent means, ignored Paris, the critics, and the buying public. Cézanne worked to capture the best of both artistic worlds: the instantaneity of Impressionism and the realistic depth and solidity of earlier styles.

Paul Gauguin ("go-GAN," 1848–1903) was a stockbroker who chucked it all to become a painter. Like Cézanne, he left the artsy folk of proud Paris for inspiration in simple surroundings. He spent time with van Gogh in southern France, but after Vincent attacked him in a fit of artistic rage, Paul sailed for Tahiti.

Cézanne, **Still Life with Basket of Apples,** *1894 (Art Institute of Chicago). Cézanne painted numerous still lifes in his experiments with form and composition. He once remarked that nature reveals itself in the geometric forms of cylinders, spheres, and cones. This painting includes cylindrical biscuits, spherical apples, and a conical bottle.*

Gauguin, **Arearea** *(Pleasantries) (Orsay Museum, Paris)*

Gauguin's bright, bold paintings of native scenes hit Europe like a ripe mango. He used "primitive" techniques—simple outlines, sharply contrasting colors, and a flat, two-dimensional look—to create a naive and naturally expressive style that inspired many 20th-century artists.

Van Gogh

Vincent van Gogh (pronounced "van-GO," or "van-GOCK" by the Dutch and the snooty, 1853–1890) used Impressionist techniques powered with passion. Painting what he felt as well as what he saw, his art truly reflects his life.

Vincent's early life was religious, not artistic. Disillusioned with the shallow values of the modern world, he served as a lay preacher for poor coal miners. In his late twenties, he channeled that religious vision and spiritual intensity into his art.

After learning from the Impressionists in Paris, he moved to southern France to cloister himself in nature and his art. He did most of his great paintings there in the space of three years. They show the extreme loneliness, the emotional ecstasy, and the spiritual struggles he went through. Several times his work was interrupted by mental illness.

Van Gogh, **Self-Portrait,** *1890 (detail) (Orsay Museum, Paris). With swirling brush-strokes, Vincent charged Impressionism with emotion. His canvases take you through the rapids of his life.*

Van Gogh, **The Potato Eaters,** *1885 (Van Gogh Museum, Amsterdam). Vincent worked with the poorest of the poor. He understood their dark, dreary world and painted it with dignity.*

Finally, believing that insanity was destroying his creative abilities, he killed himself.

Van Gogh's art is an oil-on-canvas translation of his soul, his genius, and his emotions. The subjects were simple—common people and landscapes. His style was untrained and crude. By distorting and exaggerating certain colors and details, he gave his work spirit and emotions.

Van Gogh's love of the common man shines through in his painting. His subjects seem to glow with, as he put it, "that something of the eternal which the halo used to symbolize."

In his landscape *Road with Cypress Trees,* we see a simple, peaceful scene "van Gogh-ed" into a stormy sea of turbulence and emotion. He uses the strong, thick brush-strokes and bright colors of the Impressionists not to capture the light of the scene but to churn it up with emotion. Waves of wheat and flames of trees vibrate with an inner force that van Gogh believed inhabits all things.

Perhaps the best examples of van Gogh's art are his self-portraits. These show the man as well as his talent. Haunted and haunting, we see in his burning eyes the passionate love of all things and the desire to paint them on canvas.

*Van Gogh, **Sunflowers**, 1888 (National Gallery, London [other versions elsewhere]). Two years after painting these sunflowers, the artist killed himself. Vincent van gone.*

Europe's van Gogh treasure chest is the great Van Gogh Museum in Amsterdam (next to the Rijksmuseum). His art is well displayed, in chronological order, with each of his artistic stages related to events in his personal life. It's one of Europe's most enjoyable museums.

Impressionist and Post-Impressionist Sights

France
  - Orsay Museum, Paris
  - Rodin Museum, Paris
  - Marmotten Museum (Monet), Paris
  - Orangerie Museum (more Monet), Paris
  - Monet's garden, Giverny, near Paris
  - Toulouse-Lautrec Museum, Albi
  - Arles, St. Remy, and Auvers, while without Vincent sights as such, are towns that inspired van Gogh.

Britain
  - Tate Gallery, London
  - National Gallery, London

Netherlands
  - Van Gogh Museum, Amsterdam
  - Kroller-Muller Museum (van Gogh), Arnhem

Europe in the 20th Century

Contemporary Europe is just as exciting as historic Europe and shouldn't take a back seat to Old Regime palaces and ancient ruins. While most of the sights tourists chase in Europe date back to before the 20th century, an understanding of our tumultuous age is important in understanding Europe's number one tourist attraction—its people.

The 20th century began with the sort of easy happiness and nonchalance of a summer barbecue. The average European in 1910 felt very lucky to be living during those prosperous and peaceful times.

Behind the scenes, however, tension was growing. Germany's late entry onto the European economic game board caused competitive rivalries. Tension mounted as Germany grabbed for its "place in the sun." Germany understood that capitalist economies need colonial sources of raw materials and marketplaces for finished products. By the time Germany arrived, most of the underdeveloped world was already controlled by other European powers.

There was a scramble for alliances across Europe. No one wanted to be left without an ally, so most countries dove headlong into an international game of "Let's Make a Deal." Alliances were secret, often conflicting, and no one knew for sure exactly where anyone else stood.

The modern nationalities of Europe were awakening, and particularly in the vast Hapsburg Empire, national groups were working aggressively for independence.

World War I

Beneath its placid exterior, Europe was ready to explode. The spark that set things off was the assassination of Archduke Ferdinand. The heir to the Hapsburg throne was shot by a Serbian nationalist in 1914. The Hapsburg government, which ruled Austria, jumped at the opportunity to crush the troublesome Serbs.

One by one, Europe's nations were drawn by alliance into this regional dispute. Each had a self-serving interest. Russia, slavic Serbia's big brother, aided Serbia. Germany gave Austria a curious "blank check" of support. Germany knew that Russia was about to complete a new railroad mobilization plan that would give Russia first-strike capabilities. Many speculate that Germany thought a war sooner, while Russia was still slow to mobilize, was preferable to a war later, when Russia would be better prepared.

EUROPE IN 1914

NORWAY
FINLAND
SWEDEN
NORTH SEA
DENMARK
GREAT BRITAIN
RUSSIA
ATLANTIC
NETH. GERMAN EMPIRE
POLAND
BELG.
OCEAN
FRANCE
AUSTRIA
SWITZ.
HUNGARY
RUM.
PORTUGAL
Sarajevo • SERBIA
BLACK SEA
SPAIN
BULG.
ITALY
ALB.
TURKEY (OTTOMAN EMPIRE)
MEDITERRANEAN
GREECE
SPANISH MOROCCO
SEA

⊞ ALLIES BASIS: TRIPLE ENTENTE (1907)
▤ CENTRAL POWERS BASIS: TRIPLE ALLIANCE (1882)
▨ ITALY (LEFT CENTRAL POWERS & JOINED ALLIES 1915)
☐ NEUTRAL

But when Austria attacked Serbia and the Russians mobilized, Germany invaded . . . France! France was allied to Russia, and Germany hoped to wipe out France by surprise rather than risk getting embroiled in a two-front war.

Well, it didn't work out quite the way Germany planned. Flank, flank, flank, from the Alps to the Atlantic, the Franco-German stalemate that became the Western Front dug in. Soldiers dug trenches to duck machine-gun bullets. France and Germany settled into a battle of attrition, in which the political and military leaders of opposing nations decide to bash their heads against each other, each knowing it will suffer horrific losses but calculating that the other will bleed white and drop first.

For four years, generals waved their swords and wave after wave of troops climbed out of their trenches and fell into their graves. On many occasions, France lost 70,000 people in one day. That's more than the U.S. lost in the entire Vietnam War. By 1918, half of all the men in France between the ages of 15 and 30 were casualties.

Too often, military leaders are the heroes of previous wars who underestimate the new war technology. In World War I, that technology was the machine gun, a tool so awesome that a newspaper columnist of the day called it the "peacekeeper" because no civilized commander could send his boys into its fire.

Russia and Germany fought a mobile and bloody war with the help of trains on the Eastern Front. Meanwhile, Austria had trouble with the stubborn Serbs.

Europe dove into the "War to End All Wars" expecting a quick finish. It took four bloody years for the Allies (France, England, Russia, and, ultimately, the United States) to defeat Germany and Austria. By the 1919 signing of the Treaty of Versailles, 9 million of the war's 65 million soldiers were dead. Germany lay crushed and saddled with demoralizing war debts. Once-mighty Austria was reduced to a poor, tiny, landlocked country with a navy of three police boats on the Danube. France was finished as a superpower. Europe lay dazed and horrified at the unthinkable which had just happened.

With a little study you could fill a whole tour with World War I and World War II sights. In northern France and Alsace, you can tour bits of the Maginot Line and visit emotionally moving memorials at famous battle sights such as Verdun, near Reims.

After the war, the map of Europe was re-drawn. The old ruling families of Germany, Russia, and Austria and the Ottoman rulers of present-day Turkey were finished. New, democratic nations drew borders along cultural and ethnic boundaries, defining Finland, Austria, Hungary, Czechoslovakia, Poland, Yugoslavia, Latvia, Estonia, and Lithuania. Germany handed over the provinces of Alsace and Lorraine to France.

Compared with war-ravaged Europe, the United States was a dominant, seemingly boundless superpower. By 1929, it boasted a whopping 42 percent of the entire world's industrial output.

Between the Wars: Totalitarianism

After World War I, the big question was: Would Germany be democratic or Communist? Russia had wrapped up its revolution and become the Soviet Union. According to Marxist theory, industrial-based Germany was the perfect candidate to lead the world into communism. But the victorious Allies (the United States, Great Britain, and France) managed to install the Western-style Weimar government, and the German Communist party was literally buried in one night when the top 1,000 Communists, including leaders Rosa Luxembourg and Karl Liebknecht, were shot.

The many German people who figured they could have hung on and won the war associated their "stab in the back" Western government with the hated Treaty of Versailles. Although the Weimar government was technically a modern constitutional democracy, behind the scenes ticked the old ruling order—the army and industrialists—scheming to reverse the war's outcome and revive Germany as Europe's foremost power. Many people view World War II as the logical continuation and conclusion of World War I, and the misguided Treaty of Versailles as the intermission.

Mussolini

Meanwhile, in Italy, a violent, melodramatic nationalism and an anti-intellectual movement called "fascism" were born. Benito Mussolini led the Fascist party, stressing unity and authority. Capitalizing on Italy's corrupt government, miserable economy, and high unemployment, he rose easily to power. As in Germany a few years later, the rich and the businessmen believed fascism to be distasteful but supported it as the only alternative to Europe's rising red tide of communism.

In 1922, Mussolini took the reins of government. Il Duce went straight to work, filling the government with Fascists, organizing the strongman *squadrisi* to "encourage" Italians to support him, and building a strong, super-nationalistic, self-sufficient Fascist Italy.

This **stamp from Ethiopia,** licked by Mussolini in 1935, shows the Fascist alliance of Hitler and the Italian dictator. The slogan reads: "Two peoples, one war."

Although Mussolini's government had its problems, it was the only strong rule under which Italy has functioned in this century. As a tourist, you'll drive on a system of super-freeways commissioned by Il Duce's government. Many of Rome's buildings, including the Olympic Games complex and the futuristic suburb of EUR, are Fascist in style. EUR, 10 minutes by subway from Rome's Colosseum, with its bold and powerful architecture, is worth exploring.

Hitler

The roots of Adolf Hitler's success lay in Germany's anger. After World War I, when Germans hated the Treaty of Versailles and the Weimar government and when hyper-inflation ripped up Germany's moral fabric, Hitler and his party leaped into the news. When the value of the mark dropped from 4 marks = U.S.$1 to 4 trillion marks = U.S.$1 in 1923, the hardworking German middle class lost faith in society. All debts, savings, and retirement funds were wiped out. (It took a wheelbarrow full of paper marks to buy a pretzel.) People were ready to believe the promises of a charismatic madman.

Nazi campaign poster. This political ad tells voters they can free Germany from its chains—by voting for Hitler.

Like Mussolini, Hitler expertly capitalized on society's problems; when he couldn't find a solution, he found a scapegoat. His party boomed until Germany did. When Germany entered its happy-go-lucky cabaret years in the mid-1920s, people wrote off Hitler and other political extremists as fringe lunatics.

When the Great Depression hit in 1929, Hitler rose again. With his political genius, terror tactics, scapegoating of the Jews, and the support of the rich elite of the day (who saw fascism as the only defense against communism), Hitler became Germany's dictator.

In 1933, he proclaimed that his "Third Reich" would last a thousand years. (The first two

Nazi mass meeting, 1937. *Fifty thousand Nazis attend a rally to hear Hitler rant and rave in a setting with the air of a grandiose Hollywood epic. Like Napoleon before him, Hitler dreamed of a reunited Roman Empire.*

reichs were pre-World War I Germany, 1871–1918, and the medieval Holy Roman Empire.) Hitler's agenda was to turn Germany into a monolithic slab of nationalistic rock. There were to be no states, no classes, no questions, and no alternative to the Nazi party. There was to be only Germany. The Nazi party was purged, the Gestapo kept the flags waving, unmarked graves and concentration camps were filled with dissenters, and Nazism became the religion of state.

In his own frothing way, Hitler was a genius. Germany prospered. The economy boomed and everyone was employed. Complete self-sufficiency (necessary to wage a world war) was right around the corner.

Nazi propaganda. *Translation: "Judaism is criminal." Signs like this were common in Hitler's Germany. Someone had to take the blame for Germany's problems, and the Jews were a traditional scapegoat.*

It was clear to Germany that more "living room" was justified. Hitler said, "Space must be fought for and maintained. People who are lazy have no right to the soil. Soil is for he who tills it and protects it. If a nation loses in the defense of its soil, then the individual loses. There is no higher justice that decrees that a people must starve. There is only power, and power creates justice. . . . Parliaments do not create all of the rights on the earth; force also creates rights. The question is whether we wish to live or die. We have more right to soil than all the other nations because we are so thickly populated. I am of the opinion that in this respect, too, the principle can be applied; God helps him who helps himself."

And the German people marched in lockstep.

Franco and Spain's Civil War

From 1936 to 1939, Spain was torn to pieces in a struggle between left-wing Republicans and right-wing Nationalists. After the "Popular Front" (a left-wing coalition) gained power in 1936, right-wing general Francisco Franco led an uprising which became the Spanish Civil War.

The Nationalists (Franco's fascist Falange party) were supported by Hitler and Mussolini from abroad and the army, police, and civil guard at home. The (Spanish) Republicans were befriended by idealists, writers, workers groups, intellectuals, socialists, and the like. Russia supported them until Stalin got fed up with their ideological independence. Volunteers from many countries formed the International Brigades about which Ernest Hemingway wrote.

This was the first modern war. Hitler enjoyed trying out WWII-style bombing. Guernica, the town flattened by fascist bombs, was immortalized by Picasso's famous painting (which was moved into Spain only after Franco's death). The war was brutal, with brothers killing brothers, entire villages being slaughtered, and half a million dead.

It's a wonder that the ragtag Republicans held out against Franco and his well-disciplined and well-stocked Nationalists for three years. Franco's 1939 victory was followed by more bloody reprisals.

Franco's isolationism allowed him to remain neutral in WWII, and to rule Spain until his death in 1975. He was succeeded by King Juan Carlos, who opened Spain up to the democracy it enjoys today.

A 450-foot-tall concrete cross marks the "Valley of the Fallen," a giant mausoleum carved into a hillside outside Madrid. Dug mostly by Republican prisoners, it commemorates the 500,000 dead of Spain's Civil War. Franco's tomb is the centerpiece.

Totalitarianism

Totalitarianism was big in the 1930s, gaining power in Germany, Italy, Spain, and the USSR. In *The Origins of Totalitarianism*, Hannah Arendt describes this harsh form of government:

> The very ethics of totalitarianism were violent and neo-pagan. It declared that men should live dangerously, avoid the flabby weakness of too much thought, throw themselves with red-blooded vigor into a life of action. The new regimes all instituted youth movements. They appealed to a kind of juvenile idealism, in which young people believed that by joining some kind of squad, donning some kind of uniform, and getting into the fresh air they contributed to a great moral resurgence of their country. Young men were taught to value their bodies but not their minds, to be tough and hard, to regard mass gymnastics as patriotic demonstrations, and camping trips as a preparation for the world of the future. Young women were taught to breed large families without complaint, to be content in the kitchen, and to look with awe upon their virile mates. The body-cult flourished while the mind decayed. The ideal was to turn the German people into a race of splendid animals, pink-cheeked, Nordic, and upstanding. Contrariwise, euthanasia was adopted for the insane and was proposed for the aged. Later, in World War II, when the Nazis overran Eastern Europe, they committed Jews to the gas chambers, destroying some 6,000,000 human beings by the most scientific methods. Animals were animals; one bred the kind one wanted and killed the kind one did not.

Fascist art and architecture from Mussolini's planned futuristic suburb, EUR (a short subway ride from downtown Rome)

Dachau Concentration Camp, *b. 1933, near Munich, Germany. The 20th century saw slaughter and suffering on an unprecedented scale. Modern totalitarian governments proved they could turn people into meaningless numbers.*

World War II

The peace in Europe following the shortsighted Treaty of Versailles was unstable. It couldn't last—World War II was inevitable. Future historians will probably refer to the two "world wars" of this century as one long war with a troubled intermission.

While most of Europe between the wars was pacifist and isolationist, Hitler waged a careful campaign of "gradual encroachment." Each year he ranted and raved and threatened to go wild. When he would take just a little, the world felt relieved and hoped he was satisfied.

But even the most naive pacifist couldn't ignore Germany's invasion of Poland in 1939. England and France declared war and it was one big pigpile all over again.

WW II EUROPE
(1942: THE HEIGHT OF AXIS POWER)
- Axis nations
- Axis-controlled
- Allies
- Neutral nations

World War II, Fascist, and Nazi Sights

Germany
- Kaiser Wilhelm Memorial Church, Berlin
- Kathe-Kollwitz Museum, Berlin
- Hitler's Eagle's Nest, Berchtesgaden
- Haus der Kunst (exterior), Munich
- Dachau Concentration Camp (near Munich)
- Buchenwald Concentration Camp, Buchenwald

Austria
- Mauthausen Concentration Camp, Mauthausen

Britain
- Cabinet War Rooms, London
- Imperial War Museum, London

Italy
- Mussolini's planned city, EUR, Rome

France
- D-Day landing sights, Normandy
- Bayeux WWII museum, Normandy
- Deportation Monument (behind Notre Dame), Paris
- Oradour sur Glane (bombed and burned memorial ghost city), near Limoges

Netherlands
- Anne Frank's House, Amsterdam
- Corrie Ten Boom's "Hiding Place," Haarlem

Poland
- Auschwitz Concentration Camp, Auschwitz

Czech Republic
- Jewish Archives and Museum, Prague

Norway
- Nazi-Resistance Museum, Oslo

Denmark
- Nazi-Resistance Museum, Copenhagen

Speculating on Heroic Death, *1934 (Dachau Museum). The artist predicts the coming world war.*

For Hitler, 1940 was a good year. By April he controlled Austria, Poland, Czechoslovakia, Denmark, and Norway. In May, impatient at his "slow" progress, Hitler launched his ingenious Blitzkrieg ("lightning war"). Attacking swiftly by land and air, the Nazis conquered the Netherlands, Belgium, and France within seven weeks. By mid-1940, Hitler held most of central and northern Europe.

In April 1940, Winston Churchill took the English helm, offering "nothing but blood, toil, tears, and sweat . . . but a faith in ultimate victory." He successfully inspired and led England through the desperate Battle of Britain (July 1940), when German bombers almost leveled London.

Frustrated by British planes and the English Channel, Hitler turned eastward and sank his iron teeth deep into vast Russia. The Soviets suffered, but a harsh winter and the Russian "scorched earth" policy thwarted the Nazis just as they had foiled Napoleon's army 130 years earlier.

The war raged in Africa. And in Asia, Japan grabbed a million square miles. After Japan's unprovoked attack on Pearl Harbor in 1941, the United States joined in the melee. America's fresh forces and underestimated industrial might turned the tide.

The Allies took North Africa and invaded Italy. They crossed the English Channel to Normandy on D-Day (June 6, 1944), gaining a vital toehold in France from which to attack Germany. And Russia made great advances in the East. In 1944, the Allies gained complete air control of German skies, bombing its cities almost at will. By May 1945, Hitler was dead and Germany lay quiet, smoldering, and exhausted.

The tourist today sees very few sights produced by the world wars—what is important is what the tourist doesn't see. You won't see the wonders of Dresden, Germany, at one time one of the most beautiful medieval cities in Europe. You won't see the lovely original old towns of Berlin, Köln, or Rotterdam. Air raids leveled these cities during World War II, and the survivors rebuilt them in a modern style.

Europe Since 1945

World War II left much of Europe in ruins. Even before the shooting stopped, it was evident that a post-war world would be bipolar, dominated by an American sphere and a Soviet sphere. Scrambling to pick up the broken pieces of earlier powers, each side did what it could to grab the technology and great minds of Germany and turn former enemies into economic and political allies.

The Soviets "liberated" the Eastern European nations from the Nazis, installing Moscow-trained governments in each capital. The "Iron Curtain" fell, ushering in a 45-year period of strict Soviet control over the nations it figured it needed as a buffer zone against another attack from the West.

Germany and its capital city, Berlin, were split between the four victorious allied powers: France, Britain, the USA and the USSR. While three of the allied sectors worked amicably together and became West Germany and West Berlin, the Soviet sectors fell behind the Iron Curtain. Southern Germany, or Bavaria, was the American sector, which may explain why America's clichéd image of Germany is Bavarian.

The United States, learning from the mistakes of World War I's Treaty of Versailles that a healthy Germany is safer than a wounded Germany, funded the rebuilding of Western Europe with a huge and effective aid program called the Marshall Plan. Western Europe's economy lurched and then boomed while Eastern Europe lagged under its controlled Soviet-style economy. The NATO (West) and Warsaw Pact (East) alliances were formed.

The Cold War began. The USSR blockaded West Berlin (1948). With the help of an American airlift, this island of the capitalist West remained free to provide a painful contrast to the bleak Eastern economies. (The West German government subsidized this contrast by providing many perks—tax breaks, cheap flights, draft deferments, and so on to anyone who would live, travel, and work in West Berlin.) The USSR, under the guise of a Warsaw Pact peacekeeping force, crushed revolutions in Hungary (1956) and Czechoslovakia (1968). To keep their people in, the East German government built in 1961 what it called the "anti-fascist barrier"—what we called the Berlin Wall.

Caught between two superpowers and sitting on nuclear arsenals capable of destroying Europe's windmills, castles, pubs, and people many times over, Europe was tense. With many one-legged pensioners and tombstone-covered hills as reminders, Europe knew the reality of war. As "evil empire" rhetoric raged between the flagbearers of the planet's two most aggressive ideologies, many Europeans feared their homeland would be the fighting ground for World War III.

But in the 1980s, the Cold War began to thaw. The rise of the Polish labor movement, Solidarity, under Lech Walesa made a powerful impression on workers across Eastern Europe. Then in 1985 came Mikhail Gorbachev, the first modern, truly post-Stalin, post-World War II Soviet leader. His reforms and personal charisma made him the man of the decade. "I 'heart' Gorby" pins were common across the Warsaw Pact countries as the Soviet leader ended the Brezhnev doctrine, saying, basically, if you want to split and do your own thing economically, good luck, but we'll need to maintain foreign policy control (as in Finland) for defensive purposes.

Driving an economic machine that didn't work and with its fuel tank on "E," the USSR fought and lost a war of economic attrition with the USA. While America was left deeply in debt, the Soviet Union collapsed (as it would have anyway, given time).

And, like dominoes, the tumultuous revolutions of 1989 and 1990 toppled Communist regime after Communist regime across Eastern Europe. East German Communist leaders were tried and convicted for abuse of power and corruption. The dictator of Romania and his wife were executed. A playwright became the president of Czechoslovakia. Every time we turned around, another nation raised its grass-roots to the sky, tossed out its outdated Communist party, and threatened to join the Eurail club. It was exciting to live in 1989, a year that will be on our children's history tests.

Travel in Eastern Europe? Things are wide open and a lifetime of pent-up entrepreneurial spirit has been unleashed, offering the visitor no shortage of tour guides, bed and breakfast places, and travel thrills. East Germany is being assimilated into the sleeker West (with typical German tenderness). Berlin is shuffling itself back together with building projects that would have made Hitler proud. Prague, the best-preserved Baroque city in Europe, is the darling of East European tourism with as many tourist crowds as Salzburg or Edinburgh. Further east (Bulgaria, Romania, the Ukraine), things get more depressing, bleak, and relatively lawless. Despite their rich cultures and warm, curious people, these countries are in desperate times economically and the average traveler might not enjoy the challenge of traveling here. The five most accessible and livable cities of the former Soviet Union (St. Petersburg, Moscow, Tallinn, Riga, and Vilnius) are also the most enjoyable for visitors. Budget independent travel through these cities is far easier now than it was five years ago.

Meanwhile, in Western Europe, countries have been working out other problems. No European country has perfect homogeneity. Small nationalities without a nation are struggling for independence, or survival. France, for instance, has the Basques, the Corsicans, and the Celtic people of Brittany, many of whom see themselves as un-French parts of a French empire ruled from Paris. The George

Washingtons and Nathan Hales of these small, neglected nationalities are making news in Europe. Terrorism filled headlines throughout the 1970s and 1980s, and there's no reason to think that patriots will stop regretting that they have only one life to give for their countries.

A silent victim of modern times, the environment, finally gained attention in the 1980s. The Green party, whose platform was primarily environmental, raised issues many chose not to see in spite of the diseased forests, dead rivers, and radioactive reindeer in their midst. Nuclear accidents, acid rain, ozone problems, and chemical spills are awakening a continent notorious for treating its Mediterranean Sea like its own private cesspool. Even politicians tied to the teats of big business are beginning to realize that you can't exploit the poor on an uninhabitable planet.

20th-Century Art: Reflecting a World in Turmoil

Why is modern art so bizarre? Better to ask: Why is the modern world so bizarre? The world changed by leaps, bounds, and somersaults during the 20th century. Strange as some art might seem, it's often an honest representation of our strange world.

The world wars devastated Europe. No one could have foreseen the extent of the slaughter. People, especially artists, were shocked, disgusted, and disillusioned. As old moral values were challenged by the horror of war and our rapidly changing society, so were artistic ones.

Twentieth-century art is such a confusing pile of styles and theories that only one generalization can be made: little of it looks like the real world. But you can't judge art simply by how well it copies reality. Artists distort the real world intentionally. Especially in 20th-century art, some of the messiest and least-organized-looking works ("My 4-year-old coulda done that!") are sophisticated, based on complex theories requiring knowledge of many art styles. If you don't understand it, you can't judge it. Learn about art first, understand the artist's purpose, and then you can appreciate or criticize with gusto.

Basically, modern artists portray the "real" world in two different ways, expressive or abstract. Expressive art is like van Gogh's. It depicts the real world but distorts things to make them express an emotion. Abstract art abandons the visible world altogether, making basic lines and patches of color that reflect not real objects but a more basic beauty. Other 20th-century styles such as Cubism, Primitivism, and the combo style of abstract-expressionism, are variations on these two basic themes.

PHOTO-REALISM
OP ART
Pollock
ABST. EXPR.
Lichtenstein
POP ART
Warhol
PURE ABSTRACT.
MASS MEDIA SOURCES
Picasso
Kirchner
Nolde   Kokoschka
Duchamp
Kandinsky
DADA
Leger Miró Braque
Klee
Chagall
GERM. EXPR.
SURREALISM
Mondrian
FANTASY
Matisse
Dali
Roualt
GEOMETRY
CUBISM
FAUVISM
ABSTRACTION
EXPRESSIONISM
Munch
Modern Art
—A GROWTH DIAGRAM—
Seurat   Van Gogh
Cézanne Gauguin
PRIMITIVISM
POST-IMPRESSIONISM
DCH
PRIMITIVE SOURCES
Renoir IMPRESSIONISM
Monet   Degas
OLD   MASTERS

Expressionism

The best example of the "expressive" distortion of reality is a style called, believe-it-or-not, "expressionism." Expressionism carries van Gogh's emotionalism to the extreme. In *The Scream*, Norwegian artist Edvard Munch ("MOONK," 1863–1944) bends and twists everything into a landscape of unexplained terror. We "hear" the scream in the lines of the canvas rising up from the twisted body, through the terrified skull, and out to the sky, echoing until it fills the entire nightmare world of the painting.

We can appreciate the power of modern art by comparing *The Scream* to an earlier work, Gericault's *Raft of the Medusa* (page 202).

Both are a terror on canvas. But while Gericault's terror arises from a realistic portrayal of a grotesque event, Munch simply distorts the appearance of an everyday scene so we see it in a more powerful way, from a different emotional perspective.

Expressionism flourished in Germany from 1905 through 1935. Artists showed the horror and injustice of the war years they experienced. The garish colors, twisted lines, and masklike faces stress emotion over realism.

Munch, **The Scream,** *1893 (Edvard Munch Museum, Oslo). Norwegian Munch led the way into the artistic movement aptly called "expressionism." These artists distorted reality to express the horror of the modern world. The Munch museum in Oslo is excellent.*

Abstract Art

The second strain of 20th-century art, "abstraction," is less understood than the "expressive" distortion employed by Munch and van Gogh. Abstraction is simplification.

Since a tree, for instance, can never be painted with all its infinite details, all art is to some extent an abstraction, or simplification, of the real world. For so many generations, artists had denied this fact, trying to make their two-dimensional canvases look as real as the three-dimensional world they painted. But by the 20th century, the camera had been accepted as the captor of reality. Artists began to accept the abstract and artificial nature of paintings. In fact, they emphasized and enjoyed this abstraction to the extent of neglecting the subject itself. They were free to experiment with the building blocks of realistic art: lines, colors, and shapes. Not concerned with representing the real world, this art is called "non-representational."

Abstract pondering

Abstract artists are free, like children with a set of brightly colored building blocks. Rather than use the blocks to build a house or some recognizable object, children are fascinated by the blocks themselves. Like children, abstract artists spend hours organizing patterns that are pleasing for their own sake, not because they add up to something else. But unlike children, abstract artists generally have years of training with which to plan the best arrangement of the "blocks."

To appreciate and judge modern art, the viewer needs to know the rules, especially if the art can't be compared to reality.

Cézanne, **The Card Players,** *1892*

Van Doesburg, **Card Players,** *1916*

Here is a progression of realism to abstraction based on Cézanne's post-Impressionist painting (top left), which is more or less realistic. Top right: The figures are flattened, the canvas reduced to a composition of geometric shapes. The subject matter is still apparent. Below right: Simplified into a jumble of puzzle pieces, the card players are barely recognizable. The blocks of line and color themselves become the subject.

Van Doesburg, **Card Players,** *1917*

Abstract Art = Visual Music

It's helpful to compare abstract art to pure instrumental music. Some music is designed to imitate a sound heard in nature, such as a storm or a bird's call. Other music is intended to express an emotion, such as the sadness caused by the death of a friend. But most music is the perfect audio equivalent of abstract visual art. It simply plays with the beautiful "shapes and colors" of sound, the harmonious relationship of tones. Our ears don't demand to know what the sounds are supposed to represent. Our ears are better than our eyes at accepting abstract beauty.

Abstract art explores the relationships of lines and colors. The rules of these relationships are visible to the trained eye just as the rules of music are audible to the trained ear. But to the average viewer (or listener), abstract art (or music) is to be enjoyed, not analyzed. Music is enjoyable even if you don't understand the meter and scale on which it's built. The same is true of visual abstract art—it's just plain nice to look at. (Notice the similarity between the titles of abstract art-works and musical compositions: *Composition with Red, Yellow and Blue*, "Sonata for Piano and Violin No. 1.")

Abstract artists have been criticized for avoiding reality—for playing with their building blocks and making patterns that only they can understand. Artists such as Piet Mondrian, Paul Klee, and Wassily Kandinsky have replied that what they paint is reality, not the fleeting reality of the visible world that changes and passes away, but the eternal and unchanging world of geometrical relationships. The abstract artist simplifies the world into timeless shapes and colors. Are your eyes as open-minded as your ears?

Kandinsky, **Composition 238: Bright Circle,** *1921. Reality is tossed out the window as the artist calls on us to enjoy more basic shapes and colors. We hope this is right side up.*

Primitives and Wild Beasts

"Primitivism" is a return to the simplified (and therefore abstract) style

used in prehistoric cave paintings and stylized, early Greek art.
Primitivists tried to paint the
world through the eyes of primitive people, with a calculated
crudeness. Paul Gauguin was
their inspiration. Gauguin rejected the sterile, modern, industrial world (and its sterile art) for
the expressive and magical power
of primitive images.

Rousseau, **War,** *1894 (Orsay Gallery, Paris)*

The Fauves (French for "wild
beasts," pronounced "foavs")
shocked the modern-art world
with their exuberant use of elements of primitive art: strong
outlines; bright, barbaric colors;
and two-dimensional flatness.
The Fauves distorted the visible
world so we could see it through
more primitive eyes.

Their leader was Henri
Matisse ("mah-TEES," 1869–
1954), a master of simplicity.
Each of his subjects is boiled
down to its essential details and
portrayed with a few simple
lines and colors.

Even though Matisse's work
looks crude, his classical training is obvious. The "flat," primitive look is actually carefully

Matisse simplifies reality so we can see it better through primitive eyes. The two-dimensional flatness shows Gauguin's influence.

planned 3–D. The bright colors that seem so bizarre are purposely
placed to balance the composition. And despite the few lines, his figures are accurate and expressive.

Picasso and Cubism

Pablo Picasso's long, prolific career spans several art styles. Picasso
(1881–1973), an innovator, provides us with prime examples of
many things characteristic of 20th-century art.

Picasso, **Science and Charity,** *1897 (Picasso Museum, Barcelona). As a teenager, Picasso painted realistically.*

When he was 19, Picasso moved from Barcelona to Paris to be where the artistic action was. (An exciting collection of his early works is displayed in his house in Barcelona.) Picasso's early paintings of beggars and other social outcasts are touching examples of expressionism done with the sympathy and understanding of an artist who felt, perhaps, as much an outcast as his subjects. These early works were from his Blue Period (around 1905), so called because their dominant color matches their melancholy mood.

Picasso was jolted out of his Blue Period by the abstract methods of the Fauves. Fascinated but not satisfied with the Fauvist 2–D treat-

Picasso, **The Frugal Meal,** *1904 (Museum of Modern Art, New York). He then explored beyond what the eye sees, evolving through several stages. This stage was melancholy, a style of expressionism called Picasso's "Blue Period."*

Picasso, **Seated Nude,** *1909 (Tate Gallery, London). During a frenzied period in Paris with painting buddy Georges Braque, Picasso jumbled realism into a new art style, "Cubism."*

ment of 3–D, Picasso played with the "building blocks" of line and color to find new ways to reconstruct the real world on canvas.

In about 1910, after an orgy of artistic exploration, Picasso and his friend Georges Braque found a new way to portray their world. This was Cubism, so called because the painting looks as though it was built with blocks. Cubism is like breaking a vase and arranging the broken pieces on a flat surface. In Picasso's work, chunks of light and shadow seem to stand out in 3–D, like shards of broken glass reflecting light.

Picasso was still tied to the visible world. The anatomy might be jumbled, but it's all there. Picasso shattered the real world, then pieced it back together on canvas in his own way.

In his monumental mural *Guernica,* Picasso blends the abstract and the expressive. In the 1930s, Nazi-backed Spanish fascists destroyed the Spanish town of Guernica. Picasso captured the horror of the event, not through a realistic portrayal but through expressive images.

The ambiguous, abstract nature of *Guernica* elevates the painting to a statement about all wars. There are some clearly recognizable images of the agony of war: the grieving mother with her dead child (a modern *Pietà*); the dying warrior clutching a broken sword; the twisted horse's head. But the real power of the work comes from the disjointed anatomy typical of early Cubist works, as if the bombs had shattered every belief and decimated every moral principle, leaving civilization in a confused heap of rubble.

Picasso, **Guernica**, *1937 (Centro de Arte Reina Sofia, Madrid). This master-piece combines Cubism, surrealism, and abstractionism in black, gray, and white to show the terror of the Fascist air raid on a defenseless town during the Spanish Civil War. Today it is a virtual national monument of Spain and a comment on the futility and horror of war in general.*

Guernica, Spain's national work of art, spent the Franco years in exile. Today it's the powerful centerpiece of the Reina Sofia Museum in Madrid, a few blocks from the Prado museum.

Dada

The Jazz Age of the 1920s, when Europe tried to drown the memory of the war in wine and cynicism, produced Dadaism. The name was intentionally nonsensical and childish to poke fun at the pompous art styles, theories, and -isms of prewar times. The one rule of the Dada theory is that there are no rules. The *Mona Lisa* with a mustache, a snow shovel signed by the artist, a collage of shredded paper dropped on a canvas—these were the Dadaists' contribution to Art, a summation of the rebelliousness and disgust of the Roaring Twenties.

If a snow shovel is art, what is art? With mass production, the lines began to blur. Handmade art became an economic dinosaur as it became possible for rich people to buy beautiful objects and furnishings right off the production line. Artists found themselves on the outside of an industrial society that was interested more in utility than in aesthetics.

Without patrons to please, modern artists had no one to please but themselves and fellow artists. They turned to subjects interesting to the highly educated—studies in color, brushwork, and textures. Originality and innovation became more important than beauty.

*Duchamp, **Fountain**, 1917. Marcel Duchamp, the daddy of Dada, placed this urinal in a New York exhibit. By taking a common object, giving it a title, and calling it art, he makes us think about the object in a new way.*

Modern artists face the same challenge as Michelangelo's successors: to be original at all costs. If you can't please the public, shock it.

Surrealism and Beyond

Dada's successor for shock value was surrealism. (The name implies "beyond realism," as if reality isn't weird enough already.) Inspired by the psychiatric theories of Sigmund Freud, surrealism explores the inner world of the subconscious mind. The canvases of Salvador Dali are primal, troubling "dreamscapes." In dreams, objects appear in weird combinations, constantly changing in shape and meaning. A woman becomes a cat, the cat has a trainpass, the cat is the train . . .

Marc Chagall ("shuh-GAWL," 1887–1985), although not a surrealist, used the same scrambling of images. Raised in Russia, Chagall mixed a rich borscht of Russian folk images, Jewish motifs, and Christian messages. His colorful paintings are a stimulating fantasy of mostly weightless images. The Chagall museum in Nice, designed by the artist himself, is a delight.

While surrealists painted recognizable objects (though often in a twisted or unusual setting), other artists produced purely abstract works. As Europe struggled to rebuild and recover after World War II, the focus of art shifted to the United States.

Pop Art

"Pop Art" of the 1950s and 1960s, like Dada of the Jazz Age, challenges the old rules of what constitutes art. The everyday toothpastes, soup cans, comic books, and advertisements of commercial society are displayed as art. The viewer sees these objects in a new way, reflecting on the value our society places on them.

Chagall, **Self-Portrait with Seven Fingers,** *1912 (Stedelijk Museum, Amsterdam)*

Dali, **The Persistence of Memory,** *1931 (Museum of Modern Art, New York). This first-ever look at "flex time" sums up the surrealists' attempt to shock us by taking familiar objects and placing them in an unfamiliar context.*

Lichtenstein, **Whaam!***, 1963 (Tate Gallery, London). A child's comic book becomes a 70-square-foot piece of art: Pop Art. What would Raphael think?*

Modern artists experiment with modern materials. From initial experimentation with Cubist collages, artists began replacing paint with all kinds of things. The resulting mixed-media creations stimulate all the senses—in some cases, even smell—and fuse the mediums of painting and sculpture.

Painting has been the most dynamic of the visual arts in this century, but sculpture followed some of the same trends. The primitivism of the Fauves influenced Constantin Brancusi, whose sculptures are the equivalent of Matisse's "minimal" paintings. Brancusi altered the shape of the original stone only slightly.

Author Gene Openshaw "getting into" modern art (Pompidou Gallery, Paris)

Modern Art Sights

Spain
- Picasso Museum, Barcelona
- *Guernica*, Reina Sofia Museum, Madrid
- Dali Museum, Figueres

France
- Picasso Museum, Paris
- Pompidou Gallery, Paris
- Grimaldi-Picasso Museum, Antibes
- Marc Chagall National Museum, Nice
- Foundation Maeght, St. Paul, French Riviera
- Many galleries on the French Riviera (Matisse, Chagall, Picasso)

Germany
- Wallraf-Richartz Museum, Köln

Netherlands:
- Stedelijk Museum, Amsterdam
- Kroller-Muller Museum, near Arnhem

Britain
- Tate Gallery, London

Italy
- Guggenheim Gallery, Venice

Denmark
- Louisiana Museum, north of Copenhagen

Norway
- Munch Museum (Expressionism), Oslo

Switzerland
- Kunst Museum (lots of Paul Klee), Bern
- Art of the Criminally Insane (Collection de l'Art Brut), Lausanne

Sweden
- Modern Art Museum, Stockholm

Anywhere in Europe: Commercial galleries sell contemporary art. Temporary exhibits abound; often, one wing of a museum is reserved just for temporary exhibits. Check local periodical entertainment guides, tourist information offices, and posters around town.

Modern Architecture

"Form follows function" was the catchphrase of early 20th-century architecture. While painters and sculptors have to concern themselves primarily with how good their artwork looks (its form), architects must also be concerned with how their buildings work (function).

At the turn of the century, the ready availability of steel frames, reinforced concrete, and high-quality, mass-produced glass gave architects the tools to build almost any style of building they wanted. Architects began stripping buildings down to their barest structural elements, letting the function dictate the form.

The international style that developed in the 1920s followed the lead of the Bauhaus, a German art school. This blocky building emphasized industrial design and functionalism in architecture. Rectangular outlines, flat roofs, no ornamentation, white walls, and lots of glass were Bauhaus favorites. When the Nazis closed the Bauhaus, its director moved to the United States; tall, boxlike, steel-and-glass skyscrapers soon became the standard U.S. urban skyline.

As architects dealt with the large-scale reconstruction of European cities flattened by World War II, they busied themselves with plans for towns, housing, and schools. Rotterdam and Köln are two of many cities rebuilt from scratch after the war.

Contemporary European architecture has branched in several directions. An extreme example of form following function is the Georges Pompidou Center in Paris. This huge, exoskeletal structure drapes its "guts" on the outside. All plumbing, heating ducts, and

*Gropius, **Bauhaus**, 1925, Dessau, Germany. Modern architecture focused on function over good looks. This purely geometric building set the style for almost every skyscraper since.*

***Pompidou Center,** b. 1977, Paris. With its guts color-coded and draped on the outside, the interior of this Parisian cultural center is filled with modern art galleries and exhibits.*

wiring are brightly color coded and in full view, freeing the interior space for its expansive modern art museum.

Le Corbusier, who said "a house is a machine for living in," was a major force in 20th-century European architecture. An innovative leader in city planning, he popularized putting buildings on pillars to create space below. After Le Corbusier, governmental buildings were no longer built to look like Neoclassical temples. One church he designed, in Ronchamp, France, has become a pilgrimage site for students of architecture.

Munich's buildings for the 1972 Olympic Games are an interesting experiment in tent forms. Across the street, the BMW headquarters and museum occupy a futuristic, cylindrical, glass skyscraper.

Scandinavian architects such as Alvar Aalto from Finland developed their own style based on simplicity and clean lines. These traits

*Le Corbusier, **Chapel,** 1954, Ronchamp, France. A far cry from Gothic, this highly expressive church (located atop a hill in the Vosges Mountains) is one of the gems of modern architecture.*

Modern Architecture Sights

Finland
- Temppeliaukio Church, Helsinki
- Tapiola (planned suburb), Helsinki
- Works of Alvar Aalto (museum), Jyvaskyla

Sweden
- Vallingby and Farsta (planned suburbs), Stockholm

France
- The "Cube" at La Defense, Paris
- Forum/Les Halles shopping mall, Paris
- Pyramid Entrance to Louvre and attached mall, Paris
- Georges Pompidou Center, Paris
- Chapel at Ronchamp, France

Italy
- Termini Train Station, Rome

Germany
- Berlin housing projects (Kreuzberg district), Berlin

Austria
- Hundertwasser Haus, Vienna

Netherlands
- Rotterdam, the whole city

I. M. Pei's Pyramid entry to the Louvre, 1990, Paris

carry over into the Scandinavian furniture and lighting designs popular in America today.

The streets of Europe's cities are becoming "people places." Most large cities (such as Copenhagen, Florence, and Munich) have traffic-free pedestrian areas full of shops and cafés, providing perfect opportunities for that great European pastime—people-watching.

Faced with ever-dwindling space, rising populations, and dynamic societal changes, European architects and city planners have come up with some creative ideas. Today's architecture is—as it has been from the caveman to Egypt and from Rome to the Renaissance—a product of available materials and technology, climate, and the needs of the people.

A United Europe?

As Europe grapples with problems concerning the environment, terrorism, politics and competition in a global market, it has recognized the growing necessity of speaking, trading, and legislating with one voice. Today the question of a united Europe is no longer "if," but "when."

In 1948, Belgium, the Netherlands, and Luxembourg (BeNeLux) united economically to compete with the bigger countries. Later, the European Coal and Steel Community (founded by Germany, France, Italy, and the BeNeLux nations) quickly showed that the free trade concept was a winner.

In 1957, these six countries expanded their agreement to include agricultural products, further linking their economies. Interdependence was up, especially between two former arch-enemies, Germany and France. Their affiliation became known as the Common Market.

The Common Market was joined by Great Britain, Ireland, Denmark, Greece, Spain, and Portugal. In the mid-1990s, Austria, Sweden, and Finland became members, while Norway voted against membership. Today this European Union (EU) bustles with 15 states and over 370 million producer/consumers.

In 1992, all commercial borders between EU nations were dissolved. In the mid-1990s, passport controls for citizens and tourists were eliminated as well. Today the EU has one common passport and one uniform driver's license. A common European currency unit called the ECU is used for intra-EU trade. Plans for a unified currency are in the works.

The economic success of the EU, the demands of continental problems like acid rain that know no borders, and the pressure to compete in a global market against the Americas and Asia have convinced most Europeans that some degree of unification is a good idea. But many issues remain unresolved, including the status of foreign guest workers and refugees, who increasingly find themselves the targets of racism and even violence. Also there remains great debate about what to do in terms of a unified defense force. This became apparent during the unrest in the former Yugoslavia.

The opening of the English Channel Tunnel (the Chunnel) in 1995 was one high-profile example of how Europe is growing together physically—in ways unimaginable just a decade ago. The world's longest tunnels are under construction as Norway tames its rugged environment. Denmark is bridging its islands. Bullet trains from Sweden to Spain are lacing together capitals. Europe is charging confidently into an age where there are only neighbors. This is great news for both Europeans and us tourists.

Free trade throughout Europe is obviously worth pursuing, but just how far should unification go? Many worry about the homogenization of the cultures as well as the impact of "party crashers" coming in from the poorer eastern fringe of Europe. What impact will a freer Eastern Europe have, with its pent-up capacity to consume and produce? What about the reunification of Germany, which has in itself created a new economic superpower? What about the foreign policy of a united Europe?

Germany, France, and Benelux seem gung-ho for a serious union. France figures the only way not to be dominated by a unified Germany is to join forces with it. Britain and Scandinavia are reluctant and cautious. The core countries are leery of the economic drag southern countries might bring to a united Europe. Poor countries in the east don't want to be shut out.

Many expect the unification of Europe to include a series of widening circles, with a core union functioning almost as a single country, a second circle containing Great Britain, a wider circle containing Austria, Scandinavia, and Switzerland, and an outermost circle letting

AIDS poster. *Uniting, but with caution, Europe looks to the future.*

Turkey and Eastern Europe in on some of the trade fun. Sadly, the fate of Russia is still an unknown.

The challenge for the EU is to maintain the cultural diversity that makes Europe so unique and vital while taking the logical steps to ensure Europe's health as an economic force in the 21st century. _Vive la différence!_

The Superpower Bowl		
Region	_Population_	_Rough GNP_
EU	370 million	5 trillion
U.S.	260 million	6 trillion
Japan	125 million	2.5 trillion

As you feel the fjords and caress the castles, remember that Europe is alive—coping, groping, and more interested in its future than in its past.

As visitors, we often forget that quaintness, cute thatched-roof houses, and yodeling are not concerns of the average European. Sure, it's exciting to find odd remnants of Europe's Old World that somehow missed the 20th-century bus. But much of what we see touted as the "real thing" culturally is actually a cultural cliché kept alive for the tourists. As you travel, seek out contemporary Europe as well as its past. Educate yourself about the concerns and issues of today.

As the world hurtles past 100 billion McDonald's hamburgers served, Europe is looking more and more like the United States. It seems that when all the wrinkled old ladies in black are gone, they are destined to be replaced by Coca-Cola, skyscrapers, fast food, computers, and the global pop culture.

The most encouraging aspect of our future is that as the world grows smaller, more people will travel and rub shoulders. As this happens and we begin to view our globe as the home of 6 billion equally precious people, we'll all feel a little less American, British, Japanese, French, or whatever, and a little more like a member of humankind.

The lessons of history apply even today. It's easy to think that we are in a grand new age with no precedent, one that follows no rules. But every generation has thought that of their era, and we're just the latest in a long line of "pioneers."

History is happening now, and plenty of excitement awaits. If we see ourselves in historical perspective, grasp how yesterday shaped today, and learn less from the news media and more from our travels, we will better understand and shape the events of tomorrow.

Part II
Tangents

Britain

Ancient Britain

The Isle of Britain was a mysterious challenge to General Julius Caesar as he prepared for his invasion. Curtained in mist, separated from the civilized Continent by an arm of the ocean, peopled by strange, savage tribes who painted themselves blue and sacrificed human beings to their gods—this was nearly all that was known of merry olde England when Caesar set sail in 55 B.C. to conquer it.

The 45-year-old general had conquered Gaul (modern France), but wanted one more conquest to impress the folks back home so that when he returned to Rome they would invite him to rule the empire. His invading ships approached Dover to find the cliffs lined with screaming, war-painted, spear-carrying Britons. After beaching, Caesar led a swift charge, driving the Britons back. The Romans huddled near the coast and waited for reinforcements, which were delayed by stormy weather. They were harassed by daring native soldiers driving war chariots, who would dash up to the camp balanced on the yoke, wreak havoc, and ride away.

As soon as new ships arrived, a weary Caesar packed up and returned to Gaul. His conquest of 200 meters of beach was hailed as a triumph in Rome; the Senate proclaimed an unprecedented twenty days of public thanksgiving.

The next year, better prepared, Caesar tried again, this time marching inland as far as modern London. He won battles, took hostages, exacted tribute, and made treaties. He left England having brought the mysterious land into its first contact with "civilization."

Celts (500 B.C.–A.D. 43)
The Celtics (pronounced KELL-tiks, except in Boston) Caesar found weren't as barbarous as he had expected. There were perhaps 100,000 Britons scattered in small, isolated tribes. A number of

towns had 500 people; present-day Colchester, with 1,000, was the largest. Still, most were rural farming/hunting/herding tribes united under a local chieftain. People didn't travel or trade much and most buildings were small and made of wood.

The Celts (who included Gaels, Picts, Scots, and many smaller tribes) migrated to England and Ireland from the Continent beginning around 500 B.C. They conquered and blended with the prehistoric inhabitants (those even-more-mysterious people who built Stonehenge with huge rocks quarried 100 miles away and traded goods as far as ancient Greece). The Celtic language survives today in modern Gaelic (Scotland), Erse (Ireland), Welsh (guess), and Breton (Western France). About half of present-day Great Britain is of Celtic-Pictish blood.

The Celts' nasty reputation in the Roman mind came from the Druids. These witch-doctor priests presided over rituals to appease the gods, spirits, and demons that inhabited the countryside. There were ghosts and spirits everywhere; one could feel them in the gloom of a dark forest or in the power of a rushing waterfall. The Druids, painted blue, sacrificed and decapitated animals and occasionally humans, offering the head to a local god or to one of the more powerful fertility or war gods. Then they tore the body apart, using the disposition of the guts to predict the future. They also practiced voodoo magic, cursing someone by making a statue of the person and then mutilating it.

The Romans, tolerant as they were, drew the line at Druidism. Because the Druids were also tribal aristocrats trying to preserve tradition, they posed a political threat to the Romans. The Druids maintained power for a century after Caesar's brief invasions.

Romans (A.D. 43–500)

Then, in A.D. 43, the Emperor Claudius ordered a massive invasion that overwhelmed the courageous but outmatched Celts. Claudius personally rode north from Rome for the victory procession through Colchester, accompanied by the Praetorian Guard, a host of Roman aristocrats, and the imperial elephant corps to impress the natives. The Romans had arrived.

Claudius left after two weeks with the simple order, "Conquer the rest." It took forty years, but finally all the lowland areas of England and Wales, plus lower Scotland, were in Roman hands, where they would remain for four centuries. The fiercely independent herdsmen of the Scottish highlands, though nominally Roman, never were assimilated into "civilized" Roman society (and, some would say, have yet to be assimilated into British society).

The conquest wasn't without resistance. In A.D. 60, after a dispute at modern-day Colchester, Roman soldiers took the Celtic palace, flogged the queen, raped her daughters, and seized the royal treasury. The outraged Celts banded together under Queen Boadicea and set out burning and looting Roman towns. The rebels took "Londinium" (London), burned it to the ground, and offered the Romanized inhabitants as human sacrifices to the Celtic god of war. Blood-hungry with success, the rebellion spread. It took months for the Romans to quiet the Celts. The winter was a bleak one for Britain as the Romans wreaked violent revenge. To escape reprisal, Boadicea and her family took poison. (Boadicea is honored with a statue across the street from Big Ben, in London.)

The Romans learned a lesson, however, and instituted policies to keep the Celts happy. Government was in the hands of a Roman, but he allowed local chieftains to retain power as long as they cooperated with him. Local customs and religious practices were generally accepted.

Around their forts, the Romans planned towns in the familiar Roman pattern: a rectangular street plan with the forum (marketplace) and basilica (courthouse) in the center, temples, baths, and a piped water system. Later, earthwork walls were built, defining their growth limit through the Middle Ages. Some towns such as Corinium (today's Cirencester) and Aquae Sulis (modern Bath) grew to have over 1,000 inhabitants.

To connect towns and forts and to facilitate trade and communication, the Romans built roads, many of which still stand. Latin was taught, and soon it was as popular (in urban centers) as Celtic. When marriage was legalized for Roman soldiers, they often married local girls, and their sons grew up to join the ranks. The line between "Roman" and "Briton" grew fuzzier and fuzzier. By A.D. 200, the urban centers of southeast England were as "civilized" as any part of the empire. The population of Roman Britain grew to 2 million.

Londinium was the Roman center of the country, the capital, trade center, and the hub of the road system. It was surrounded by a stone wall (parts of which are still visible near the Tower of London). From here, Britain traded with the Continent, exporting wool, metals, hunting dogs, corn, and oysters. In return, they got all the luxuries of the Roman world: pottery, wine, glassware, lamps, jewelry, silverware, furniture, and the latest clothing fashions.

The northern tribes of Scotland weren't very impressed with what the Romans had to offer, preferring independence to the niceties of Latin culture. Roman soldiers had to protect their settlements from periodic raids by the highlanders. They conquered as far north as the present border of Scotland and then built a wall. Hadrian's Wall (built while Hadrian was emperor, around A.D. 130) stands 20 feet high and 8 feet thick (wide enough to hold a chariot), stretching from coast to coast across northern England. It was manned by 20,000 soldiers in forts spaced 1 mile apart ("mile castles") all along the wall. For more than three centuries it kept the Scots at bay, and much of it stands today, a tribute to Roman military engineering.

(Hadrian's Wall is worth a visit. The best-preserved section is in Northumberland near the town of Hexham. A youth hostel called Once Brewed is just a short walk from Housesteads Fort, a Roman mile castle with the best museum about the wall.)

Christianity arrived with the Romans. Rome, generally tolerant of local religions, accepted many of the local Druid gods, giving them new Latin names. (The superstitious Roman soldiers, assigned to a distant outpost near a dreary forest, were careful not to offend any fierce spirits that might have dwelled there.) The sterile Roman religion with its abstract gods and reverence for the state didn't really do it for the locals, so the Britons, like many Romans throughout the empire, turned to Eastern religions such as Mithraism, the Cult of Isis, and Christianity.

Legend has it that Christianity was brought by Joseph of Arimathea, the man who paid for Jesus' burial, and that he converted the Britons with a miracle: he planted his staff in the ground and it took root, becoming a thorn tree in Glastonbury that is said to bloom every Christmas.

Christianity became a powerful force—probably the number-one religion during the Roman occupation. But Celtic, Roman, and Eastern religions were also a part of Roman Britain. As late as A.D. 400, Celtic temples were built; many Druidic rituals survived among the peasants until modern times.

As Rome fell, so fell Roman Britain. The combination of internal decay and external enemies that caused Rome's collapse forced them to slowly withdraw troops and administrators from Britain. Over the centuries, even the Roman governors and generals had become Britonized, and drifted away from Rome. Some generals went so far as to secede from the empire, declaring themselves kings of Britain. Without Rome's strength and organization, the island was easy prey for invaders. In A.D. 409, the emperor in Rome was forced to completely abandon Britain.

The Anglo-Saxons (A.D. 400–800)

The invaders came from Germany and Denmark, tribes called Angles, Saxons, Jutes (and worse names by the Britons). They came not as conquerors but as refugees, leaving behind crowded, bleak homelands for the fertile farmlands of Britain. As early as A.D. 250, small groups in longboats began arriving on the northeast coast. The Roman Britons fought them off when they could and tolerated them when they couldn't. As Roman support waned, the invasion/migrations increased. The sixth century saw the Anglo-Saxons pushing the Celts and Romanized Britons westward. This is the period of the real King Arthur, most likely a Christian Romanized British general valiantly fighting the invading tribes.

By 600, the southeast part of the island was "Angle-land" (England), the land of the Angles. The Roman world slowly crumbled; the towns dwindled, and the roads fell into disuse. The invaders were a rough, savage people compared to the Romans, with no central government or economy. Each tribe had its own chief and council of elders. The society was bound by a code of hierarchy and personal loyalty similar to that of the later medieval feudal system.

England had entered the Dark Ages. The economy was weak, life was harsh, and justice was severe. The "wergild," a system worked out to financially compensate relatives for people murdered in feuds, gives us a look at the value placed on human life in those harsh times. If a noble was killed, the murderer's clan had to pay the victim's clan 1,200 shillings; a knight was worth 300; a free peasant, 200; killing a serf required no recompense at all. Women of equal position were worth less than their male counterparts. Hmmm.

The Anglo-Saxon pagan religion replaced Christianity in many places. Some of these Norse gods are familiar to us today: Tiw, Woden (King of the Gods), Thor (with his hammer), Frig. Not familiar? How about "Tiw's-day," "Woden's-day," "Thor's-day," and "Frig's-day." They also celebrated a spring festival to the goddess Eostre (Easter).

Christianity re-entered England with missionaries from both Ireland and Rome. When the Saxon King Aethelbert of Kent was converted (around 600), the tide was turned. Within a hundred years, England was again mostly Christian, though not by much. Pagans continued to rule in many kingdoms throughout the Dark Ages.

One of the Christian kings, Offa (around 780), brought some stability to the warring Anglo-Saxon tribes. The time of peace brought a
renaissance of learning, and the English language took its earliest
form. The poem "Beowulf," written in England but incorporating
Norse mythology, was written at this time. (You can see a manuscript
in the British Museum, London.) Offa printed coins with his portrait
on them, advancing the notion that the many Anglo-Saxon tribes
were part of a single nation. He also built a trench to separate England
from the Celtic Welsh. Offa's Dike, running the length of the English-
Welsh border, is a popular hike.

Only Two Invasions to Go (A.D. 800–1066)

True unity didn't come until after another set of invasions—this time
from the Vikings, the Anglo-Saxons' distant cousins from Denmark.
The two groups warred, made peace, and mingled during the next
few centuries. This was the period of rulers with names such as
Harold Harefoot, Eric Bloodaxe, Edgar the Peacock, Ethelred the
Unready, and Edward the Confessor (Edward commissioned
Westminster Abbey).

The stew of peoples that make up present-day England was nearly
complete—from prehistory to the Celts, the Romans, the Anglo-
Saxons, and finally the Danes. Next came the Normans, from northern France (present-day Normandy). William the Conqueror invaded
from across the channel, defeating Saxon King Harold at the Battle of
Hastings (1066). This battle marks England's escape from the Dark
Ages and her entry into the High Middle Ages.

English Kings and Queens

*"For God's sake, let us sit upon the ground and tell sad stories of the
death of kings . . . "*

Shakespeare, *Richard II*

The history of England's royalty is full of violence, corruption, treason, sex, scandal, power, and greed. Remarkably, the country survived its rulers.

England's Alfred the Great

Alfred (849–899), an enlightened and compassionate ruler, is considered the first king of a united "England." He rallied the scattered
Anglo-Saxon tribes of England to ward off the Viking invaders. After

establishing peace, he turned to matters closer to his heart. Having had an older brother, he never expected to become king, so he studied poetry and Latin. He even visited Rome in his teens.

When he became king, he reformed the government and built schools that taught English as well as Latin. Alfred deserves his reputation as the model English king—strong, learned, and kind.

French Kings: The Normans

William the Conqueror crossed the channel from Normandy and defeated the Saxon forces at Hastings. He was crowned king of England on Christmas Day 1066, in London's Westminster Abbey, where future kings and queens would be crowned. A harsh but efficient ruler, he united the British lords and established a feudal society. (Construction of the Tower of London, where so many leaders were later executed, was begun during William's reign.)

William and his Norman successors were never very popular with the common people. They were foreign invaders who spoke French and followed French customs.

The Tower of London, *1077–1097. The prison and execution site for those accused of crimes against the monarchy. Admission tickets include a very informative and entertaining tour by a Beefeater. (Executions available by reservation only.)*

His son William II, called "Rufus" (the Red) because of his ruddy complexion, was even less well liked. A vain, arbitrary tyrant, he made no attempt to mix with the English people. He died in a hunting accident—an arrow in the back. His brother Henry just happened to be in the hunting party, behind him. Henry immediately rode to Winchester, seized the treasury, and was crowned king the next day.

More French Kings: Angevins

The French kings expanded their empire. By the time Henry II took power (1154) at the age of 21, his Angevin Empire stretched from Scotland to northern Spain. His long and hard-fought rule consolidated the empire.

Henry was a good soldier, a fair diplomat, well read (for a king), and possessed of restless energy and a violent temper. The beginning of his reign was marked by optimism. He and his wife Eleanor, a beautiful and accomplished lady of the time, established a court where chivalrous knights, ladies, troubadours, and scholars met. Henry built numerous castles throughout the empire.

But then things went bad, and it seemed as though everyone in the world was fighting Henry. He waged war with the Welsh, the Scots, and French rebels. He quarreled with English barons over taxes. His sons, supported by Eleanor, tried to overthrow him. Perhaps the most painful betrayal was that of his close friend and adviser, Thomas Becket, whom he had appointed Archbishop of Canterbury. When Becket's strong, independent policy threatened the king's power, Henry's knights murdered Becket in Canterbury Cathedral. Becket became an instant martyr to the English people, and the cathedral became a popular pilgrimage site.

Henry II died a broken man, and his son Richard the Lionhearted assumed power. Richard was the model of a chivalrous knight—a good soldier, a poet, a musician, and a handsome, valiant Crusader. He was also a Frenchman. He hated England. (He once said, "I would sell London if I could find a buyer.") During his ten-year reign, he spent only six months in the country he ruled.

Everyone hated Richard's successor, his brother John Lackland. Everyone. He is unanimously considered the worst king England ever had. Devious and weak, he had an uncanny ability to make enemies of everyone—barons, popes, the English, and the French. He murdered his own nephew in a drunken rage. He waged war in France and lost miserably. The Angevin Empire collapsed under his rule. He overtaxed and bullied the English barons. All in all, he was very much the evil King John of the Robin Hood legend—perhaps the one true character in the myth.

John's place in history was assured by fixing his seal to the Magna Carta (Great Charter) forced on him by unhappy barons. This was the first step of many in English history to limit the power of kings and increase that of the nobles and common people. (The Magna Carta is on display in the British Museum, London.)

Royalty on the Rocks:
The Troublesome Centuries (1200–1400)

The next two centuries gave Shakespeare enough regicide, rebellion, and treason for eight plays. In that time, four kings were murdered, two died in battle, civil wars were rampant, and two family lines of kings were overthrown.

Edward II, a tyrant, was opposed by Roger Mortimer, his wife's lover. Edward was captured and murdered in a manner so brutal that to describe it would exceed this book's standard of good taste. Well, okay, if you insist. Suffice it to say that a red-hot poker, Edward's backside, and a thrusting motion were involved. Ooh.

His son Edward III (reigned 1327–1377) avenged his father's death in a relatively civilized manner, by merely having Mortimer hanged, drawn, and quartered. Edward's good rule (aided by his chivalrous son, the famous "Black Prince") included early victories in the Hundred Years' War with the French, in which England initially conquered, and then slowly lost, France.

The next monarch, Richard II (reigned 1377–1399), ruled poorly and was finally overthrown by an upstart baron who locked him in the Tower of London. The long line of French-English kings came to an end.

The House of Lancaster

Henry IV, the Usurper (reigned 1399–1413), of the house of Lancaster, was the first completely English king—the son of English parents who spoke no French. Handsome, athletic, a musician and scholar, he invited poet Geoffrey Chaucer to his court. Yet like so many others, when he died he was bitter and broken, worn out by years of opposition and civil war.

His son, the "Prince Hal" of Shakespeare's plays, was said to have lived a misspent youth, carousing, gambling, and thieving with commoners and prostitutes. Whether true or not, when he became Henry V he was cold, stern, and very capable. His victory at the Battle of Agincourt (1415) put most of France back under English rule.

All of Hal's gains became losses in the weak hands of Henry VI, whose attempts to hold France were foiled by a young French peasant woman, Joan of Arc. She claimed to hear voices of saints and angels who told her where to lead the French armies. She was eventually captured and burned as a witch by the English, but not before the French had gained an upper hand in the war.

War of the Roses

The inept Henry VI of the Lancaster family was opposed by the York family, and a long civil war broke out—the "War of the Roses," named for the white (York) and red (Lancaster) roses that the families used as their symbols. Edward IV, a York, locked Henry in the Tower of London, later executing him. Edward died young, at the age of 40, reportedly worn out by his sexual excesses.

Two of Edward's excesses survived him, but not by much. His sons, the heirs to the throne, were kidnapped and murdered in the Tower of London by Richard III (Edward's own brother), and both houses decided the bloody war had to end. When a petty noble from the house of Tudor defeated Richard's armies and killed him in battle, all of England was prepared to rally round him as the new king. Henry VII was crowned, a diplomatic marriage was arranged, and England was united.

Tudor Rule, 1485–1603

Henry VII (reigned 1485–1509) was shrewd and efficient; he was England's first "modern" chief executive. He united the country and built up a huge treasury. (To protect himself from traitors, he established a royal bodyguard, the Beefeaters.)

His 18-year-old son inherited a nation that was solvent, strong, and at peace.

Henry VIII (reigned 1509–1547) was the English version of a Renaissance prince—tall, handsome, athletic, a poet and musician, and well read in secular learning and theology. He was charismatic but could also be arrogant, cruel, gluttonous, erratic, and paranoid.

The most notorious event of Henry VIII's reign was the break with the Catholic Church (and his establishment of the nearly identical Church of England). This arose over the Catholic Church's refusal to grant him a divorce from his first wife, Catherine of Aragon (the daughter of Ferdinand and Isabella of Spain) and to sanction his subsequent marriage to the beautiful and lively Anne Boleyn. Henry was determined to get a wife who could give him a son. For whatever reasons—love, desire for an heir, diplomacy, or sheer lust—Henry went through six wives, divorcing, imprisoning, or beheading them when they no longer served his purpose.

Henry faced enemies in England over his break with Catholicism, and he dealt with them characteristically—with the axe. Among those beheaded at the Tower for holding fast to their convictions was

Henry VIII, _by Hans Holbein_

Thomas More, Henry's chancellor and author of the famous political tract, "Utopia."

While the Reformation wars raged on the Continent, England was having religious troubles of its own. After the brief but weak reign of Henry's long-awaited male heir, the stage was set for Henry's daughters.

Mary I (reigned 1553–1558), the daughter of his first wife, Catherine, had her mother's fanatic Spanish Catholic devotion (the same kind that gave us the Inquisition). She was convinced her mission was to return England to the Roman church—come Hell or high water. Neither came but in her zeal, she ordered burned at the stake over 300 men, women, and teenagers, and ordered the execution of the innocent, 17-year-old Lady Jane Grey (a rival for the throne) in 1554. Compared with the tens of thousands killed in other countries it seems like nothing, but it shocked the English enough that they turned their backs on Catholicism for good and nicknamed their queen "Bloody Mary."

Mary's successor, Elizabeth I (1558–1603), Henry's daughter by the fiery Anne Boleyn, had absorbed the lesson of religious fanaticism. She was a Protestant with a broad Renaissance education. Her tolerant policies and prudent nature brought peace at home and victory abroad, making England a true European power for the first time. Among other conquests, Elizabeth subdued Ireland, beginning that country's centuries of struggle for independence.

The English navy defeated the famed Spanish Armada and soon ruled the waves. Explorers and traders probed the New World and

Elizabeth I, 1558–1603

Asia, bringing back spoils and luxury goods. (Sir Walter Raleigh introduced tobacco from America to a skeptical Queen Elizabeth.)

Elizabeth was golden-haired, prudent, and a "Virgin Queen," but her cousin Mary, Queen of Scots, was dark, lively, and a lover of dance, music, and men. Mary (not "Bloody Mary"), a Catholic from the Stuart family, represented the opposition to Elizabeth and the Protestant regime. After Mary was implicated in an anti-crown plot, Elizabeth imprisoned her for 19 long years. But Mary never bowed. Fat, wrinkled, and wearing a wig to cover her balding head, she was finally led to the execution block.

The Elizabethan era was England's High Renaissance, especially in literature. Shakespeare, Raleigh, John Donne, Christopher Marlowe, and many others shaped the course of English literature and the English language itself. (The British Museum in London has letters and manuscripts by England's great writers.)

The Stuarts and Civil War

When Elizabeth died, presumably still a virgin and definitely without an heir, the Tudor throne passed to the Stuarts—to James, son of Mary, Queen of Scots. James I (reigned 1603–1625) was vain and arrogant, a "foreigner" (from Scotland), and a Catholic to boot, who succeeded in alienating both the English people and Parliament.

James insisted that he ruled by "divine right" and was therefore above Parliament and human laws. The one lasting achievement of his reign was the King James version of the Bible, a landmark translation in both theology and literature, the culmination of the Elizabethan Renaissance.

It's said that James steered the ship of state toward the rocks and then left his son to wreck it. Throughout the 17th century, the haughty Catholic Stuart kings were at odds with Parliament until Parliament got fed up, rebelled, and established a "constitutional monarchy" that limited, by law, the king's power.

Charles I (reigned 1625–1649) was his father's son in every way, but even more so: he was pompous, vain, anti-Protestant, and anti-Parliament. When Parliament refused to grant him more money, he dissolved the body for over ten years. Parliament (which was made up mostly of nobles) responded by raising its own army and declaring war on the king. Their leader, Oliver Cromwell, vowed, "We will cut off the King's head with the crown on it." Civil war had begun.

Parliament defeated the troops loyal to the king, deposed him, and set up a Commonwealth ruled by itself. Charles was executed as Cromwell had promised.

Cromwell, a Puritan gentleman-farmer elected to Parliament, soon assumed the powers of a dictator. He was very capable, religiously tolerant, and kept a steady hand in a troubled time. However, he himself suspended Parliament, a la Charles, when it disagreed with him.

When Cromwell died, in order to prevent another civil war in the struggle for power, Parliament invited Charles II to reign—on the condition that he follow rules it set out.

(The French experienced a similar cycle 130 years later. The royalty abused its power; Parliament took matters into its own bloody hands, beheading the king. After a dictator's enlightened but harsh rule, the king was invited back and allowed to rule with constitutional or parliamentarian limitations.)

Charles II and Restoration

The "Restoration" of the monarchy (1660) was reason to celebrate in England. After decades of civil war and Puritan rule (with all the negative things "puritan" implies), it was nice to have the pomp, ceremony, luxury, and even decadence of the Stuart kings. Charles II (1660–1685) had spent his exile in the magnificent court of Louis XIV. He returned to London with the latest fashions.

Charles had a series of dazzling mistresses who shocked the Puritan Parliament and titillated the public. (There were so many, most of them Catholics, that one of them took to identifying herself: "I'm the Protestant whore.")

During Charles' reign, London was devastated by a plague and burned to the ground in the Great Fire of 1666. The rebuilding, lead by architect Christopher Wren, reflects Charles' Baroque influence (from Versailles).

Charles' brother, James II, lived up to the Stuart name by persecuting Protestants and plotting against Parliament. He was thrown out in the "Glorious Revolution." Parliament invited James' daughter and her husband to rule again, according to the dictates of Parliament. William and Mary were succeeded by the unremarkable Queen Anne.

The House of Hanover

In 1714, the Stuart line was exhausted and so were the English people, worn out by religious strife. Parliament chose the king least likely to stir up trouble, George I (reigned 1714–1721) of Germany. George was 54 years old, spoke no English, and had no interest in politics. His chancellor, Sir Robert Walpole, essentially ran the country. George II (1727–1760) was the sequel to this bland state of affairs.

George III (1760–1820) was the first truly English ruler in 50 years. He took the throne with high hopes and then ran right into the American Revolutionary War, the French Revolution, and Napoleon. The world changed too fast for him, and in 1810, he slipped into madness. England was left with "an old, mad, blind, despised and dying king" (as the poet Shelley put it).

But England was changing rapidly, the Industrial Revolution was creating a whole new society, and England's monarchy knew it would meet the same fate as its French counterpart if it didn't modernize.

Victoria

Fortunately, along came Queen Victoria (reign 1837–1901), the first of England's modern figurehead monarchs. She had little interest and less influence in government. Her husband, Prince Albert, took some part in promoting science and industry (especially in organizing the Great Exhibition of 1851), but after his death things were run by Parliament and prime ministers (Disraeli and Gladstone).

Victoria was under 5 feet tall but radiated a regal aura. She was strong, bearing nine children, whom she married off to other European royal houses. (Kaiser Wilhelm and Tsarina Alexandra of World War I fame were her grandchildren.) She hated Georgian excesses and was notoriously prudish (hence, our word "Victorian").

The Victorian period saw England rise to its zenith. Its colonial empire was the largest in the world and its technology was the envy of Europe, yet its pockets of poverty were worse than those of many of its colonies.

Victoria's son, Edward VII (reign 1901–1910), was born and raised in the lap of Victorian luxury but never quite grew up, assuming the throne as a "child" of 60. The Edwardian period before World War I was the last golden (though fading) age of English optimism and civility. The horrors of the Great War shattered that forever.

The House of Windsor

One of your authors mixing it up with Princess Di as Charles looks on.

Edward's son, George V of Windsor, ruled in the "modern" style (subservient to law and Parliament) until 1936, when he was succeeded by his son, Edward VIII. Edward (the Duke of Windsor), in the most-talked-about action of modern royalty, abdicated the throne to marry a commoner, twice-divorced American Mrs. Wallis Warfield Simpson. Edward's brother, George VI, ruled until his popular daughter, Elizabeth II, took the throne in 1952 with her husband, Phillip Mountbatten, Duke of Edinburgh. Charles, Prince of Wales (of *National Enquirer* fame), waits to be our generation's entry in the parade of English kings and queens.

As you travel through England, you'll hear plenty of news about Charles, Lady Di, their royal rug-rats, and the British royalty of today. If you're alert and even if you're not, there's a good chance you'll get at least a fleeting glimpse of England's busy first family. Although their kings and queens don't come cheap and are only figureheads, most British seem to thoroughly enjoy having a royal family.

Victorian London

"It was the best of times, it was the worst of times . . . "
Charles Dickens, *A Tale of Two Cities*

Dickens' words best describe his own city of London in the 1800s. With 4 million people, it was the world's largest. It was the busiest, the richest, the most productive; the hub of the most industrialized nation on earth; and the capital of a colonial empire that covered

*The British Empire of the 19th century was the biggest, richest, and most powerful in history. Here, **John Bull** (the British Uncle Sam) is selfishly holding his swollen colonial empire.*

nearly one-fourth of the world's land surface. But the seamy underside of London was like a Third World country—dirty, poor, disease-ridden, and dangerous.

This contrast was everywhere. You could buy any commodity in the world on London's docks and lose it to a thief just as quickly. It was the center of industrial growth, yet it was choked with coal dust and industrial filth. London hosted the lavish social life of Prince Edward as well as thousands of homeless urchins begging, stealing, and sleeping in the streets. Palaces and townhouses contrasted with sagging tenements; well-lit cafés opposed seedy pubs where the poor indulged in one of their few affordable pastimes, drunkenness.

This was the Victorian period—that is, it occurred within the time of Queen Victoria (1837–1901). Victoria's husband, Prince Albert of Germany, was handsome, intelligent, progressive, and extremely proper. Victoria adored him. He was the quintessential gentleman.

The Great Exhibition and London's Growth

It was one of Albert's projects that spurred London's remarkable growth. He was fascinated with science and technology and proposed a Great Exhibition "uniting the industry and art of all nations"—in other words, a World's Fair. Held in 1851 in Hyde Park, it was the talk of Europe.

More than 6 million visitors jammed London's streets. The main attraction was the amazing Crystal Palace, an iron and glass structure with 300,000 windowpanes, covering 19 square acres—the symbol of the new and glorious Industrial Age. The Exhibition was a smashing success, and many visitors returned to settle down in London.

The Victorian Age was a building time: the Houses of Parliament, the Law Courts on the Strand, railroad stations (to accommodate a revolutionary form of transportation), churches, office buildings, and townhouses went up. Unfortunately, this abundance of building was not accompanied by a similar abundance of good taste. Most were designed in a rather bland neo-Gothic or Neoclassical style. The one truly Victorian style was the use of ornamental ironwork, inspired by Joseph Paxton's Crystal Palace. There was wrought iron everywhere; everything had a railing, whether needed or not.

On a typical business day, London traffic moved as fast as the narrow streets would allow. Double-decker buses—horse-drawn in those days—were as vital as their big red cousins of today. Efficient, two-wheeled, horse-drawn cabs sped recklessly through the streets. And the bicycle brought new mobility. On the streets were merchants of all kinds, many of whom sang songs to advertise their wares: the popular muffin-man, ringing his bell to attract children at tea time; the quack doctor hawking his Elixir of Life; the fishmonger; the delivery boy; the lamplighter, prostitute, pickpocket, and bobby.

The Rich

On the busy streets, London looked like a real melting pot of humanity, but Victorian society was rigidly hierarchical: rich, middle class, and poor. The rich spent part of their time on their country estates, coming to London only for "the season," an annual period of socializing and parties. The main purpose of these events was to pretend to have fun while arranging marriages for the children. Most marriages were business deals involving large dowries.

Every rich family had servants. The husband and wife each had personal attendants to dress them, advise them, and keep their social calendar. Besides these, there were the cooks and maids. Cleanliness, like godliness, was a priority.

The Middle Class

The middle-class families, while trying to keep up with the wealthy, were strongly influenced by the example of Victoria and Albert. The royal couple was the model of domestic happiness—proper, hardworking, and devoted to their many children. So it was throughout middle-class London. The wife was lord and master of the house; the husband was lord and master of the wife. He came home from work to find his slippers and velvet jacket warming by the fire. After dinner he'd play with the kids, do some reading aloud, listen to his wife play the piano, and go to bed early.

One of the characteristics of the Victorian Age was the advance of the middle class. They lived in nice homes equipped with that newfangled invention, the toilet. They were well-educated and infected with Albert's interest in science and the arts. The popularity of Dickens' works attests to this; his stories were serialized in pulp magazines that reached literally millions of people.

The Poor

Progress did not trickle down to London's wretched lower classes, however. Even before Reagan, the upper classes were oblivious to the lifestyle of the urban poor. The lower class lived in a different world, one that the upper class didn't care to know about. In the East End, people lived in decaying, crowded buildings crawling with rats. Whereas a middle-class family of ten (most Victorians had large families) lived in a spacious, ten-room house, the poorest lived ten to a single room. Human waste lined the streets.

London's poor

The gas lighting hardly cut through the dark on foggy nights in narrow alleyways where cutthroats lurked. Brothels, gambling dens, and pubs were these districts' major businesses.

Work was scarce. A man might haul garbage, shovel coal, or make deliveries, but that was about it. Women and children labored in the factories for pennies. For those in debt, there was the workhouse, which was much like a prison work camp. For some, the alternatives were drunkenness or the Queen's Army. Recruiting sergeants stood outside the pubs with shillings in their hands as bait for the down-and-out.

Private charities did little good. It wasn't until major government reforms at the end of the century that the slums got some relief. The reforming spirit got a boost from the writings of Dickens, a poor boy who made good but never forgot where he came from.

But all the classes in Victorian London had one thing in common— a spirit of optimism. There was a vitality to the city that even the poor felt. There was a sense that technology could bring about a better life for all, that hard work and right living would be rewarded just as surely as laziness and vice would be punished. London was a busy, hard-driving, shrewd city that maintained an outer face of gentility, grace, and good cheer.

Europeans: A Babel of Tongues

Imagine the confusion if the citizens of each state in the United States spoke their own language. Europe is like that now, but it wasn't always.

Europe's languages can be arranged into a family tree. Most of them have the same grandparents and resemble each other more or less like you resemble your brothers, sisters, and cousins. Occasionally, an oddball uncle sneaks in who no one can explain, but most languages have common roots.

LANGUAGE TREE

An understanding of how these languages relate to one another can help boost you over the language barrier. The following generalities are useful:

1. Knowing Greek and Latin roots used in our language broadens your English vocabulary and helps you make educated guesses at the meaning of words in other languages.

2. The most valuable second languages to know in Europe are German, French, and Spanish. English is the most widely spoken language in Europe.

3. As you can see from the tree, the dominant European family branches are the Romance and Germanic language clans.

Romance Countries: Italy, France, Spain, and Portugal

The Romance family evolved out of Latin, the language of the Roman Empire ("Romance" comes from "Roman"). Few of us know Latin, but knowing any of the modern Romance languages helps with the others. For example, your high-school Spanish will help you with Italian and Portuguese words. (But speaking Spanish to Italians will get you nowhere.)

French, after English, is the most popular second language in Central Europe and the Mediterranean world. In Morocco and other former French colonies, French is the standard second language. Colonial background determines the second language (and sometimes even the first language) of countries all over the world.

Germanic Countries: Germany, Scandinavia, and England

The Germanic languages, though influenced by Latin, are a product of the native tribes of northern Europe—people the ancient Romans called "barbarians" because of the crude sound of their language.

German is the handiest second language in Northern and Eastern Europe. It's spoken by all Germans and Austrians and most Swiss. You'll also find German-speaking enclaves in Italy, the Czech Republic, Slovenia, Romania, and other nearby countries. The many Turks who have worked in Germany speak German.

The people of Holland and northern Belgium speak Dutch (called Flemish in Belgium), which is very closely related to German. While Dutch is not Deutsch, a Hamburger or Frankfurter can almost read an Amsterdam newspaper.

The Scandinavians (except the Finns) can read each other's magazines and enjoy their neighbors' TV shows. If you speak one Scandinavian language, you can get by in all the Scandinavian countries. Any young or educated Scandinavian speaks several languages. English is the second-language choice and is spoken better here than anywhere else on the Continent.

Although Norwegians, Danes, and Swedes can understand each other (at least as well as Shakespeare could have understood Charlie Brown), the Finns, who are "Scandinavian" only geographically, have not even a hint of "Ya sure, yu betcha" in their language. Finnish, like Hungarian and Estonian, was somehow smuggled into Europe from distant Central Asia. More Finns speak Swedish than English.

English is technically a Germanic language—though sometimes it seems that we share half our words with French.

Multilingual Regions

Linguistic boundaries are never as cut and dried as political borders. Europe has several officially multilingual states and generally fuzzy borders.

Switzerland speaks four languages: 67 percent of the people speak Swiss German; 20 percent speak French; 12 percent speak Italian; and 1 percent speak Romansch, a language related to ancient Latin. The Romansch-speakers live in remote southeastern Switzerland.

Cereal in 14 languages

Alsace, another bilingual culture, is a French province on the German border. This chunk of land, whose ownership has often been disputed, happens to lie between the Rhine River (which the French claim is the natural boundary) and the Vosges Mountains (which the Germans claim God created to divide these two peoples). Its people have been dragged through the mud during several French-German tug-of-wars. For the time being, it's a part of France. Still, German works better than English here.

Belgium waffles, linguistically, with the southern half speaking French (the Walloons) and the other half speaking Flemish, or Dutch. Brussels, like Belgium itself, is legally bilingual, but the French in Belgium, like those in Switzerland and Canada, often feel tongue-tied and linguistically abused.

Their problems pale, however, beside the linguistic and demographic mess in much of Eastern Europe. The people of Poland, Bulgaria, Slovakia, and Serbia are Slavic and speak languages related to Russian. You'll meet many English-speaking people in the East. For a generation, it's been that region's linguistic window on the West.

Dying Tongues

The Basques, struggling to survive in the area where Spain, France, and the Atlantic all touch, are well aware that every year five languages die on our planet and that the cards are stacked against isolated groups like theirs.

England is surrounded by a "Celtic Crescent." In Wales, Scotland, Ireland, and Brittany (western France), you'll find bits and pieces of the old Celtic language. These survive mostly as a symbol of national spirit and local determination not to be completely subjugated culturally (as has occurred politically) by England or France. Seek out those diehard remnants of the old culture in militant bookstores (fronts for the autonomy movement in Brittany), Gaelic or folk pubs, and the Gaeltachts (districts, mostly in Western Ireland, where the old culture is preserved by the government).

Small linguistic groups, such as those who speak Flemish or Norwegian, are quicker to jump on the English bandwagon. It's crucial for these cultures to know a major language, and ours is the most major. These cultures are melting more and more into the English sphere of linguistic influence, while large groups such as the Spanish, French, and Germans can get by without embracing English so readily.

Whose Story Is History?

The world's 358 richest people have a net worth greater than the annual wage of the poorest 45% of the world's people. The U.S., with 5 percent of the world's population, controls about one-third of its wealth. And, as they say in London (before stepping off the "tube"), "mind the gap." It's growing.

With all the chaos and suffering on this planet, it's comforting to believe the rich got that way fair and square. Erik Dammann, Norwegian philosopher and author of *Future in Our Hands*, takes a *campesino's* view, arguing that the rich give history a comfortable spin.

When Columbus discovered America, the world's biggest and one of its most beautiful and sophisticated cities was Tenochtitlan, present-day Mexico City. Built out over a large lake with a population of about half a million, it looked a lot like Amsterdam. There were goldsmiths, chemists, barbers, public baths, and bustling marketplaces. Pre-Columbian Mexico had a system of paved roads, aqueducts, suspension bridges, police, a criminal code and court system, doctors capable of performing skull surgery, and a king elected by a council. Hernán Cortés, the Spanish conquistador who conquered present-day Mexico, wrote, "Discipline and high principles prevail everywhere. People are well-educated and, as far as I can tell, the form of government resembles that of Pisa or Venice." This is the Mexico that the Europeans "discovered" and destroyed 500 years ago. Mexicans don't celebrate Columbus Day.

Many areas of Africa, Latin America, and Asia were just as morally, ethically, and technically developed as Europe before our culture expanded. In A.D. 400, while most of Europe was still in skins, Africans wore Indian cotton and Chinese silk. In 1500, the top industry in Timbuktu was books. Africa had intricate networks of roads, large cities, irrigation projects, and lots of trade. During these days, when European nations exchanged ambassadors with their African counterparts, they expressed much respect for African governments, crafts, and societies. By the 1800s, when artifacts from these same civilizations were brought to Europe, they were thought to be from Atlantis or ancient Greece. By this time we had "learned" that Africans were incapable of creating objects of such quality. School books labeled Africa "the dark continent."

In 1498, Vasco da Gama discovered the route to India with the help of Arab sailors and also of maps and directions from friendly African merchants along the way. The Indian Ocean already had a busy, well-balanced, and stable system of trade among Indians, Chinese, Arabs, and Africans. These people used boats much bigger than those the Portuguese had arrived in, and their boats were equipped with tools such as quadrants and compasses.

Europeans were usually received warmly. They saw incredible wealth and spent the next 400 years taking it. Entire cultures vanished as hundreds of millions were enslaved. Literate and stable societies were colonized, raped, and left illiterate and with no basis for development. (Before Indonesia and Algeria were colonized by Europeans, their populations were 90 percent literate. When the Europeans were done with them, the colonies were left with their independence and 90 percent illiteracy.) Thousands of tons of gold were brought to Europe. All this gave Europe and the United States the resources, surplus wealth, land, and manpower to undergo the most rapid development in history—at the expense of the rest of the world. The inertia from this period still exists today, and the wealth continues to trickle up.

How did this happen? The Europeans were powered by greed and a love of gold. Exploration was a "for-profit" activity. And the cultures the Europeans met were just no match for Western tactics. For instance, African generals always left rear openings so their enemies could retreat if necessary. Battles were normally started in the afternoon so that the weaker side could retreat under the cover of darkness. Before the battle, opposing sides partied together.

In our culture, "all is fair in love and war." The first president of the United States won fame and a decisive victory by attacking on a Christmas Eve when his enemy was drunk and unprepared.

Within a few years of da Gama's famous voyage, Portugal controlled the Indian Ocean and had destroyed the 500-year-old cultures of East Africa. European memory of a destroyed civilization vanishes conveniently with that culture.

For the next nearly 400 years, the slave trade powered much of the European/American economy. A super-profitable triangular trade system brought slaves from Africa to America and minerals and natural wealth from America to Europe. This fueled Europe's Industrial Revolution. Huge ports such as Liverpool grew up and boomed with the slave industry. During this period, the industrial basis of European/American economic power in the 20th century was established.

While only about 15 million slaves reached America alive, conservative estimates say Africa lost 50 million of its strongest young men through the European and American slave trade. For 400 years of demoralizing slavery, Africa received only the opportunity to buy European products.

African cultures crumbled and were comfortably forgotten. What was left had no confidence and almost no hope. (Some say that slave traders were only capitalizing on an existing institution of inter-African slavery. But slavery in Africa before the Europeans arrived was closer to feudal European serfdom. Only with European aggressiveness did slavery become big business.) In the 1800s, as slavery became unprofitable, the immorality of it was recognized.

Europe's leaders met in Berlin and divided up Africa by drawing lines on the map. Cultural and linguistic boundaries were ignored. Looting Africa of its mineral wealth, colonial powers racked up annual profits of from 50 to 500 percent.

Shortly after its discovery, Central America was given to Spain by Pope Alexander. The ensuing destruction of Mexico from 1519 to 1521 by Cortés and a handful of mercenaries is a fascinating story of greed and power.

According to pre-Columbian Mexico's religion, their Messiah, Quetzalcoatl, was due to arrive wearing a beard and riding a horse (two things very unusual to these people) during the very year Cortés arrived, a bearded man on a horse. Thinking Cortés was Quetzalcoatl, the Mexicans warmly welcomed the Spaniard with 2,000 heavy pieces of gold. Montezuma, the Mexican leader, greeted Cortés, saying, "O Lord, our Lord . . . at last you have come to this land, to your own land and to Mexico your own city. Sit down on your mat, upon your throne which I have kept for you . . . Welcome to our land. Rest yourself now. Rest here for a while. Rest in our palace—together with your princes, your exalted companions, and all the others."

Cortés must have thought to himself, "This is really great!" He and his men were taken into the king's palace and were so impressed with all the gold and riches that they arrested Montezuma, destroyed the palace, and took all its riches.

Doubting the divinity of Cortés, the citizens asked him to leave and welcomed him to take their treasure with him. But Cortés wanted complete control, so the battle began and the Spaniards destroyed the civilization: 100,000 were killed, and the libraries, temples, art, and literature of this culture were lost forever. Today Montezuma is remembered for his "Halls" and as a kind of diarrhea.

Twelve years later, under the Spaniard Francisco Pizarro, gold-hungry Europe moved into South America. Europeans looted for 100 years before mining was even necessary. The Indians were beasts of burden. A hundred years of war and new diseases cut Mexico's population by 50 percent. As local populations shrank, Africans were imported to fill in. By 1800, about half of the populations of Venezuela and Brazil were Africans imported by European businessmen.

For 300 years, Spain milked Latin America until, in the early 1800s, independence was won. Then in 1824, British Foreign Minister Channing declared, "Latin America has won its freedom. If we play our cards right, this part of the world will be ours!" France, Britain, and the United States moved in, if not politically, then economically. Today, the outcome of a U.S. presidential election has a greater impact on the people of Central America than it does on the people of North America.

And the story continues. They say the wise learn from history. The value of what they learn depends on the quality of the history they study. Whose story is history?

Art Appreciation

"Only through art can we get outside ourselves and know another's view of the universe."

—Marcel Proust

To Know Art Is to Love Him

Getting to know art is like getting to know another person. First impressions mean a lot, but true understanding takes time. And you're more likely to become friends if you have an open mind.

In art, as with people, "Don't criticize what you can't understand." Learn about it first. Then you can really run it into the ground.

Most works of art show two things—the physical subject and the mood or message the artist is conveying. Artists can change or distort reality (the actual subject matter) to enhance the mood. When we know why reality is distorted, we can see the world through the artist's perspective, emotions, eyes—or maybe corrective lenses.

Knowing a little something about artists' lives makes their art more interesting and sometimes easier to understand. Find out where the artist was and what the inspiration was for a certain painting. A simple painting of crows in a wheat field takes on new meaning when you know that, shortly after painting it, van Gogh shot himself.

Techniques

Artists know what catches your eye. They use this knowledge to punch the right emotional buttons to get their message across. (Modern advertisers have made a science of this.) Here are some of the techniques used to attract your attention and produce an emotional response.

Composition

Composition, the layout of the main figures, is the skeleton of the work. Imagine a painter planning out a scene on grid-lined graph paper, calculating how big the main characters will be and where to place them. Let's say the artist decides to arrange the figures into a geometrical pattern, say a pyramid like this:

It doesn't look like much in rough form, but flesh out this skeleton composition with neat lines and real-life colors and you have

Raphael's **La Belle Jardiniere**

Raphael's _La Belle Jardiniere_. The geometrical composition is what makes the picture so harmonious and pleasing to the eye.

Look at the skeleton pattern. Notice how much forethought went into the composition, how orderly and pleasing the shapes are. Imagine the rough shapes colored in. It would look something like modern art, no? Can you see the appeal of abstract art, which uses the same rules of composition, line, and color but doesn't portray real-life subjects?

Line

The eye will naturally follow the curve of a line until it's broken by a line running in another direction. The artist uses this eye movement to create movement and rhythm in the scene which, in turn, creates a mood of tension or rest in the viewer. At their own pace, trained artists guide you from one figure to the next.

Grünewald's **Isenheim Altarpiece**

In the _Isenheim Altarpiece_, Grünewald directs all the motion toward Christ's agonized face. From John's pointing finger, your eye travels to the face, up Christ's arm to the crossbar, out to the end, down to the grieving figures at the left, down their slanted bodies to the kneeling Mary, and up her arm, pointing again to Christ's head. Grünewald moves our attention full circle, always returning to the central figure of Jesus, where the lines intersect.

Perspective

Lines are governed by the laws of perspective—the science of painting three-dimensional objects on a two-dimensional surface. When you draw receding lines to turn a square into a 3–D box, you've followed the laws of perspective. If the lines of the box were continued, they'd eventually converge on the horizon at what is called the "vanishing point."

Da Vinci's **Last Supper**

Using perspective and the vanishing point, an artist can place the viewer of a painting right in the middle of the action. Think of the picture frame as a window through which you are viewing the painted scene. Where are you in relation to the main figures? The artist lets you know, subconsciously, with the vanishing point.

The vanishing point is also the compositional center of the work. In Leonardo's famous *Last Supper*, the lines converge at the center of the canvas, which is the emotional focus: Christ's head. All the linear motion flows to and from this center of calm.

Color

Color is the flesh on the compositional skeleton, bringing the figures to life. It too plays a role in bringing order to art. The artist can make the picture peaceful by using harmonious colors or tense by using colors that clash.

Red, yellow, and blue are the primary colors; we get the rest by blending these three. Red is associated with passion, action, intensity,

Mantegna, **Dead Christ,** *1466
(Pinacoteca di Brera, Milan). This
Renaissance experiment in extreme
foreshortening brings the viewer
right to the scene of the action. The
psychological effect of seeing the
body from this intimate viewpoint is
exciting.*

and (as designers of fast-food menus know) hunger. Yellow is
warmth, the sun, peace. Blue is melancholy, thoughtful, the sea and
sky. Some colors complement each other (red and green), while others contrast (yellow and orange). The various combinations and
moods available to the artist are endless.

Some painters make broad outlines of figures, then fill them in with
smooth color (like a coloring book). Giotto demonstrated this technique. Monet, however, used almost no outlines whatsoever. His
paintings are more like a mosaic of minute patches of color applied
by quick strokes of the brush.

Understanding Is Appreciation

When people, admitting their ignorance of art, say, "But I know what
I like," they usually mean, "I like what I know." It's easier to like
something that's familiar and understood. Baseball is the most boring
game in the world if you don't understand the rules or players. Good
wine is best appreciated by people who've made a point of understanding the art of wine-making. You can't appreciate the classic lines
of a '56 Chevy if you don't know a Volvo from an Edsel. If you like
what you know, you can usually increase your liking by simply
increasing your knowing.

When you understand an artist's intention and techniques, you can appreciate the work even if you don't like the result. In baseball, you can appreciate a well-turned double play even if you don't like it (it made your team lose). In art, you may not like what was painted—it might be an unusual, startling, or bland scene—but you might appreciate the artist's composition or use of line and color.

Learn as much as you can about art history, artists, styles, theories, and so on, but remember that the best aid to art appreciation is simply an open mind.

Check out an art book with nice color prints from the library. Relax in your favorite chair. Light a fire. Open some wine or something. Then, alone or with a friend, leaf slowly through the book. Don't bother much with names, dates, or commentary. Just look for a painting or two you like. Play a game where you pick your favorite from each chapter, and then compare notes with a friend. (If, after two glasses of wine, you still can't find anything you like, don't push it. Turn on the TV.)

Once you find a painting that speaks your name, ask yourself why you like it. Is it the bright colors? The story it tells? The emotional effect on you? Does it make you feel good? Or sad? Or angry? Any reason for liking art is a good one. Just try to recognize what it is. Look for other works by an artist you like. If you like a similar work, maybe that means you like that style. What do the two works have in common?

Assume that the artist put a lot of thought and sweat into the artwork and is happy with the result. Try to understand why.

Museum-going

Europe is a treasure chest of great art. Many of the world's greatest museums will be a part of your trip. Here are a few hints on how to get the most out of these museums.

Pre-trip studying makes the art more fun. It's a waste to visit Rome or Greece or Egypt with no background in the art of those civilizations. I remember touring the National Museum of Archaeology in Athens as an obligation and being quite bored. I was convinced that those who looked as if they were enjoying it were actually just faking it. Two years later, after taking a class in ancient art history, that same museum was a fascinating trip into the world of Pericles and Socrates, all because of some background knowledge.

A common misconception is that great museums have only great art. A museum such as Paris' Louvre is so big (the building was, at

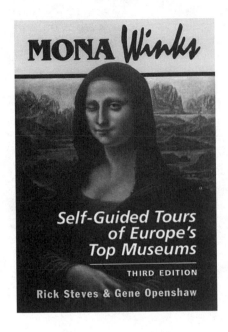

Mona Winks: Self-Guided Tours of Europe's Top Museums. *By Rick Steves and Gene Openshaw.*

one time, the largest in Europe), you can't possibly cover everything properly in one visit, so don't try. Be selective. Use a guide or guidebook to show you what is considered the best two hours of viewing in a museum. Brief guide pamphlets recommending a basic visit are available in most of Europe's museums. With this selective strategy, you'll appreciate the highlights while you are fresh. For me, museum-going is the hardest work I do in Europe, and I'm good for two, maybe three hours. Assuming that's your limit too, we've written *Mona Winks* (Santa Fe, N.M.: John Muir Publications, 1995), a collection of two-hour self-guided tours through Europe's twenty greatest museums.

If you are especially interested in one piece of art, spend a half-hour studying it and listening to each passing tour guide tell his or her story about *David* or *Mona Lisa* or whatever. The guides do their own research and each one comes up with different information to share. There's really nothing wrong with this sort of tour freeloading. Just don't stand in the front and ask a lot of questions. Many museums offer fine (and often free) tours, either of the general collection or with a particular focus. Call the museum in advance to learn what's scheduled. Most museums also have fine coffee shops or cafeterias to punctuate longer visits.

Before leaving, thumb through a museum guidebook index or look through the postcards to make sure you haven't missed anything of importance to you.

Most museums are closed one day during the week. Your local guidebook or tourist information should know when. Free admission days are usually the most crowded. It may be worth the entrance fee to avoid the crowds. While arriving late can be a fine way to avoid the summer heat and crowds, many museum ticket offices close 45 minutes before the museum does. If you'll be in a museum till the very end, visit the extremities first; these are the places likely to be shut down early as the museum staff begins sweeping the art-lovers out.

Art Patronage

It's only recently that artists have claimed the right to paint just what they want, just how they want it. In the ancient world, artists had a low social status and were expected to do as they were told. Anyone who worked with his hands was simply a common laborer, like a bricklayer. The ancient Egyptians, with their need for funerary art, encouraged painters and sculptors and paid them well for their services but never gave them any special respect. Architects had higher social status; they worked with their heads, not their hands. Imhotep, who designed the first pyramid in 2650 B.C., was actually deified.

In early Greece, most artists were slaves. Gradually, though, artists gained respect. By the Golden Age, they had begun to sign their works, rising above the level of the anonymous craftsman. Still, even the great sculptor Phidias was criticized for vanity when he tried to include his self-portrait (and that of Pericles) in one of his works on the Acropolis.

By the time of Alexander the Great (about 300 B.C.), however, artists were freer to express their individual tastes. For the first time private patrons financed artists to make works that were merely pleasing to look at. Artists became respected and admired in the community. Alexander showered wealth and favors on his favorites. He was so pleased with a painting that he once offered the great artist Apelles one of his own mistresses.

The more practical Romans thought their artists should be paid but not pampered. As Seneca put it, "Art should be enjoyed—artists should be disdained." Nevertheless, their society gave artists plenty of work: government buildings, temples, monuments to emperors and conquerors, coins, household goods, graven images of gods, and portraits. Roman artists were treated as anonymous skilled craftsmen who couldn't compare with the classical Greeks. Rich Romans were most interested in buying copies of Greek masterpieces.

With the fall of Rome and the resulting economic and cultural decline, there were no strong states and few wealthy individuals. What little art remained was in the hands of the church. Monks illustrated manuscripts of the Bible and sacred writings. Virtually the only market for a lay artist was in churches and monasteries. "Lodges" of journeymen masons, carvers, sculptors, and the like traveled from town to town building religious structures.

Artists fought for economic security against the unstable patronage of the Middle Ages by forming guilds. Half union, half co-op, guilds trained artists, regulated quality standards (as well as moral standards), and served as middlemen between the artists and prospective buyers. In a sense, the guild often was the artist's patron: it told him where and when to work and gave him his percentage of the fee when the completed product was approved. As late as 1570 in Italy, artists were required to be members of a guild.

The guild underlined the artist's role as craftsman. The Guild of St. Luke, in Holland, included painters, carvers, and goldsmiths as well as plumbers, slate-layers, printers, and lantern-makers. Most commissions were collaborations between guild members: one covered the walls, another painted a design on them, another carved the ornaments, and so on.

As Europe prospered, so did artists. Individual artists were in high demand and art flourished. We see the same pattern throughout history: a culture prospers by economic or military expansion, creating a class of patrons with a taste for decoration. In ancient Egypt this class was the ruling kings and priests, who used art to maintain the political and religious status quo. Greece and Rome added a new class of wealthy people who appreciated art apart from its propaganda purposes. (Although Rome was still very much into art as propaganda, as you see in all its commemorative statues and triumphal arches.) In the early Middle Ages, the church was virtually the only patron, producing art only for its limited, spiritual purposes.

During the Italian Renaissance, all three patrons (church, state, and private individuals) used their growing wealth to compete for a few artists. This climate of healthy competition not only made artists wealthy, famous, and respected, but it also, for the first time in history, allowed them freedom to create art on their own terms (within the structure of their commission), not solely according to the patron's specifications. With Michelangelo, the modern idea of the artist as a divinely inspired genius had arrived. Self-portraits were becoming more common.

Patronage and artist prestige reached its height during the Baroque period. Rubens and Bernini lived like princes, courted by kings, cardinals, and intellectuals alike.

In the Northern European countries, a large middle class of merchants and bankers controlled the wealth. Steady patronage by the church and monarch was not available because the North was Protestant and more democratic. Northern artists had to turn to scenes that would interest the buying public: landscapes, domestic scenes, humorous incidents. They still did some made-to-order works, but more and more they began to complete works for display at trade fairs, hoping to find buyers. This set the precedent for modern patronage.

In the time of absolute monarchs such as Louis XIV of France, artists were compelled to work for the king alone. Louis established the Royal Academy to train young artists for his service. They had less independence than their counterparts in free-market Holland and England but more formal training and financial security. France soon became the center of European art.

The Modern, Independent Artist

The French Revolution was the (symbolic if not final) end of the "Old Regime" of church, state, and aristocrats which had financed most of Europe's great art since the Middle Ages. Artists became more and more independent. They turned away from the propaganda art of church and kings, and even from so-called lovers of freedom such as Napoleon.

In the 19th century, art retreated into the museums and galleries. Artists didn't wait for a specific commission to decorate a particular palace, church, or public square. Instead, they created what they wanted, then looked for a place to exhibit it. The Impressionists had to arrange their own exhibitions when the conservative galleries refused their controversial work. Some artists (such as Cézanne) rejected all outside patronage or official schooling by financing themselves or by simply refusing to sacrifice their artistic principles to the demands of the buying public. The bohemian artist, starving but not selling out, was born.

Of course, some forms of official patronage have filled the vacuum. Churches still commission artists and architects (the church at Ronchamp, France, by Le Corbusier is one modern example). And governments are some of the steadiest sources of support for an artist.

Until recently, Eastern European countries used art for propaganda purposes, with huge monuments and murals dedicated to Marxist leaders and ideals. And patronage is moving away from art for art's sake; large corporations fund the arts for public relations purposes and tax write-offs. Art-buying has also become a major investment area for businessmen with no interest in the art itself.

As you enjoy Europe's art, wonder who paid for it and why. One thing is for sure: it wasn't designed to embellish a museum. Some person or organization probably employed that artist for a particular self-serving purpose. Today, happily, the greatest art of our civilization fills Europe's great museums, and that art serves the public.

Common Subjects and Symbols in Art

In a quick jaunt through any church, palace, or museum, you're bound to see many of the same subjects painted and sculpted in different ways by different artists. A little knowledge (a dangerous thing, but we'll trust you) of these common themes helps you appreciate the art much more.

The inspiration for most European art comes from the Bible and Greek/Roman mythology. For general background, read the Book of Matthew in the New Testament (about 35 pages long) and a children's book of Greek myths. (The Christian Themes and Symbols section was written by Mike McGregor.)

Christian Themes and Symbols

Jesus of Nazareth (c. 4 B.C.–A.D. 29)

The life of Jesus is the most popular source of material for artists. Here's a thumbnail sketch.

Born in a stable under miraculous circumstances, Jesus was visited by shepherds and Wise Men. His religious mission had earlier been announced to his mother, Mary, by the angel Gabriel. He was raised to be a carpenter, but even at an early age he proved his teaching powers.

At 30, he left home to preach the word of God, choosing 12 disciples, or apostles. He preached, performed miracles, healed people, and antagonized the religious establishment.

On a visit to Jerusalem, Jesus celebrated Jewish Passover with his disciples. Later that night he was arrested by the Roman and Jewish authorities, betrayed by one of his own followers. Arraigned before

Medieval: This 14th-century crucifix concentrates on the agony of Christ—His twisted, tortured body and drooping head.

Renaissance: Masaccio's Christ is solid, serene, and triumphant—part of a majestic architectural setting presided over by God the Father.

Baroque: Rubens captures the drama and human emotion of the moment with the expression on Christ's face and the rippling energy of the surrounding figures.

Modern: Rouault breaks the scene into its basic geometrical "abstract" forms. The only emotion is in the tilt of Christ's head. The heavy outlines and blocks of color are almost a return to medieval stained glass.

the Jewish elders and the Roman governor, Pilate, and mocked and whipped by Roman soldiers, he was given a crown of thorns and sentenced to die by crucifixion. They made Jesus carry his own cross to the execution site.

Crucifixion was a Roman specialty. The victim often hung for days before dying. The Romans stabbed Jesus in the side for good measure. Above the cross were the Roman initials I.N.R.I. for Jesus of Nazareth King (Rex) of the Jews. Mary was comforted at the foot of the cross by John, one of the disciples. After Jesus' death, his body was taken down and placed in a tomb.

After three days, Jesus came alive again and visited many of his friends and disciples. Finally, he ascended into heaven.

Popular Bible Topics in Art

Old Testament
The Old Testament tells the history of the Israelite people, from the creation of the world to the coming of Jesus. Michelangelo painted nine of these first ten on the ceiling of the Sistine Chapel at the Vatican in Rome:
- **God divides light from darkness** (Gen. 1:3–5).
- **God creates the sun and moon** (Gen. 1:14–18).
- **God separates water from earth** (Gen. 1:9–10).
- **Creation of man** (Gen. 2:7).
- **Creation of woman** (Gen. 2:21–22).
- **Original sin**—A serpent convinces Eve to eat the one fruit God told her not to, and she in turn convinces Adam to have a bite. This is the first sin, and Adam and Eve are banished from the garden (Gen. 3:1–24).
- **Cain and Abel**—Adam and Eve have two sons. Abel becomes a keeper of sheep and Cain, a farmer. Both make sacrifices to God, but God accepts only Abel's sacrifice. Cain becomes angry, kills his brother, and is banished forever (Gen. 4:11–12).
- **The Flood**—Upset with His creation, God causes a flood to destroy virtually all of humankind (Gen. 6:5–7, Gen. 7:11–24).
- **Noah's sacrifice**—After surviving the flood, Noah builds an altar and offers a sacrifice to the Lord (Gen. 8:20).
- **Noah's drunkenness**—Noah's sons respectfully cover their naked father (Gen. 9:20–23).
- **Abraham sacrifices Isaac**—God makes a pact with the wanderer Abraham, promising him many descendants even though he is old

and his wife is childless. Abraham believes God, and his faith is rewarded by the birth of his son, Isaac. But then God tests Abraham's faith by asking him to sacrifice Isaac. Abraham intends to obey, but God stops him just before he kills Isaac. Isaac becomes the father of the Jewish nation; one of his descendants is Jesus (Gen. 22:1–18).

• **Exodus from Egypt**—The people of Israel are captives of the Egyptians, but Moses rises up to lead them to freedom. Inspired by God, Moses parts the Red Sea to allow his people to escape quickly from the Egyptians (Exodus 14:16–30). The Jews are promised a new land, but because they disobey God they are first forced to wander in the desert for 40 years (Exodus 1–19).

• **Moses and the Bronze Serpent**—The people of Israel disobey God again while they wander in the desert, so God sends snakes to bite them. He tells Moses, though, to make a bronze snake and put it on a pole, and that all who keep their eyes on it will live (Numbers 21:4–9).

• **Moses and the Ten Commandments**—In order to tell the people of Israel how He wants them to live, God gives Moses on Mt. Sinai ten "thou-shalt-nots" written on tablets of stone (Exodus 20:1–17).

• **David and Goliath**—The people of Israel are challenged in battle by the Philistines, who have a mighty giant warrior, Goliath. Of all the Israelis, only a young shepherd boy named David is bold enough to fight him (David later becomes king). David uses rocks and a sling-shot to bring Goliath down, then cuts off the giant's head (1 Samuel 17:1–51).

New Testament

• **Annunciation**—The angel Gabriel announces the birth of a son, Jesus, to Mary (Luke 1:26–38).

• **Madonna and Child**—Mary and the baby Jesus (Luke 2:6–7).

• **Holy Family**—Mary and Jesus with Mary's husband, Joseph, mother Anne, or others. When two children are shown, they're usually Jesus and Johnny the Baptist.

• **Adoration of the Magi**—Three wise kings follow a bright star from the East and bow down to worship the baby Jesus (Matt. 2:1–12). Tradition says that one king was from Ethiopia; he is usually depicted having black skin.

• **Flight to Egypt**—Mary's husband, Joseph, is warned to flee from King Herod. Herod, wanting to be sure that the newborn boy (Jesus) predicted to be greater than himself will die, has ordered that all male infants be killed. Joseph and Mary take Jesus to Egypt (Matt. 2:13–23).

• **Slaughter of the Innocents**—King Herod kills the children in and around Bethlehem, where Jesus was born (Matt. 2:16–18).

• **Baptism of Jesus**—John the Baptist pours water over Jesus in the Jordan River as a symbol of cleansing. God the Father is represented in the scene as an eye or a voice, and God the Holy Spirit is represented as a dove (Matt. 3:13–17).

• **Resurrection of Lazarus**—Jesus raises his friend Lazarus from the dead (John 11:1–45).

• **Last Supper**—Jesus celebrates the Jewish festival of Passover by having one final meal with his disciples. That same night he was arrested (Mark 14:1–31, John 13:1–17:26).

• **Garden of Gethsemane**—Jesus is arrested while praying in a garden (Mark 14:32–53).

• **Crucifixion**—Jesus is nailed to a cross and dies (Matt. 27:27–54, Mark 15:16–39, John 19:16–37).

• **Pietà**—Mother Mary with the dead body of Jesus (no clear reference).

• **Resurrection**—On the third day after his burial, Jesus rises from the dead and appears to many people, including his mother, Mary Magdalene, his disciples, and two men on the road to Emmaus (Matt. 28, Mark 16, Luke 24, John 20–21).

• **Ascension**—Jesus leaves the earth by rising into the clouds (ascending) to return to his rightful place beside his Father in heaven (Acts 1:9–11).

• **The Last Judgment**—Jesus returns to the earth to sort out the good people and the bad. Angels float the good to heaven and demons drag the bad to hell. Bodies rise from their graves to find out how they will fare (Revelations).

• **Assumption of the Virgin**—Angels hoist Mary up through the clouds to heaven (no Biblical reference).

The Saints
Holy people were venerated by the European faithful. Though we don't know what they really looked like, we can tell who's who by their symbols.

• **Peter**—The most important saint, a disciple of Jesus. The name Peter means "rock." Jesus said, "On this rock I will build my church." St. Peter's Basilica, in Rome, is built upon the grave of St. Peter. Usually shown in middle age with a bushy beard, keys, or an upside-down cross in hand (symbolic of his crucifixion).

• **Paul**—The second most important saint, Paul was primarily responsible for establishing Christianity through his missionary

Peter was crucified upside down

journeys. He wrote half of the books of the New Testament. Shown bald-headed and bearded, gripping a sword and a book.

• **Matthew, Mark, Luke, and John** (The Four Evangelists)— Wrote the first four books of the New Testament, which chronicle the life of Christ. Symbols: Matthew, an angel with a book; Mark, a lion; Luke, a winged bull; and John, an eagle with a book.

• **John the Baptist**—Shown as an emaciated prophet dressed in animal skins, carrying a long cross, a lamb, and often a scroll bearing the words *Ecce Homo* ("Behold the man," referring to Christ crowned with thorns). Spent many years preaching that Jesus was coming into the world, then eventually baptized him. After objecting to Herod's marriage to his own brother's wife, John was imprisoned by Herod. At the request of Herod's stepdaughter, John was beheaded. (Matthew 14:3–12)

• **Mary Magdalene**—A prostitute whom Jesus forgave of her sins, she became a follower of Jesus and was at the cross when he died. Usually shown having long hair and carrying a jar of ointment.

• **Michael, the Archangel**— Shown in armor, with a sword, standing over or fighting with a dragon; also sometimes shown with a set of scales. The most important of the angels, Michael cast Satan out of heaven and will one day blow the waking trumpet and lead the forces of Good at the last great battle on Judgment Day.

• **Anne**—The mother of the Virgin Mary, the grandmother of

Martin Schongauer, **Temptation of St. Anthony,** *c. 1490 (National Library, Paris). This early Christian saint (c. 300) was legendary for his ascetic desert life and the temptations he endured.*

Jesus, shown with the Virgin Mary and usually also with the baby Jesus.

• **Francis of Assisi**—A medieval monk noted for his vow of poverty and love of God. The most important monk of all time, Francis founded the Franciscan order and lived in Assisi, Italy. He is usually shown in brown Franciscan habit, on his knees, with a winged Christ in the sky sending down the stigmata (the nail marks from Jesus' body appearing on Francis' body).

• **Sebastian**—A soldier in the army of Roman emperor Diocletian. Diocletian loved Sebastian, but when he learned Sebastian was a Christian, Diocletian ordered him tied to a tree and shot with arrows. Legend says Sebastian survived to confront Diocletian . . . only to then be beaten to death with clubs. Usually depicted naked, tied to a tree, and pierced by arrows.

St. Sebastian is shown pierced with arrows, the symbol of his martyrdom.

• **George**—The subject of many legends, George saved a town from a dragon to which the townspeople were sacrificing their children. He was a chivalrous knight, usually shown on horseback spearing a dragon while the king's daughter, Cleodolinda (who was in the sacrificial on-deck circle), looks on.

• **Jerome**—A hermit, he translated the Hebrew Bible into Latin producing the Vulgate, the standard text of the Catholic Church through modern times. His symbols vary, but he is often shown with a lion, from whose foot he extracted a thorn.

• **Bartholomew**—A first century A.D. missionary. Tradition says he was captured in Armenia and flayed alive, then crucified for being a Christian. Bartholomew is usually shown with a book and knife or holding his skin. He is sometimes depicted being skinned.

Michelangelo, **The Last Judgment** *(detail) (Sistine Chapel, Vatican Museum). The Christian martyr St. Bartholomew was skinned alive. Here he bears the face of Michelangelo.*

• **Denis**—Sent by the pope on a missionary journey to Paris, Denis became the first bishop of Paris and was eventually beheaded there for his faith. You'll see him all over Paris holding his head in his hands.

• **Theresa**—In the 16th century, she reformed the Carmelite monastic order and wrote many religious works. Theresa is usually shown with her heart pierced by an angel's arrow, or in ecstasy while praising God.

• **Christopher (the patron saint of us travelers)**—A third-century man who went out in search of someone to serve, he wandered aimlessly for years and ended up ferrying people across a river while waiting for Christ to appear to him. Christ finally appeared as a child whom Christopher carried across the river. Shown as a giant carrying a child and holding a staff.

These stories are found in pictures and stained glass in churches throughout Europe. The masses were usually illiterate, so church paintings were their Bible.

Much Christian art is symbolic. During medieval times, every animal, fruit, flower, color, and number had some meaning. Apes symbolized man's baser nature; bees were a symbol of industriousness (busy as a . . .); a lamb was a sacrificial animal (like Jesus); a dolphin carried the soul of the blessed to heaven. Mythical beasts had meaning, too: dragons (Satan), griffins (power), unicorns (purity), and phoenixes (resurrection). Numbers had symbolic meaning: 7 was a lot, 77 was a heck of a lot.

It's interesting to compare two different paintings or stained glass of the same subject. There are literally thousands of crucifixions, but no two are the same. Some artists concentrate on Jesus' agony, some on his serenity. For some, it's a gruesome moment of defeat, for others, a glorious triumph over sin.

Jesus is portrayed in different ways to emphasize different virtues. In one picture he is the Good Shepherd, a handsome, kindly young man caring for people as a shepherd cares for his sheep. In another he is a wise teacher. Or he might be a king, crowned in majesty. He may even be a warrior. These differences tell a lot about how people viewed the Christian message at the time of the painting.

Jesus taught with parables and performed miracles, both of which are common features in works of art. Look for the Prodigal Son (Luke 15:11–32), the Good Samaritan (Luke 10:30–37), Jesus walking on water (Matthew 14:25–27), and Jesus changing the water into wine (John 2:1–11). Only Jesus is shown with a cross on his halo.

If you see a face in a crowd of saints, church fathers, and Bible figures that you don't recognize, chances are it doesn't really belong in such holy company, anyway. Patrons of works often insisted that they be included in the work praising the Virgin Mary or what have you. If money couldn't buy them a spot in heaven, at least it could put them in a picture of heaven.

The Stars of Greek and Roman Mythology

The Greek gods were bigger-than-life human beings. They quarreled, boasted, loved, and hated just as mortals do, yet they controlled the fates of humankind. Classical mythology tells how the gods dealt with each other and with the mortals who asked them for favors. (The Greeks must have enjoyed hearing their own weaknesses glamorized, just as we do through our Hollywood stars.)

Later, the Romans adopted most of the Greeks' gods and gave them new names. Still later, Renaissance artists revived them, using them as symbols of Christian virtues and vices. After centuries of painting the same old God, it must have been a great sense of freedom to paint new ones and a whole pantheon of them, to boot.

In your museum-going you're likely to see Prometheus discovering fire or in chains, Hades capturing Persephone, Pandora opening the box, Jason and the Golden Fleece, Midas and his Goldfinger touch, the Battle of the Centaurs, the Battle of the Amazons, Leda and the Swan, and on and on. Here are the most important Greek gods and how to recognize them (Roman name in parentheses):

• **Zeus (Jupiter)**—Ruled as King of the Gods in their court on Mount Olympus. He divided up his realm among his sisters, brothers, and children. Bearded, sometimes carries a spear. Zeus had a nasty habit of turning himself into some earthly form to hustle unsuspecting females. You're just as likely to see him portrayed as a bull, a cloud, a swan, or a shower of gold as in his majestic human body.

• **Hera (Juno)**—Wife of Zeus.

• **Poseidon (Neptune)**—King of the Sea. Holds a trident.

• **Hades (Pluto)**—King of the Underworld. Bearded and sad, carries a staff.

• **Apollo**—Ruler of the Sun, God of Music and Poetry. Drives the sun's flaming chariot across the sky each day. Major symbol is the sun.

• **Hermes (Mercury)**—Messenger of the Gods. His helmet and shoes have wings. Delivers a lot of flowers these days.

Diana the Huntress *(Orsay Gallery, Paris)*

• **Ares (Mars)**—God of War. Dresses in war garb and carries a spear.

• **Dionysus (Bacchus)**—God of Wine and college fraternities. Holds grapes, wears a toga and a wreath of laurel leaves. Sometimes shown as a chubby little boy.

• **Athena (Minerva)**—Goddess of Wisdom. A virgin, born from the head of Zeus. Carries a spear.

• **Artemis (Diana)**—Goddess of the Moon and Hunting. Carries a bow and arrow.

• **Aphrodite (Venus)**—Goddess of Love and Beauty. Often shown partially naked, with Cupid nearby.

• **Eros (Cupid)**—God of Desire. Usually shown as a baby with wings, wielding a bow and aphrodisiac-tipped arrows.

Other characters and miscellaneous beasts:

• **Pan (Faun)**—A lesser god of shepherds. Top half man, bottom half goat. Carries a pan flute.

• **Hercules**—Son of Zeus born to a mortal woman. Strongest man in the world. Performed many feats of strength. Often wears a lion's skin.

• **Odysseus (Ulysses)**—Homer's *Odyssey* tells the story of Ulysses' ten-year journey home from the Trojan War.

• **Helen of Troy**—The most beautiful woman in the world. Her kidnapping started the Trojan War, the subject of the *Iliad*. Hers is "the face that launched a thousand ships."
• **Satyr**—Top half man, bottom half goat. Horny.
• **Centaur**—Top half man, bottom half horse. Wise.
• **Griffin**—Winged, lion-like beast.
• **Harpy**—Bird with female human head and seductive voice.
• **Medusa**—Woman with hair of snakes and a face that, when glimpsed, turns people to stone. Slain by Perseus.
• **Pegasus**—Winged horse.
• **Minotaur**—Beast with the head of a bull. Lived in the labyrinth in the palace on Crete.

Even if you know zero about art, if you know who's in a painting and what they're doing, your interest level jumps 50 percent. Learn something about Christian and classical mythology, and your museum-going will be more fun.

Historical Scenes

Modern artists, in search of new subjects, turned to famous scenes from history, trying to capture the glory or emotion of the moment. In the early 1800s, Romantic artists tapped the patriotic fervor of their audiences with scenes of heroics against oppressors. Goya's *Third of May–1808* shows the murderous execution of Spanish nationals by Napoleon's troops. Delacroix painted a battle scene from a French anti-monarchy uprising which now graces the French 100-franc note. J. L. David, a Neoclassicist, chronicled (and "romanticized") the French Revolution and reign of Napoleon.

Still Lifes

Scholars debate whether "art imitates life" or "life imitates art," but to a great extent, "art imitates art." Artists will often choose a subject already done by many previous artists in order to carry on and extend the tradition both to learn from earlier masters' versions and to try something new.

Perhaps the best example is the "still life," a painting of a set

Claesz, **Still Life** *(Rijksmuseum, Amsterdam)*

of motionless, common objects: fruit, cups, a knife, a chair, curtains, and so on. It's a simple form, often undertaken by students practicing their drawing and simple composition, yet many great artists have shown their ingenuity by turning it into great art. Each successive artist is challenged to make the old style and familiar items new again.

Landscapes

Certain artists, such as Canaletto and Constable, concentrated on paintings of places: landscapes, seascapes, domestic and rural scenes. The same place may be completely different in two different paintings, so it is interesting to compare each artist's approach.

El Greco, **Landscape of Toledo**

Baroque artists often decorated churches with an appropriate landscape—heaven. Ceilings seem to open up to the sky, gloriously busy with angels, chariots, and winged babies (called *putti*).

Portraits

Portraits are, of course, supposed to be accurate renditions of the posers, but many try to glorify their subjects. Two particular types of portrait sculpture are the "bust" (neck and head only) and "equestrian" (riding a horse).

The "nude" is another kind of portrait, concerned more with the shape of the body than specific identifying features. A good nude does not necessarily have the most beautiful body. It's up to the artist to pose the body just right, reclining or standing, to capture the most interesting and harmonious lines.

A classical style, the *contrapposto* (Italian for "counterpoise") is a painting or sculpture of someone standing, resting their weight on one leg. (Michelangelo's *David* is contrapposto.) The faint S-like curve of the body attracts the eye as much as any individual body features.

Music Appreciation

Music, like all art forms, is shaped by the cultural mood and environment of the time. It's easy to trace the course of musical history as it marches arm in arm with painting, architecture, philosophy, lifestyles, and sculpture from Baroque to Neoclassical to Romantic to Impressionistic and into the no-holds-barred artistic world of our century.

As we trace this evolution of musical styles through post-Renaissance history, let's use this section as a review of the progression of art styles in general since the Baroque days of Louis, Bernini, and Bach.

The Baroque world was controlled exuberance, glory to man and his God-blessed accomplishments. Music, like art, was brilliant, bright, alive, and decorated with trills, flutters, and ornamentation like the powdered wigged, perfumed, and elegantly gowned musicians who wrote and performed it.

But the frills rested on a strong foundation. While a two-part Bach invention, Handel's "Messiah," or a Scarlatti sonata may sparkle with bright and happy ornaments, they are carefully based on a solid mathematical structure. An analysis of Bach's work shows many patterns, staircase-type series, and a grand plan, tying all the musical ribbons and bows together. Bach, Handel, and Scarlatti, all born in 1685, were the great musical masters of the Baroque period.

In the late 18th century, the Neoclassical movement took art as well as music back to pure, clean basics. It was a stern reaction to the "clutter" of Baroque. Buildings were built with clean, true domes, circles, and squares. The age of reason had arrived, and beauty was simple. A good example of how music played along with the Neoclassical movement is found in the art of Mozart. Neoclassical music is called simply "classical." A classical composer, Mozart wrote pieces of powerfully simple beauty. Grand and frilly were out. The better a Mozart sonata is played, the easier it sounds. Classical music, like the dome on our Capitol, is a search for basic, pure beauty. Its beauty lies in its simplicity.

In the 1800s, reason and logic were dethroned and Nature and Emotion became a religion. Music's grand metronome had swung back again. The Romantics were awestruck by the wonders of nature and happy victims of its power and immensity. Grieg's fjord hideaway, Verdi's nationalism, and Chopin's battered heart all inspired the masterpieces of this Romantic era. They expressed emotions—good and bad—for the sake of emotions. Orchestras grew in size to add more punch. A series of pieces by Chopin, Wagner, or Schumann can take you through an emotional wringer. The pieces, often with names reflecting their heartfelt stories ("Ase's Death," "Pleading Child," "Raindrops Prelude," "Dreaming"), want to affect the listener strongly rather than merely to entertain.

As painting reached beyond mere realism, we enter the Impressionist era. While Monet and Renoir were catching sunbeams, leafy reflections, and the fuzzy warmth of that second glass of wine, composers such as Debussy and Ravel were doing the same thing on the keyboard or with orchestras. Artists struggled to capture basic shapes, colors, and moods. A blue moment, a fleeting rainbow, or an enchanted cathedral were targets of the artist's mind, the painter's brush, the composer's pen, and the conductor's baton. Debussy is Monet for your ears. (And for the more musical, Monet is Debussy for your eyes.)

In the 20th century, artists are abandoning reality, exploring new frontiers that know no rules, and choosing personally stimulating works of artistic esoterica over pleasing the people. Paintings are abstract, and music is atonal.

Atonal music is freed from tonality and worry about "what key are we in?" There is no key, meter, or consistent beat pattern (such as 2/4 or 3/4 time). The only real rule is that artists should not be bound by the rules of others.

But atonality is as difficult for our ears as abstraction is for our eyes. We're taught to need art to portray something real, just as we need music to stick to a key. The great composer and pianist Franz Liszt knew the power of tonality. And so did his wife. To get him out of bed in the morning, she would play the first seven notes of a scale: do re mi fa so la ti . . . He would toss aside the covers, run to the piano, and play that last necessary note . . . do. Liszt was a tonal guy. Good morning.

Appendix

Best of Europe Sightseeing Lists

Europe's Top Museums and Cultural Experiences

(Self-guided tours covered in our *Mona Winks* book)
British Museum, London
National Gallery, London
Tate Gallery, London
The Louvre, Paris
The Orsay Museum, Paris
Pompidou Modern Art Museum, Paris
Historic Paris Walk
Versailles, Paris
Rijksmuseum, Amsterdam
Van Gogh Museum, Amsterdam
St. Mark's and the Doge's Palace, Venice
Accademia, Venice
The Renaissance Walk, Florence
Uffizi Gallery, Florence
Bargello, Florence
A Walk Through Ancient Rome
St. Peter's, Rome
The Vatican Museum, Rome
The Prado, Madrid

Rick's Favorite Works of Art

Garden of Delights, Bosch, Prado
Isenheim Altarpiece, Grünewald, Colmar
Primavera, Botticelli, Florence
Guernica, Picasso, Madrid
Pietà, Michelangelo, Vatican
David, Michelangelo, Florence
Sistine Chapel (ceiling and *The Last Judgment*), Michelangelo,
   Vatican
School of Athens, Raphael, Vatican Museum
Virgin of the Roses, Schongauer, Colmar
Sainte Chapelle church, Paris
St. John the Baptist, Donatello, Venice
Self-Portrait, Dürer, Prado
Hand of God, Milles, Stockholm
Pietà Rondanini, Michelangelo, Milan
The Orsay Museum building, Paris
Temppeliaukio church, Helsinki

Gene's "Lucky 13" Picks (with apologies to no one)

Isenheim Altarpiece, Grünewald, Colmar
The Tempest, Giorgione, Venice
Head of Christ Mosaic, Dafni, Greece
Interior of My Studio, Courbet, Louvre
Burial of Count Orgaz, El Greco, Toledo, Spain
School of Athens, Raphael, Vatican Museum
Moses, Michelangelo, San Pietro in Vincoli, Rome
Last Supper, Leonardo, Milan
Intrigue, James Ensor, Royal Museum, Antwerp
Descent from the Cross, Roger van der Weyden, Prado
Grande Odalisque, Ingres, Louvre
Jacob Wrestling with the Angel, Gauguin, National Gallery,
   Edinburgh
St. Francis in Ecstasy, G. Bellini, New York

Most Overrated Sights

Manneken-Pis, Brussels
Stonehenge, England
Atonium, Brussels
Athens, Greece

Glockenspiel, Munich (actually, glockenspiels in general)
The Little Mermaid, Copenhagen
Hitler's Bunker, Berlin
Spanish Steps and Trevi Fountain, Rome
Blarney Stone, Ireland
Land's End, England
Loch Ness Monster, Scotland
Cannes
Champs-Elysses, Paris' hamburger row

Most Underrated Sights

Ostia Antica, Rome's ancient port
Bath, England's finest city
Toledo Cathedral Sacristy, Spanish Renaissance
Chantilly Château, near Paris
Vaux-le-Vicomte château, near Paris
Schatzkammer (Treasury), Vienna
Bern
Pisa Baptistery and Church (not Tower)

Most Underrated Museums

Vatican Museum (before the Sistine Chapel)
Unterlinden Museum (*Isenheim Altarpiece* and more), Colmar
Chagall Museum, Nice
Groeninge Museum, Brugge
York Castle Museum, York
Costume Museum, Bath
Fitzwilliam Museum, Cambridge
Museo del Duomo (Donatello and Michelangelo), Florence
Museo de Santa Cruz (El Greco), Toledo
Kunstmuseum (modern, Klee), Bern
Kroller-Muller (van Gogh), Arnhem, Netherlands

Offbeat Europe

Paris sewers tour
A million skeletons in Paris Catacombs
Parco dei Mostri, cement monster park near Viterbo, Italy
L'Art Brut (art of the criminally insane), Lausanne, Switzerland
Legoland, Bilund, Denmark
Porthmeirion (Italian city), Wales
Homage to Stravinsky fountain (near Pompidou center), Paris

Hundertwasser Haus, Vienna
Capuchin crypts (bones), Rome and Palermo, Italy
Medieval Crime and Punishment Museum, Rothenburg, Germany

Favorite Festivals

Salzburg Music Festival, end of July through August
Edinburgh, late August–early September
Munich beerhalls, June 1–May 31
Oktoberfest, late September to early October, Munich
Each country's national holiday (like French Bastille day, July 14
 and Swiss Independence day, August 1)
Palio, Siena, Italy (July 2 and August 16)
Carnevale, Venice (February)
Fasching, Germany (especially Köln), February
Kinderfest, Dinkelsbuhl, Germany (mid-July)

Favorite Churches

Charlemagne's chapel, Aachen
Sacré-Coeur, Paris
St. Peter's, Vatican
Toledo Cathedral, Toledo
Sainte Chapelle, Paris
Orvieto, Italy

Best Evening Scenes

Flamenco and *paseo* street scenes, Seville
La Dolce Vita stroll, Via del Corso, Rome
Passegiata/Paseo, almost every Italian/Spanish town in evening
Piazza Navona, Rome
Mathauser's Beerhall, Munich
Jazz clubs, Paris
"Pub Crawl," back streets of Venice
Empty St. Mark's Square at midnight, Venice
Tivoli, Copenhagen
Any Italian hill town after the tour buses leave
Breakwater, Vernazza, Cinque Terre, Italy

Musical Sights

State Opera Houses, Vienna, Milan, and Paris
Mozart's birthhouse, Salzburg
Musée Carnavalet (Chopin), Paris

Ringve musical history museum, Trondheim, Norway
Beethoven's birthhouse, Bonn
Europe's greatest organs: Passau (Germany), Haarlem (Holland)
Beatles Museum, Liverpool
Grieg home, Troldhaugen, Bergen, Norway

Royal Jewels

Crown Jewels, Tower of London
Schatzkammer, Vienna and Munich
Apollo Gallery, Louvre, Paris

Cemeteries

Capuchin crypts (oodles of bones), Rome and Palermo
Pére Lachaise (Chopin, Jim Morrison, Edith Piaf, Oscar Wilde)
Central Cemetery (Beethoven, Brahms, Mozart, etc.), Vienna
U.S. cemeteries in Normandy (France) and Bastogne (Belgium)
Bone chapel, Hallstatt, Austria

Sports and Games Sights

Olympics museums, Innsbruck and Lausanne
Olympic Stadium, Berlin, Athens
Olympic Village, Munich
Ski jumps in Innsbruck, Garmisch
Ski museum, Holmenkollen ski jump, Oslo
Hurling match, anywhere, Ireland
Hang gliders and parasailers, throughout the Alps (especially
   Chamonix, Tegelberg near Füssen, and the Schilthorn)
Luge rides near Reutte, in Tirol (Austria) and Chamonix (France)
Autoworld museum, Brussels
Casinos in Baden-Baden (Germany) and Monte Carlo

Assorted Military Sights

The medieval armory, Graz, Austria
Musée de l'Armee, Invalides, Paris
Medieval Crime and Punishment Museum, Rothenburg
Valley of the Fallen, near Madrid
Wasa, Swedish warship, Stockholm
Armory (medieval weapons), Doge's Palace, Venice
Gibraltar
Waterloo (fans only), Brussels, Belgium
Imperial War Museum, London

Artist Timeline: 1300—1985

Artists and Dates

Bernini (bayr-NEE-nee), 1598–1680: Baroque grandeur.

Blake, William, 1757–1827: Mystical visions.

Bosch, Hieronymous (bosh), 1450–1516: Crowded, bizarre scenes.

Botticelli, Sandro (bott-i-CHELL-ee), 1445–1510: Delicate Renaissance beauty.

Braque, Georges (brock), 1882–1963: Cubist pioneer.

Brunelleschi, Filippo (broon-uh-LESS-key), 1377–1446: First great Renaissance architect.

Bruegel, Pieter (BROY-gull), c. 1525–1569: Netherlands, peasant scenes.

Caravaggio (car-rah-VAH-jee-oh), 1573–1610: Shocking ultra-realism.

Cézanne, Paul (say-ZAH), 1839–1906: Bridged Impressionism and Cubism.

Chagall, Marc (sha-GALL), 1887–1985: Fiddlers on roofs, magical realism.

da Vinci, Leonardo (dah VINCH-ee), 1452–1519: A well-rounded Renaissance genius who also painted.

Dali, Salvador (DAH-lee), 1904–1989: Father of Surrealism.

Degas, Edgar (day-GAH), 1834–1917: Impressionist snapshots, dancers.

Donatello, (doh-na-TELL-oh), c. 1386–1466: Early Renaissance sculptor.

Dürer, Albrecht (DEWR-er), 1471–1528: Renaissance symmetry with German detail; "the Leonardo of the north."

El Greco (el GREK-oh), 1541–1614: Spiritual scenes, elongated bodies.

Fra Angelico (frah an-JELL-i-co), 1387–1455: Renaissance techniques, medieval piety.

Gauguin, Paul (go-GAN), 1848–1903: Primitivism, native scenes, bright colors.

Giorgione (jor-JONE-ee), 1477–1510: Venetian Renaissance, mysterious beauty.

Giotto (ZHOTT-oh), 1266–1337: Proto-Renaissance painter (3-D) in medieval times.

Goya, Francisco (GOY-ah), 1746–1828: Three stages—frilly court painter, political rebel, dark stage.

Hals, Frans (halls), 1581–1666: Snapshot portraits of Dutch merchants.

Ingres, Jean Auguste Dominique (ANG-gruh), 1780–1867: Neoclassical painter.

Manet, Edouard (man-NAY), 1823–1883: Forerunner of Impressionist rebels.

Mantegna, Andrea (mahn-TAYN-ya), 1431–1506: Renaissance 3–D and "sculptural" painting.

Matisse, Henri (mah-TEES), 1869–1954: Decorative "wallpaper," bright colors.

Michelangelo (mee-kell-AN-jell-oh), 1475–1564: Earth's greatest sculptor and one of its greatest painters.

Mondrian, Piet (manh-dree-ahn), 1872–1944: Abstract, geometrical canvases.

Monet, Claude (moh-NAY), 1840–1926: Father of Impressionism.

Picasso, Pablo (pee-KAHSS-oh), 1881–1973: Master of many modern styles, especially Cubism.

Raphael (roff-eye-ELL), 1483–1520: Epitome of the Renaissance—balance, realism, beauty.

Rembrandt (REM-brant), 1606–1669: Greatest Dutch painter, brown canvases, dramatic lighting.

Renoir, Auguste (ren-WAH), 1841–1919: Impressionist style, idealized beauty, pastels.

Rodin, Auguste (roh-DAN), 1840–1917: Classical statues with rough "Impressionist" finish.

Rubens, Peter Paul (REW-buns), 1577–1640: Baroque, fleshy women, violent scenes.

Steen, Jan (steen), 1626–1679: Slice-of-life everyday Dutch scenes.

Tiepolo, Giovanni Battista (tee-EPP-o-lo), 1696–1770: 3–D illusions on ceilings.

Tintoretto (tin-toh-RETT-oh), 1518–1594: Venetian Renaissance plus drama.

Titian (TEESH-un), 1477–1576: Greatest Venetian Renaissance painter.

Turner, Joseph Mallord William, 1775–1851: Messy "Proto-Impressionist" scenes of nature.

Uccello, Paolo (oo-CHELL-oh), 1396–1475: Early 3–D experiments.

Van Eyck, Jan (van IKE), 1390–1441: Northern detail.

Van Gogh, Vincent (van GO, or, more correctly, van GOCK), 1853–1890: Impressionist style plus emotion.

Velázquez, Diego (vel-LAHSS-kes), 1599–1660: Objective Spanish court portraits.

Vermeer, Jan (vayr-MEER), 1632–1675: Quiet Dutch art, highlighting everyday details.

Veronese, Paolo (vayr-oh-NAY-zee), 1528–1588: Huge, colorful scenes with Venetian Renaissance backgrounds.

A New Enlightenment Through Travel

Thomas Jefferson said, "Travel makes you wiser but less happy." "Less happy" is a good thing. It's the growing pains of a broadening perspective. After viewing our culture from a coffeehouse in Vienna or a village in Tuscany, I've found truths that didn't match those I always assumed were "self-evident" and "God-given." And flying home gives me a healthy dose of culture shock in reverse. You know how I love Europe. But I haven't told you about my most prized souvenir—a new way of thinking.

The "land of the free" has a powerful religion—materialism. Its sophisticated priesthood (business, media, military, and political leaders) worships unsustainable growth. Contentment and simplicity are sins. Mellow is yellow. And evil is anything steering you away from being a good producer/consumer.

Yes, greater wealth could be wonderful. But for whom? The gap between rich and poor—both within our society and among humankind in general—is growing. Regulatory, tax, and spending policies in the United States since 1982 have caused the greatest trickle-up of wealth in our nation's history. And globally, the richest 358 people now own as much as the poorest 45% of humanity put together. Designer fortifications protect the wealthy in much of the world. In the U.S. two kinds of communities are the rage: "gated communities" and prisons. The victims are the politically meek—those who don't or can't vote: the young, the poor, the environment, and the future. More and more Americans have lost hope. And when "freedom" grows at hope's expense, your children will ponder their blessings behind deadbolts.

Whoa! What happened to me? The young Republican traveled. I saw countries less wealthy than ours (but with bigger governments) where everyone had a home, enough food, and healthcare. And, like the early astronauts, I saw a planet with no boundaries—a single, tender organism painted with the faces of 6 billion equally precious people. I unpack my rucksack marveling at how politically active American Christians can believe that we're all children of God—while fighting aid for the hungry and homeless.

A new Enlightenment is needed. Just as the French "Enlightenment" led us into the modern age of science and democracy, this new Enlightenment will teach us the necessity of sustainable affluence, peaceful co-existence with other economic models, controlling nature by obeying her, and measuring prosperity by something more human than material consumption.

I hope your travels will give you a fun and relaxing vacation or adventure. I also hope they'll make you an active patriot of our planet and a voice for people in our country who will never see their names on a plane ticket.

Rick Steves

About Your Illustrious Authors

RICK STEVES (1955–2018)

Gained fame and notoriety as a guru of alternative European travel. From 1980 to 1998 he wrote and hosted the public television series *Travels in Europe with Rick Steves*, published the *Back Door Travel Newsletter*, wrote a weekly newspaper column, lectured throughout the U.S. about independent travel, organized and led "Back Door" tours of Europe, and wrote 15 travel guidebooks, including the classic *Rick Steves' Europe Through the Back Door*, which started a cult of people who insisted on washing their socks in sinks, taking showers "down the hall," and packing very, very light even when not traveling.

GENE OPENSHAW (b. 1956)

Gene is both an author and composer. After graduating from Stanford University, he promptly put his degree to work by writing joke books and performing stand-up comedy. He is currently working on an opera entitled *Matter.* Seriously.

Send Us a Postcard

It's our goal to make this book the most helpful 300-plus pages on European history and art any traveler can read. Any suggestions, criticisms, or feedback from you would really be appreciated (send to Box 2009, Edmonds, WA 98020 or e-mail to "ricksteves@aol.com"). All correspondents will receive our Back Door travel newsletter.

    Thanks, and happy travels.

—Rick

General Index

Geographical Index

A list of references by country, city, and region, for planning your trip

Rick Steves'
FREE TRAVEL NEWSLETTER/CATALOG

My Europe Through the Back Door travel company will help you travel better **because** you're on a budget — not in spite of it. Call us at (206) 771-8303, and we'll send you our **free newsletter/catalog** packed full of info on budget travel, railpasses, guidebooks, videos, travel accessories and tours.

BACK DOOR TOURS

We offer a variety of European tours for those who want to travel in the Back Door style, but without the transportation and hotel hassles. If a tour with a small group, modest Back Door accomodations, lots of physical exercise, great guides, and no tips or hidden charges sounds like your idea of fun, call us for details.

CONVERTIBLE BACK DOOR BAG $75

At 9"x21"x13" our specially designed, sturdy bag is maximum carry-on-the-plane size (fits under the seat) and your key to footloose and fancy-free travel. Made of rugged water resistant cordura nylon, it converts easily from a smart looking suitcase to a handy rucksack. It has padded hide-away shoulder straps, top and side handles, and a detachable shoulder strap (for use as a suitcase). Lockable perimeter zippers allow easy access to the roomy 2,500 cubic inch central compartment. Two large outside compartments are perfect for frequently used items. We'll even toss in a nylon stuff bag. More than 40,000 travelers have used these bags around the world. I live out of one for three months at a time. Available in black, grey, navy blue and teal green.

MONEYBELT $8

Absolutely required for European travel, our sturdy nylon, ultra-light, under-the-pants pouch is just big enough to carry your essentials (passport, airline tickets, travelers checks, gummi bears) comfortably. I won't travel without one, and neither should you. Comes in neutral beige, with a nylon zipper. One size fits all.

EUROPEAN RAILPASSES

We offer you the best prices on the full range of European railpasses, and with every Eurailpass we give you these important extras — **free:** my hour-long "How to get the most out of your railpass" video; your choice of one of my 13 country guidebooks and phrasebooks; and our sage advice on your 1-page itinerary. Call us for our free 64-page **1996 Back Door Guide to European Railpasses.**

All items are field tested by Rick Steves and completely guaranteed.
Prices are good through 1996 (maybe longer), and include shipping (allow two to three weeks).
WA residents add 8.2% tax. Sorry, no credit cards or phone orders. Send checks in US $ to:

Rick Steves' Europe Through the Back Door
120 Fourth Avenue North, PO Box 2009-A, Edmonds, WA 98020 USA
Phone: (206) 771-8303   **Fax:** (206) 771-0833   **Email:** Ricksteves@aol.com

Other Books from John Muir Publications

Travel Books by Rick Steves

Asia Through the Back Door, 400 pp. $17.95

Europe 101: History and Art for the Traveler, 352 pp. $17.95

Mona Winks: Self-Guided Tours of Europe's Top Museums, 432 pp. $18.95

Rick Steves' Baltics & Russia, 144 pp. $9.95

Rick Steves' Europe, 544 pp. $17.95

Rick Steves' France, Belgium & the Netherlands, 256 pp. $13.95

Rick Steves' Germany, Austria & Switzerland, 256 pp. $13.95

Rick Steves' Great Britain, 240 pp. $13.95

Rick Steves' Italy, 224 pp. $13.95

Rick Steves' Scandinavia, 192 pp. $13.95

Rick Steves' Spain & Portugal, 208 pp. $13.95

Rick Steves' Europe Through the Back Door, 480 pp. $18.95

Rick Steves' French Phrase Book, 176 pp. $4.95

Rick Steves' German Phrase Book, 176 pp. $4.95

Rick Steves' Italian Phrase Book, 176 pp. $4.95

Rick Steves' Spanish and Portuguese Phrase Book, 304 pp. $5.95

Rick Steves' French/German/Italian Phrase Book, 320 pp. $6.95

A Natural Destination Series

Belize: A Natural Destination, 344 pp. $16.95

Costa Rica: A Natural Destination, 400 pp. $17.95

Guatemala: A Natural Destination, 360 pp. $16.95

For Birding Enthusiasts

The Birder's Guide to Bed and Breakfasts: U.S. and Canada, 416 pp. $17.95

The Visitor's Guide to the Birds of the Central National Parks: U.S. and Canada, 400 pp. $15.95

The Visitor's Guide to the Birds of the Eastern National Parks: U.S. and Canada, 400 pp. $15.95

The Visitor's Guide to the Birds of the Rocky Mountain National Parks: U.S. and Canada, 432 pp. $15.95

Unique Travel Series

Each is 112 pages and $10.95 paper, except Georgia.

Unique Arizona

Unique California

Unique Colorado

Unique Florida

Unique Georgia (11.95)

Unique New England

Unique New Mexico

Unique Texas

Unique Washington

2 to 22 Days Itinerary Planners

2 to 22 Days in the American Southwest, 192 pp. $11.95

2 to 22 Days in Asia, 192 pp. $10.95

2 to 22 Days in Australia, 192 pp. $11.95

2 to 22 Days in California, 192 pp. $11.95

2 to 22 Days in Eastern Canada, 240 pp $11.95

2 to 22 Days in Florida, 192 pp. $11.95

2 to 22 Days Around the Great Lakes, 192 pp. $11.95

2 to 22 Days in Hawaii, 192 pp. $11.95
2 to 22 Days in New England, 192 pp. $11.95
2 to 22 Days in New Zealand, 192 pp. $11.95
2 to 22 Days in the Pacific Northwest, 192 pp. $11.95
2 to 22 Days in the Rockies, 192 pp. $11.95
2 to 22 Days in Texas, 192 pp. $11.95
2 to 22 Days in Thailand, 192 pp. $10.95

Other Terrific Travel Titles

The 100 Best Small Art Towns in America, 224 pp. $12.95
The Big Book of Adventure Travel, 384 pp. $17.95
California Public Gardens, 336 pp. $16.95
Indian America: A Traveler's Companion, 480 pp. $18.95
The People's Guide to Mexico, 608 pp. $19.95
Ranch Vacations: The Complete Guide to Guest and Resort, Fly-Fishing, and Cross-Country Skiing Ranches, 528 pp. $19.95
Understanding Europeans, 272 pp. $14.95
Undiscovered Islands of the Caribbean, 288 pp. $16.95
Watch It Made in the U.S.A.: A Visitor's Guide to the Companies that Make Your Favorite Products, 272 pp. $16.95

Automotive Titles

The Greaseless Guide to Car Care, 272 pp. $19.95
How to Keep Your Subaru Alive, 480 pp. $21.95
How to Keep Your Toyota Pickup Alive, 392 pp. $21.95
How to Keep Your VW Alive, 464 pp., $25

Kidding Around Travel Series

All are 64 pages and $9.95 paperback, except for *Kidding Around Spain*, which is 108 pages and $12.95 paperback.

Kidding Around Atlanta
Kidding Around Boston
Kidding Around Chicago
Kidding Around the Hawaiian Islands
Kidding Around London
Kidding Around Los Angeles
Kidding Around New York City
Kidding Around Paris
Kidding Around Philadelphia
Kidding Around San Diego
Kidding Around San Francisco
Kidding Around Santa Fe
Kidding Around Seattle
Kidding Around Spain
Kidding Around Washington, D.C.

Ordering Information

Please check your local bookstore for our books, or call **1-800-888-7504** to order direct and to receive a complete catalog. A shipping charge will be added to your order total.

Send all inquiries to:
John Muir Publications
P.O. Box 613
Santa Fe, NM 87504